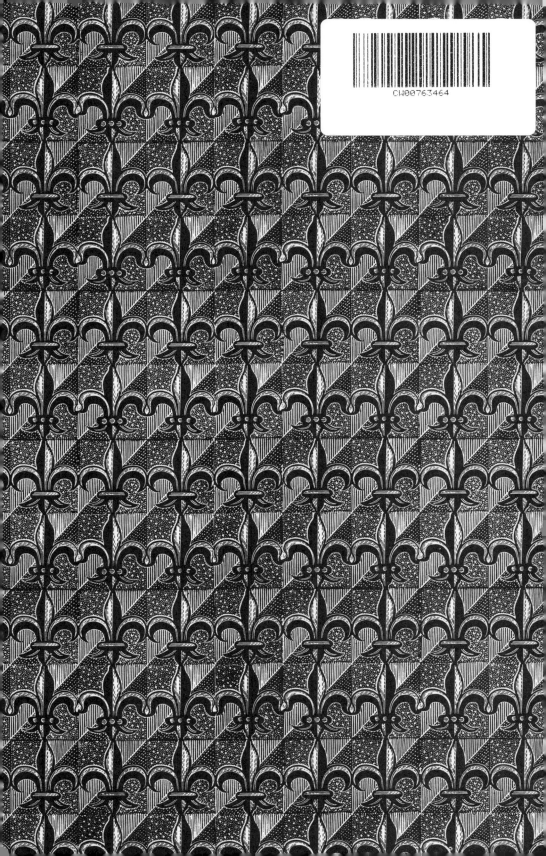
CW00763464

WALTER MONCKTON

By the same author

Norman Birkett
The Strange Death of Lord Castlereagh
Sir Patrick Hastings: His Life and Cases
Lord Reading: The Life of Rufus Isaacs
The Quiet Canadian
Cynthia
Oscar Wilde
Henry James at Home
Carson
The Londonderries
Solitary in the Ranks
The Lady Chatterley Trial
etc

— WALTER —
MONCKTON

— H. Montgomery Hyde —

SINCLAIR-STEVENSON LTD

First published in Great Britain by
Sinclair-Stevenson Limited
7/8 Kendrick Mews
London SW7 3HG, England

Copyright © 1991 by the Estate of H. Montgomery Hyde
and Richard Perceval Graves

All rights reserved. Without limiting the rights under copyright
reserved, no part of this publication may be reproduced, stored in or
introduced into a retrieval system or transmitted, in any form or by any
means (electronic, mechanical, photocopying, recording or otherwise),
without the prior written permission of both the copyright owner and the
above publisher of this book.

The right of H. Montgomery Hyde to be identified as author of
this work has been asserted by him in accordance with the
Copyright, Designs and Patents Act 1988.

British Library Cataloguing in Publication Data
A CIP catalogue record for this book is available from the British Library.

ISBN: 1 85619 045 5

Typeset by Rowland Phototypesetting Limited, Bury St Edmunds, Suffolk
Printed and bound in Great Britain by Clays Limited, St Ives plc

Contents

Acknowledgements

THE Executors of the late H. Montgomery Hyde acknowledge the kind permission of Lady Birkenhead for the use of extracts from her late husband Lord Birkenhead's biography *Walter Monckton*; of The Master and Fellows of Balliol College, Oxford, for the use of extracts from the Monckton Papers; and of Edwin Green, Group Archivist, Midland Group, for the use of extracts from the *Midbank Chronicle*.

List of Illustrations

For the loan of and permission to reproduce the photographs in this book, grateful acknowledgement is made to the following:

The Viscount Monckton of Brenchley (Harrow portrait, With Polly, Wedding, In uniform, Hunt at Fishponds, Gilbert and Valerie, Monckton Commission, The Windsors 1960)

Popperfoto (Monckton 1936, Harold Davidson, Monckton and Hawke, Monckton 1953, Lord Goddard 1958, Monckton and Biddy, Monckton 1963)

Topham Picture Library (Stanley Baldwin 1936, Duke and Duchess of Windsor, Monckton 1939, Churchill's last Cabinet 1955, Brendan Bracken 1950)

Mansell Collection (Nizam of Hyderabad)

Associated Press (Monckton and Mountbatten)

Sussex University (Inaugural address 1963)

Chapter 1

Early Years and the Great War

I

LIKE Norman Birkett, his friend and contemporary at the English Bar, Walter Monckton at one time thought of writing his memoirs. Also like Birkett, he managed to compose only a few pages; but he did succeed in outlining the form his autobiography would have taken had he been able to complete it. This 'collection of random memories', as he called it, was begun in 1940 during the Second World War, when Monckton was 48 years old and working at the Ministry of Information. 'I have had an interesting and varied life,' he began.[1]

> I dictated an account of the abdication of King Edward VIII within a week or two of the event and that was something to begin with. Then one morning in early September 1939, some few days after the beginning of this war, the King [George VI] saw me in his room at Buckingham Palace, just before I flew to Antibes to see the Duke of Windsor about his return to England, and said that I ought to write a book entitled *Odd Jobs I Have Done*. And now I have the opportunity at odd moments in the Ministry of Information during air raids or lulls in work, and I find it refreshing to plunge back into the past and live the old days once again.

Sir Walter Monckton, KCVO, as he then was, had been Attorney-General to the Duke of Windsor when he was Prince of Wales, and continued to act as the Duke's legal adviser after his abdication. The visit which he mentioned had been to the Château de la Crosse, where the Duke and Duchess were living when war broke out.

Monckton's fragment of autobiography continues:[2]

I often used to think, as I walked behind the Harcourt Buildings [in the Temple] on my way to Chambers, how much of my life was contained in the place. By 1939 for 20 years with a few very brief interludes I had spent the greater part of each working day and a good deal of many nights and of Sunday[s] there and, once I had built up my position at the Bar, I thoroughly enjoyed the life, though it was often too exacting.

I enjoyed the art of advocacy in all its stages – not only in presenting a case but the preparation (with wise and faithful devils like Colin Pearson* and Brian McKenna†) of the argument. I enjoyed advising clients, understanding and entering into their troubles, trying to win their confidence and give them the best advice and wisest counsel I could. And I had the good fortune to be consulted by a great variety. Many members of the Royal Family [including Princess Helena Victoria, Princess Marie Louise, and] a King [Edward VIII] consulted me in my Chambers, an Archbishop, Oxford University (whose standing counsel I became in 1938), the main line railway companies (whose generous retainers I held for 10 years), Embassies (including the German), stars, cricketers, County Cricket Clubs, statesmen, trade unions, local authorities, priests and crooks, police and criminals, saints and sinners, men of all colours and races, black, white and yellow, men who paid large fees and men who could pay none – all of them came to Harcourt Buildings and they all contributed to my life and my experience and I made fast friends of many of them.

But the chief joy of my life was my friendships with the Bench and Bar, and that odd but delightful race, the barristers' clerks – friendships frank and free with no jealousy and with nothing kept back. And among all these friendships none was dearer to me or more intimate than that with Stafford Cripps, especially in my last few years. I was constantly against him before all kinds of tribunals, up to the House of Lords. I learnt to respect him as far and away the best equipped and most formidable advocate of the day and he used to tell others that he did not like being against me – not (as I could have wished) for fear of my skill – but because he liked me too much! But it was good fun being against him as we never suspected each other of descending to the lower arts; we never tried to catch each other; we exchanged overnight the authorities we were going to quote the next day: and we satisfactorily helped one another to avoid mistakes in fact and law.

As soon as war was declared I went round to Stafford's chambers and discussed what was to be done. He was clear that we must both give up practice which, he said, had become 'irrelevant'. The war struck me as right, and the argument as conclusive, so we both gave up the Bar forthwith. I kept in touch with him and was later instrumental in bringing about his appointment as our Ambassador in Moscow. For I persuaded Lord Halifax

* Colin (Lord) Pearson (1899–1980) became a High Court judge and a Law Lord.
† Sir Brian McKenna (b.1905) was a High Court judge in the Queen's Bench division from 1961–1977.

[the Foreign Secretary] to ask him and me to dine in Lady Halifax's rooms in the Dorchester, and while I was happily engaged in conversation with Lady Halifax, Cripps and Halifax gradually thawed to each other and Halifax began to see that I was right in respecting and trusting Stafford.*

These words were written in the first year of the Second World War, when Walter Monckton was Director of News and Censorship at the Ministry of Information. Many other duties and offices lay ahead of him: Paymaster-General, Minister of Labour and National Service, Minister of Defence, a Viscountcy, Chairmanship of the Advisory Commission on Central Africa, and finally, for most of the last seven years of his life, Chairmanship both of the Midland Bank and of the Iraq Petroleum Company. As for his account of the abdication of King Edward VIII: he was unwilling that it should be published during his lifetime; and although parts of it are quoted in the following pages, as a whole it remains under restriction.

2

The Moncktons derived from an ancient and vigorous Yorkshire family, the lords of Monkton (now Nun-Monkton) in the West Riding of that county. It was in 1619, on becoming Rector of Hayes, that the Reverend Christopher Monketon founded the Kentish branch of the family from which Walter Monckton was descended. These Kentish Moncktons – their name acquired its 'c' in the 1700s – were respectable and well-to-do, providing a succession of clergy, surgeons, physicians, solicitors, mill-owners and the like. Christopher's son John was Vicar of Brenchley, a parish with a Saxon church where he held the living for 57 years, until his death in 1709 at the age of 89. John's son Timothy, the first Monckton surgeon of Brenchley, built a mansion in 1740 which, in honour of Admiral Vernon's capture of Porto Bello from the Spaniards in that year, was named Porto Bello House. The next Monckton of some distinction was Timothy's great-great-grandson Walter Monckton (1829–1900), a successful businessman

---

* Sir Stafford Cripps (1889–1952) was appointed Ambassador to Russia in May 1940 shortly after Churchill had become Prime Minister. He had previously visited Moscow at Halifax's instigation, being strongly in favour of improving Anglo-Soviet relations. He served in Russia for two years during the War and subsequently filled several political offices including that of Chancellor of the Exchequer in the first two post-war Labour Governments.

who owned or had interests in three paper-mills: the Basted near Borough Green, the Medway in Maidstone and above all the Roughway near Tonbridge, which had a lucrative contract to supply the Government with stamp paper. Outside business hours, Walter was active as Poor Law Guardian, magistrate, churchwarden, and President of the local Conservative association. He also had six daughters and seven sons, of whom the fifth, Frank William, was to become father of the subject of this book.[3]

Frank, an officer in the Militia, and later a Kent County Councillor, was married in 1890 to Dora Golding, a shrewd, kind-hearted woman from a well-established family with substantial farming interests. Together they set up home in Reed House, Plaxtol; and less than a year later, on 17 January 1891, their first child was born: Walter Turner Monckton, the future Viscount Monckton of Brenchley. Named Walter after his prosperous grandfather, and Turner after his grandfather's friend and partner in the Roughway mill, he was brought up at the centre of a happy and devoted family. Reed House, his birthplace, was an attractive and up-to-date grey-brick building set in the heart of the countryside, just large enough to have a billiard room, and embellished with a fine stone porch and a tower. When Walter was two years old he was joined by a sister, Dora, who was always to find him 'the kindest person in the world';[4] and when he was seven his brother Leslie was born. Two years later, in 1900, when their grandfather Walter died, they all moved into Ightham Warren, a former farmhouse which the old man had greatly extended and improved. In the meantime Frank had joined the family business, which he carried on until his death in 1924, when Ightham Warren was sold. By then Walter and Dora had houses of their own while Leslie, who had remained a bachelor, went to live in a nearby cottage.

Family life continued happily both at Reed House and later at Ightham Warren. On the surface father Frank was a strict disciplinarian: 'If I say so, it is so,' he would tell his children, 'if it is so or not!' But he had a warm heart, and Walter and the other two children adored him, as did their gentle mother. Neither Frank nor Dora rode, but at Reed House they employed grooms to look after two horses and several ponies: so it was a prosperous household, like many others in the country at the turn of the century; and with the move to Ightham Warren the children had the added benefit of 12 acres of grounds whose features included a vast lawn, great banks of rhododendrons, and many specimen trees, not to mention a tennis court.

When he was seven, in the autumn of 1898, Walter was sent to a preparatory school, The Knoll, Woburn Sands. Fortunately the headmaster, Mr E. F. M. Miller, was a clever and kindly man who would not tolerate any bullying; and he very soon formed a good opinion of his new pupil. 'I must just write a line to say how very pleased we are with your little boy,' Miller wrote to Walter's father on 21 December 1898. 'He is a capital little fellow, and I venture to predict he will do us all credit some day.'[5] Walter was never homesick, and showed from the first a quite exceptional ability to get on well with his fellow pupils. 'It would be impossible to speak too highly of him,' Miller wrote again to his father. Later he would add: 'I feel every term what a power of good his influence is. The example he sets of diligence and loyalty is invaluable.'

Walter's fondest recreations were riding and cricket, the latter becoming a major passion of his life. He was also careful with his pocket-money. 'I am sorry to say I had to get a new cap because mine was shabby,' he wrote in one letter to his father. 'When we go away to matches we have to look smart.'[6] In the autumn of 1903, when he was twelve-and-a-half years old, he became head boy at The Knoll: 'He makes a capital head boy,' wrote Miller, 'and is always to be trusted.' And in August 1904, when the time came for Walter to leave, Miller wrote that: 'It would be impossible to speak too highly of his five years here. We have never had a better boy.'[7]

Their father, for no particular reason, had decided that both Walter and Leslie should go to Harrow. Walter had been anxious to remain at The Knoll for a further period so that he could get a 'really good scholarship to Harrow', but his father did not agree, and so in September 1904 he entered Harrow where the charges in those days were £60 a year all found.

Before he left home for Harrow, Mr J. G. Moss, to whose house, Church Hill, he had been assigned, wrote to his father:[8]

> I should be glad, if some time before he comes, you will take an opportunity of warning him of the moral dangers of a large Public School. I shall speak to him myself but I like to know I have your support in this matter.

No doubt the housemaster was thinking of such dangers as homosexuality, women and drink, towards any of which a thirteen-year-old boy might be tempted. No doubt, too, Frank Monckton spoke to his son in the sense desired.

'I well remember my first day at Harrow,' Walter said afterwards. 'I felt a forlorn figure when my mother and father left me with JGM – Mr Moss, my Housemaster. The first boy to whom I was introduced was destined to become one of my greatest friends, and I shared a room with him for my first year, G. E. V. Crutchley, the great Harrow, Oxford and Middlesex cricketer.' The evening he arrived at the school, Walter recalled strolling down from Moss's house past Bill Yard, where the school roll call took place, to Stevens, a tailor opposite the headmaster's, to buy a school straw hat. 'I chose for myself in my ignorance and without hesitation a splendid straw, only to learn to my dismay that these could only be worn by cricket Flannels [members of the Harrow 1st XI]. The tailor said – and thank God, in this he was a prophet – that probably I should be able to wear one before I left.'[9]

As at The Knoll, Walter appears to have been a model pupil; and unlike Winston Churchill fifteen years before, he was never 'swished'. He began his studies in the oldest building in the school, dating from 1608, the famous Fourth Form room, the walls of which bore such names as Lord Byron, Robert Peel, R. B. Sheridan and Henry John Temple (later Lord Palmerston) carved by their owners. Also near Moss's house was Speech Room, a delightfully pillared theatre, with its semicircular tiers of seats facing a stage above which hung many colourful banners. It was here that Harrovians sung their famous school songs, of which the most celebrated, *Forty Years On*, was known as Harrow's National Anthem. Incidentally, the name of the town, Harrow-on-the-Hill, with which the school is more or less intermingled, was derived from its setting on an isolated hill overlooking London. It was an ancient settlement; and on the very summit ofthat hill stood St Mary's Church, said to have been founded by Lanfranc, created Archbishop of Canterbury by William the Conqueror.

The headmaster, the Rev. Dr Joseph Wood, previously headmaster of Tonbridge, was a distinguished but elderly classicist implacably opposed to most of the curricular changes which were then beginning to permeate the educational establishment. His famous predecessor, the Rev. J. E. C. Welldon, had been only 31 when he became headmaster; while Dr Wood was already 56 on his appointment, six years before Walter Monckton entered the school. The period was a bad patch in the school's history, since Dr Wood became an increasingly remote figure, and allowed school discipline to become lax. As a result, he presided over a decline in the number of boys from 650 to 500, and several boarding houses had to close. Moss, by contrast, was a most popular and successful housemaster; and although he too was a classical scholar, he was fond of games, and was highly regarded by the boys under his care.

Walter's progress was characteristic. Within four years he had risen to be not only an effective and popular head of his house, but also a school monitor and a respected member of the sixth form, in which he had been promoted to become one of 'The Twelve', an exclusive group of classical scholars who were taught solely by the senior classics master and the headmaster. It was during this period that Walter won an Exhibition in Classics tenable at Hertford College, Oxford. He also won school prizes for fencing, recitation and 'sound learning'. Yet he was neither priggish nor conceited, making many friends, of whom the closest was perhaps Harold Alexander, later to become Field-Marshal Viscount Alexander of Tunis. Both Walter and Harold were elected to the 1st Cricket XI in 1910, thus receiving their 'flannels'.

Walter's worst ordeal at cricket occurred during the famous 1910 Eton and Harrow match, played at Lord's, and subsequently known as 'Fowler's Match' from the name of the Eton captain Bob Fowler. Eton had 'followed on', and the Harrow XI, undefeated all season, needed only 55 runs to win. At that stage no one on either side doubted a Harrow victory. However, Fowler did marvels with his bowling, and soon had four wickets down for only 21 runs. It was now Walter Monckton's turn to bat, and even at that stage it seemed almost impossible for Harrow to lose. However, Fowler clean-bowled Walter with his second ball, which was a slow full pitch, and Walter shame-facedly made his long walk back to the pavilion.

Thereafter the Harrow wickets fell in rapid succession. With 23 runs still needed to win, Harrow's last two in were Alexander and O. B. Graham. The excitement was intense, and the cheering which followed each ball could be heard as far away as Paddington Station and London Zoo. But the Harrovians had only secured a further thirteen runs when Alexander was caught in the slips, leaving Eton the winners by nine runs.

'As Walter is leaving this term,' his housemaster wrote to his father on 1 August 1910, 'I feel I must write a few lines to tell you how sorry I am to lose him. To me personally he has been of the greatest assistance in the house, and his influence in the school has been considerable and has always been used in the right direction. It has been a great comfort to me to have such a trustworthy boy to help me. I feel sure you will be satisfied with him and that he is certain to get on well in whatever position he may be placed.'[10]

A few days later Walter Monckton said goodbye to Mr Moss. He never forgot his years at Harrow-on-the-Hill, and the songs which to him formed the essence of the school. Looking back many years later he wrote:[11]

The living breath of the Hill is in the Harrow songs. John Farmer* and Edward Bowen† caught from Harrow Hill the inspiration which the Psalmist drew from the hills that stand above Jerusalem. The life of the Hill is seen to rest on the foundation of manly love for the place, and all it stands for. In the days of the great Headmasterships‡ of the last century, the house was established, and still today it is well with the Hill.

3

Walter Monckton did not go up to Oxford as a Classics Exhibitioner at Hertford College, as he was entitled to do. Instead, in the Michaelmas term of 1910, he entered Balliol College as a Commoner. Why Balliol was chosen is not clear. It may well have been due to the influence of the Harrow headmaster, Dr Wood, who was an old Balliol man and may have considered Balliol a more intellectual institution than Hertford, as indeed it was. At all events Walter found on reaching Balliol that his surname was well known through his cousin Lionel Monckton, an extremely popular composer who had written the scores of *Our Miss Gibbs, The Quaker Girl*, and other musical comedies staged at the Gaiety Theatre, and starring his wife Gertie Millar, one of the most beautiful of the so-called Gaiety Girls.§ He also composed the music for *The Arcadians*, which began its long run when Walter was still at Oxford.

At Balliol Walter was allotted rooms on Staircase XIV, where he had the services of Geordie Bliss, said to be one of the best of the 'scouts', as these college servants were called. Walter was to spend four years as a member of Balliol, which in his time boasted the most brilliant collection of undergraduates in the university, including such outstanding individuals as Ronald Knox, Cyril Asquith, Aldous Huxley, Michael Sadleir, Philip Guedella – of whom much was

* John Farmer (1835–1901) was music teacher at the school from 1864 to 1885 when he migrated to Balliol College, Oxford, where he was organist for the rest of his life. He composed many of the Harrow school songs.

† Ernest Edward Bowen (1836–1901), who was a housemaster and pioneer of sports and games, wrote the words of many of the school songs, including the celebrated *Forty Years On*.

‡ The leading headmasters of the nineteenth century were Charles Vaughan, Montagu Butler and J. E. C. Welldon.

§ After Lionel Monckton's death in 1924, Gertie Millar, whose father was a Bradford mill worker, married the 2nd Earl of Dudley. She died in 1952.

expected (though he was later outshone by Harold Macmillan as a politician, and by L. B. Namier as an historian) – and Julian Grenfell, the future soldier-poet whose most famous poem, *Into Battle*, would be published in *The Times* in 1915 on the very day that he died of wounds in France.

The dons were equally distinguished; and Walter became particularly attached to two of them: the chaplain Neville Talbot, a delightful character who at six feet six inches not only looked larger than life, but behaved at times with a robust eccentricity; and Francis Urquhart, known affectionately as 'Sligger', a sociable history tutor and incidentally a Catholic, who entertained the undergraduates in his rooms and took them on reading parties to the Chamonix Valley in the Alps below Mont Blanc.* It was under their influence that Walter deepened his religious life, becoming an enthusiastic Anglo-Catholic; and it was in their company that he formed or developed several close friendships, including that with Neville Talbot's brother Gilbert, a Christ Church man after whom Walter was to name his only son; and Victor Mallet, with whom he went on the Sligger's reading parties.

Although not considered to be in the first rank intellectually, Walter's gift for friendship made him extraordinarily popular; and his interests were manifold: cricket and football, both of which he played for the college; membership of the Cavalry Squadron of the Officers' Training Corps; hunting – he did not keep a horse, but either used a hireling or was mounted by a rich contemporary like Fred Lawson (later Lord Burnham); membership of the Annandale Society, which held occasional riotous parties in the Bullingdon Rooms; and membership of the Union.

Walter Monckton joined the Union, that famous club and debating society, in his first term, when Guedella held the office of Librarian.[12] The custom was (as it still is) for the names both of the leading speakers and of any distinguished speakers invited to participate to appear 'on the paper', that is, on the notices of debates which were circulated and were visible in the college lodges or entrances. Those who spoke 'on the paper' wore full evening dress; and after their speeches the debate was thrown open to the rank and file of the other undergraduates present, who wore their ordinary clothes. Walter's maiden speech addressed the motion 'That this house would welcome a scheme by which membership of the Officers' Training Corps would be compulsory to resident undergraduates'. Fortunately he was called

---

* Francis Fortescue Urquhart died unmarried in 1934, aged 65. See *The Times* obituary 19 September 1934.

shortly after the principal speakers had sat down and the hall was full. Although he spoke from a sheet of notes, he had rehearsed his speech carefully and afterwards was able to copy it out and send it home. It was a considerable success, and was acclaimed as such by the undergraduate journals *Isis* and *Varsity*. On returning to his rooms after the debate, Walter wrote to his father to tell him that he had made 'a real hit', and that he was

> awfully pleased for two reasons; first I was able to get a hearing very early and the House was quite full; and secondly it will be a good start. I shall probably speak again in a fortnight, and if I can keep up tonight's form Guedella says I shall easily 'get on the paper' this term which is quite an honour worth getting.[13]

Monckton was indeed 'on the paper' early in December, when he spoke on a motion welcoming 'some system of Referendum' within the United Kingdom. From then on, his career at the Union was assured. At the end of the summer term he was elected Secretary in succession to his Balliol friend Robin Barrington-Ward, future editor of *The Times*; and he followed Barrington-Ward twice more: in the Michaelmas term of 1911 as Treasurer, and in the summer of 1912 as Librarian. His great chance, however, came on 22 November of that year, when he attended the Presidential Dinner along with two guest speakers: J. H. Campbell, former Attorney-General for Ireland, and later the Irish Lord Chancellor, Lord Glenavy; and Willie Redmond, the Irish Nationalist MP, and brother of the Nationalist leader John.

It fell to Walter Monckton to move 'That in the opinion of this House, Home Rule would be disastrous for Ireland and a danger to the Empire'; and he did it in a speech of such brilliance that in the subsequent election for President of the Union he was returned unopposed. Walter occupied the chair throughout the Hilary term of 1913; and for one debate he invited the Prince of Wales, then a Magdalen undergraduate, to attend. The Prince and the President made a favourable impression upon each other, and this occasion was the beginning of a life-long friendship. The President was already noted for his courteous and yet utterly masterful control of the house; while the Prince was described by an observer as 'small and young-looking even for his years (18) but in other ways quite "grown-up". He is quite intelligent and anxious to do the right thing – but all most naturally and unaffectedly.'[14]

However, Monckton's most remarkable hour in the Union was yet to come. He did not give up speaking after he vacated the chair; and during his successor Gilbert Talbot's Presidency, when Lloyd George, then Chancellor of the Exchequer, was the guest speaker, Walter was 'on the paper' to oppose him. When the moment came, he stood up quite fearlessly and launched a most brilliant attack upon the man who was himself one of the most notable speakers of his day. So impressed was Lloyd George that in his own speech he referred with genuine admiration to the eloquence of his opponent.

In his fourth and final year Walter shared digs with Gilbert Talbot, A. P. Herbert, and two others at 8 Longwall Street, on the edge of Magdalen Deer Park. His academic work had suffered as a result of his outside interests; but although he had only taken a Third in Honour Moderations, his first public examination, in July 1914 he secured a Second Class in Modern History. To the astonishment of most of his friends, July 1914 was also the month in which Walter was married.

Exactly two years before, Walter had become engaged to Mary (known as Polly) Colyer-Fergusson, whose father Thomas was heir to a Scotch baronetcy and whose family, at nearby Ightham Mote in Kent,* he had known since childhood. Both Gilbert Talbot and Walter's Harrovian friend Eric Long (later Viscount Long of Wraxall) were strongly opposed to the marriage, as they were aware that Walter really knew nothing of women, having had no other attachments whatever. Was not Walter's love for Polly merely an idealistic schoolboy romance? It was certainly true, as they later told their son, that Walter and Polly had been 'unofficially engaged when [Walter] was still at Harrow',[15] but the young lovers would not listen to any discouragement, and their marriage duly took place at Ightham Church on 18 July 1914.

The Bishop of Rochester officiated, assisted both by the Rector of Ightham and by Walter's former headmaster Dr Wood, who was now Vice-Dean of Rochester. Eric Long, having done all he could to prevent the marriage, was finally won over and agreed to be best man; while Polly was given away by her father. She was quite a beauty as she appeared in her wedding dress of cream satin, with a wreath

---

* Ightham Mote was a fourteenth-century moated grange with Elizabethan additions which had belonged for many centuries to the Selby family of Berwick. Dorothy, wife of Sir William Selby MP of Ightham Mote, is reputed to have deciphered the anonymous letter warning Lord Monteagle not to attend the opening of Parliament on 5 November 1605, as a 'terrible blow' would befall those present. The letter was delivered to Lord Monteagle with the result that the cellars of the Parliament house were searched and the 'Gunpowder Plot' of Guy Fawkes and his fellow conspirators to blow up the building was discovered. See Richard Church, *Kent* (1948), pp. 243-5

on her head in which orange blossom and white heather had been delightfully intertwined. Five hundred wedding guests attended the reception at Ightham Mote; and the local villagers strewed their path with flowers.

Their honeymoon was spent in Sligger Urquhart's chalet in the Haute-Savoie; but barely a fortnight after their arrival, the Great War began. The young couple immediately returned to England to await the course of events.

4

Pending military service, which he felt he should undertake, Walter decided to make an initial move towards becoming a barrister; although for a time he was uncertain whether this was the right choice, and whether he should not return to Oxford as a tutor before securing an outside teaching post. At length, through his Oxford friend Robin Barrington-Ward, he met Robin's elder brother Fred, who agreed to accept him as a pupil in his chambers at 2 Harcourt Buildings in the Temple. Meanwhile he became a student member of the Inner Temple, where he qualified by eating dinners and sitting for the necessary preliminary examinations. This he did during the next eleven months, being placed in Class III in Roman Law, Class I in Constitutional and Legal History, Class II in Criminal Law and Procedure, and Class II in Real Property and Conveyancing. At the same time he felt that he ought to be directly involved in the war effort, and so he applied to join all three services. At first he was rejected by all three on account of defective eyesight: astonishingly, because it had not in any way impaired his games-playing either as a schoolboy or as an undergraduate, it was discovered that he was almost blind in one eye. Finally in desperation he appealed to his younger brother Leslie and his cousin Lance Monckton, who were both serving in the 4th Battalion of the Queen's Own West Kent Regiment and were training in England at Tilbury Fort, hoping that like them he might be accepted as an officer in this regiment, preferably in the same battalion.

In those days it was possible for a medical officer acting alone to pass a potential recruit as fit for active service; and Leslie and Lance therefore invited both Walter and the MO to lunch with them in the Officers' Mess. It was plain to the MO that despite his handicap Walter was officer material; and once he had been mellowed with sufficient port, he explained to Walter how to pass the sight tests. He should read them with his good eye, memorise them, and then repeat the exercise with his other eye. The result of this flagrant breach of the rules was that Walter was passed into the battalion as a 2nd lieutenant. In the event he decided to use a monocle to improve the sight in his bad eye, a decision which, when combined with his unusually spruce turn-out, gave the wholly false impression, to those who did not know him, that he was a classic example of an aristocratic 'silly ass'.

In view of his passion for anything to do with horses, 2nd Lieutenant Monckton was appointed transport officer when the battalion moved to Tonbridge, not too far away from Ightham Mote for him to see his wife regularly. Before long Monckton had shown such a degree of administrative ability that when a vacancy arose he was promoted captain and appointed adjutant over the heads of several of his fellow officers: a move which caused no bad feeling, as Walter had rapidly become just as popular as he had been at Oxford. Everything was also well at home, where on 3 November 1915 his beloved Polly was safely delivered of a son.

The infant was christened Gilbert Walter Riversdale at a somewhat melancholy ceremony in the Ightham Mote chapel: melancholy because although Polly's brother Riversdale Colyer-Fergusson* was present, the other proposed godfather, Lieutenant Gilbert Talbot, had been killed at the battle of Hooge in Flanders four months previously.

Gilbert Talbot's tragic death had one striking result which is worth mentioning. In December 1915 his brother Neville got together with a Church of England chaplain, the Rev. P. T. B. Clayton (generally known as 'Tubby'), to find a rest house for the troops going to and from the Ypres Salient. Neville and Tubby Clayton found what they wanted at Poperinghe, an empty mansion which they furnished with a chapel, canteen, library and writing room. It was called Talbot House in Gilbert's memory. Tubby Clayton took charge and the place quickly became known as 'Toc H' from the initials TH in Morse signallers' language. After the war, in 1920, Clayton established a second Talbot House in London and so began the Toc H movement, which within two years had 40 branches and, by the outbreak of the Second World War, 11,000 branches in Britain, and a membership of 50,000 worldwide. Capturing the imagination of youth by its call to service and sacrifice, it was a fundamentally Christian movement of

* Riversdale Colyer-Fergusson, four years younger than Polly, was killed in action on 31 July 1917, and was posthumously awarded the Victoria Cross.

an inter-denominational nature, firmly based on the principles of honest thinking, spiritual expression, tolerance and service to others, and eventually it was incorporated by Royal Charter. Significantly, the lamp which became the symbol of Toc H was lit at the Albert Hall in 1923 by Walter Monckton's friend the Prince of Wales.*

During 1916 the 4th Battalion of the Queen's Own West Kent Regiment led a tiresomely peripatetic existence. As part of the 67th Home Counties Division, their role was to remain in England as a defence against enemy invasion; and they spent the year being moved for no apparent reason from one Kentish town to another. In July Walter found himself at Canterbury from where he wrote to Polly on the second anniversary of their wedding: 'I only hope that we shall have fifty years more in front of us even happier than these last two, and much more together.' Unfortunately this turned out to be a forlorn hope. But although Walter was later to have extra-marital affairs with several women, at this period he was punctilious in his fidelity: just as he was to be when on leave from the Western Front. So many other officers at that time enjoyed temporary liaisons in spite of their domestic obligations, feeling, often quite correctly, that it might be their last fling.

The battalion remained in England until 31 May 1917, when at long last they set sail for France. Soon they were encamped at St Nicholas between the towns of Arras and the front line to the east. 'I am out at last,' Walter wrote to his cousin Lionel, the composer,[16]

> and selfishly glad of it. I am Adjutant of our battalion. Like all other Harrovians, when it comes to the pinch your thoughts run straight back to the old school. Mixed up with it for me are Balliol and Gilbert [Talbot] and of course home. With all that behind you it ought to be pretty easy to go through with it. But it doesn't do to be over confident.

The battalion was initially attached to the 9th Division, then holding a sector of the line on the north of the River Scarpe near the St Nicholas camp. To begin with Walter and his fellow-officers were escorted to the front line by officers of the battalion whom they were

---

* It was during a visit by Tubby Clayton to my own public school (Sedbergh) that I heard him recite the lines from Lawrence Binyon's *For the Fallen* that have been quoted so often at Toc H meetings:

> They shall grow not old as we that are left grow old.
> Age shall not weary them, nor the years condemn.
> At the going down of the sun and in the morning
> We will remember them.

to relieve, to see at first-hand the dug-outs, barbed-wire, mud, and all the other features of life in the trenches.

They were fortunate that it was a relatively quiet sector, and when later they brought their own battalion up into the line, there was little fighting to be done. However, the shadow of death was very close; and in the circumstances Walter toyed with the idea of joining the Roman Catholic Church. 'There is a great attraction in going the whole Catholic stunt,' he wrote to Polly, '– then it is all over with you – nothing left to decide.' And to the Rev. Lionel Ford, the headmaster of his old school, he wrote on 17 June 1917:[17]

> Your inspiration has got to come in the last resort from Jesus Christ, and all the difficulty I have about getting religion sufficiently *personal* is gradually going away out here . . . No long faces and black clothes but a jolly buoyant devotion in these little smashed churches, and smiling padres . . . It has got all the humanity and sense of continuity of the Catholic Church.

At about the same time he sent his father an account of what he was doing in the battalion:

> . . . writing orders and messages at all hours of the day and night when I am not reading them, and being continuously on the telephone – with occasional trips round the line which, when you get used to the shells, are not as bad as I expected, but of course you don't really ever get used to the shells. But the gift of sleep is everything; I sleep in all positions, actually at the telephone sometimes when waiting for a call; in a dug-out and during shell fire; and at every possible moment, day or night, rats or no rats.

Only once did he report sick, due to the common complaint of nervous exhaustion, when he spent a week or two in a hospital behind the lines. 'He was not a robust man,' said his batman Charles Munn. 'He did not smoke or drink much, and used to be a bit of a wreck after a rowdy night with the officers. He was stronger in determination than in body. He was highly strung but did not normally show any sign of nerves. He never complained of feeling ill except from hay fever, from which he suffered abominably in the summer.'[18] As for his illnesses, he recovered quickly; and in October, after the battalion had been moved north to the Ypres Salient, he wrote to Polly that he had never felt so well. 'I am afraid I must be one of the monsters who thrive on war,' he told her. 'But I hate it all the same!'[19]

Although Walter's battalion took little part in the Third Battle of

Ypres, being in the divisional reserve, they had 30 casualties during the four days they spent in the front line at Poelcapelle. The rest of their time was spent under the direction of the Royal Engineers, in the painful construction of roads through ground which was a morass due to heavy enemy bombardment and torrential rain. The battalion's trials were increased by the use of mustard gas by the enemy; and throughout it all Walter, monocled and immaculate, was indefatigable in his attentions to his men. In November 1917, when the commanding officer went on leave, there was general delight when the popular Captain Monckton was promoted to major and given temporary command of the battalion over the head of another more senior officer. 'He really is wonderful,' wrote his cousin Lance. 'Here he is in command of the battalion and doing it jolly well.'

In January 1918 Walter was summoned back to England, where he spent ten weeks on a course for senior officers at Aldershot. This was an agreeable and somewhat unreal respite from the horrors of the Western Front, during which he was able to see Polly and Gilbert at Ightham, and put his affairs in order against the possibility of being killed on his next tour of duty in France. As it turned out he was lucky, and although he took part in further fighting he emerged from the long conflict unscathed except by a piece of shrapnel which tore his tunic, but otherwise did him little harm.

On his return to Flanders, Walter found that, following an army reorganisation by which each infantry brigade was reduced from four to three battalions, his own battalion had been disbanded, and its members dispersed. Hence Walter found himself posted, as second-in-command of a battalion, to the Duke of Wellington's Own (West Riding) Regiment. At first his elegant appearance told against him; but those who had scoffed at him as a 'dug-out wallah' had to eat their words when he appeared in the trenches on his very first night, addressing each man by name, and inquiring whether he had received his cigarette ration. Derision quickly turned to admiration, and his batman noted that when, not long afterwards, Major Monckton was transferred to the York and Lancaster Regiment, tears were shed by some of the most notorious 'hard cases' in the other ranks.

Walter's new posting was to a pioneer battalion, whose men were quickly won over by his (for an officer) unusual bravery and comradeship. A number of them had come under heavy fire as they were digging in a forward trench, and Walter immediately seized a spade and began helping them. Next, in July 1918, he was appointed as a staff officer to the 17th Division; and he remained with them until the end of the war. Meanwhile he was heartened by the news from home that on 12 September Polly had given birth to a daughter, who was christened Valerie Hamilton, the latter being a Colyer-Fergusson family name. With the Americans now on the allied side, and the Germans known to be seeking peace, Walter was further encouraged by feeling that the war must end soon. It did with the Armistice on 11 November, after which Walter received a telegram from Fred Barrington-Ward in the Temple asking him to return to chambers as soon as possible.

However, Walter had to wait to be demobilised, and in the interim became the divisional educational officer. He had often wondered whether teaching was not his true métier; and this was a role which perfectly suited his gifts. 'The education scheme goes strong,' he wrote to Polly. 'Personally I'm teaching little classes Commercial Law and big ones history. It is very pleasant work.'[20] It was also hard work, since he had to cover so many scattered areas and transport was often a problem. But it was reassuring to find that he could easily hold large audiences on such subjects as 'Richard I', 'The Duke of Wellington' and 'The Value of History'.

Accompanied by his batman, Walter left France for demobilisation in England on 5 February 1918. Before leaving, he took communion at divisional headquarters at Hallincourt with six fellow-officers including Kenneth Warner, a future Bishop, 'to mark the end of our soldiering together'.

Militarily Walter Monckton was a perfectionist. 'He was adored by his men; an absolute perfect gentleman,' said the faithful Munn, who incidentally was later to marry Valerie Monckton's nanny. 'He always had a kind word for everyone; he had no enemy. I never heard a single person say a word against him.' There can be no doubt that he thoroughly deserved the Military Cross which he was awarded three months later.

Chapter 2

The Bar and India

I

A STUDENT'S call to the Bar in those days could be accelerated if he had participated in the Great War. In Walter Monckton's case this meant that he was excused from taking the final examination. As a result he was called to the Bar at the Inner Temple on 14 May 1919. Also called that night were two of Walter's Oxford friends, A. P. (later Sir Alan) Herbert and Harry Strauss. Neither Monckton nor Strauss had read Law at Oxford, whereas Herbert had obtained First Class Honours in Jurisprudence. This induced him to point out that he was the only properly qualified lawyer of the three; and yet he was not going to practise, and indeed he went on to become a successful dramatist instead.

The chambers in 2 Harcourt Buildings were already familiar to Walter; and his return was welcomed, since it was generally believed among its members that the presence of a war veteran would restore their good name. This had suffered during the war years through the activities of Frederick Barrington-Ward, who had not enlisted, but instead had remained in the Temple, where he had acquired an immense junior practice which gave rise to the unpleasant quip that from 1914 to 1918 'the Navy kept Watch, and the Bar kept Ward'. It was said that Barrington-Ward had been much affected by the influence of the head clerk, an *eminence grise* called Colwill. There is no doubt that Barrington-Ward had very considerable talents, but he appears to have been led by Colwill into the grossest extravagance. Problems followed over unpaid income tax; and finally in 1930 (to the great distress of his younger brother Robin), this man who could have risen to be Lord Chancellor ended by accepting the relatively low judicial post of Metropolitan Magistrate.[1]

Walter began by joining the south-eastern circuit and the Kent sessions where, partly because he was locally well known, he made good progress. But what gave his practice its most substantial fillip was the fact that a few months after his call Barrington-Ward 'took silk' (i.e. became a King's Counsel), and much of his former work as a junior fell into Walter's hands. Normally most of this would have gone to the new head of chambers, Herbert du Parcq, later a Lord of Appeal. But du Parcq had given up county-court work, so all that side of the business was dealt with by Walter Monckton, who also undertook any High Court work for which du Parcq was too busy. The result was that in 1921, within two years of his call to the Bar, Walter earned £1,200 in fees.

Walter's most rewarding professional client at this time was the famous solicitor William Charles Crocker, who was impressed by the way in which he argued his cases. One of the most notable of these (though for once Monckton was unsuccessful) occurred in 1923 when a man named McCarthy was charged at Hastings with driving a car so dangerously that several people were injured. McCarthy was convicted by the Hastings magistrate; but the injured parties, in seeking damages, had instructed a firm of solicitors one of whose members turned out to be clerk to the Hastings magistrates. In the circumstances, although there was no suggestion that the clerk had acted at all improperly, an appeal was made to the Lord Chief Justice Lord Hewart, sitting in a divisional court, that the conviction should be quashed. Walter Monckton argued the case for the magistrates; but although he spoke well, the appeal succeeded and McCarthy went unpunished. It was in the hearing of this appeal that the Lord Chief Justice spoke the famous words: 'A long line of cases shows that it is not merely of some importance, but it is of fundamental importance that justice should not only be done but should manifestly and undoubtedly be seen to be done.'[2]

Crocker (who incidentally was McCarthy's solicitor) soon took the view that Walter was undermining his health by working too hard for too little reward, and should insist through his clerk upon a minimum fee for any case in which he was briefed, or any counsel's opinion which he gave. Polly and Walter were then living in a small London house in Cleveland Place, and Crocker spoke to them both. Walter required some convincing but eventually agreed that Crocker was right.[3]

By this time Walter was already doing so well that he had begun to take pupils. One of these was Robert Boothby, who was young enough to have missed the war, and who later became a celebrated politician and broadcaster. During his pupillage Boothby received an offer to join Stanley Baldwin's secretariat, Baldwin then being one of the Conservative leaders after Bonar Law and Curzon. Boothby went to see Walter Monckton in his room and, putting aside the brief on which he was working, Walter listened patiently to what he had to say. When Boothby had finished, Walter remained silent for a minute or two and then said to his pupil: 'I think you have the makings of a good criminal advocate but, unlike mine, your heart is not in the law. It is in politics. Throw your cap over the windmill, and go into politics.' That is what Bob Boothby did; and in the 1924 General Election he was returned as MP for East Aberdeenshire, a seat which he took to become the youngest member of the House of Commons, and which he held for 34 years before going to the Lords.[4]

In 1925 Walter was doing so well in his profession that he and Polly decided to give up their London home in Cleveland Place, and return to Kent. Here they acquired a piece of land on the Fairlawne estate near Ightham belonging to the Cazelet family, of whom the two most distinguished members, both Parliamentarians, were Victor and Thelma. There they built a house which they called Fishponds, taking the name from some nearby ponds which in mediaeval times had belonged to a monastery and where the monks used to catch fish. It was a red-brick house with a splendid view across a valley whose upper slopes were planted with firs, and whose lower slopes were a mass of rhododendrons and silver birches. Stables were built a little later, and then horses were bought to fill them, so that hacking and hunting were freely available to the family.

Meanwhile Walter continued to work extraordinarily hard. Crocker's advice about setting a minimum fee, instead of giving Walter and his family a more relaxed way of life, simply increased their income. It seems probable that the punishing routine which Walter set himself had much to do with personal difficulties in his marriage. By this time, sadly, Walter seems to have had a much more affectionate relationship with his daughter Valerie than with his wife. It was Valerie, for example, who accompanied him to nearby Kemsing station each morning, driven by their chauffeur Johnson, in time to catch the eight o'clock train for London. Walter would return at seven o'clock in the evening, often looking and sounding utterly worn out; but would nevertheless withdraw to his study after dinner, with only a tin of biscuits to sustain him while he worked into the early hours, thus incidentally avoiding whatever sexual difficulties were now poisoning his married life. It was often the same on Saturdays and Sundays, though Walter would sometimes try to get a day's hunting on Saturdays with the West Kent. Hunting had become his principal recreation, and Polly also hunted for a time; but then, much to Walter's disappointment, she withdrew altogether from this (to him) important area of his life.

Work went on; and as a junior Walter was naturally led to important cases by King's Counsel. Perhaps the most important of these KCs was Sir John Simon, a former Liberal law officer, who had returned to the Bar after a brief period as Home Secretary under Asquith in the war. Monckton wrote of him:[5]

> I think his mind was about the most perfect dialectical machine I ever came across. It is often said of him that he is inhuman and the hackneyed story is told of how he will greet you by your Christian name one day and not know you the next. I have the best of reasons for saying that he is capable of deep and personal sympathy: indeed no-one who has read his book about his mother would doubt it.* Still the fact remains that he seems a cool calculating machine rather than a man of flesh and blood. It is perhaps for this reason that, good as he was in all his cases, his greatest forensic achievements were in the highest courts.

Walter went on to give two examples of his being led by Simon, one in the Judicial Committee of the Privy Council and the other in the House of Lords. The first concerned the Labrador boundary dispute between Newfoundland and Canada; and the second whether or not a cricketer should be taxed on his benefit match.

The first was heard in November 1926. Besides Monckton, Simon had two other silks with him, Barrington-Ward and the Hon. W. J. Higgins, Attorney-General for Newfoundland. 'I spent a week or two with Simon at his house at Fritwell [in Oxfordshire] in the August before,' Monckton wrote afterwards. 'I had been working on the case for something like 6 years and I was horrified to find that he had hardly a bowing acquaintance with it. I still remember the long table in the room in which he worked and his opening a notebook and saying "Now tell me all about it".'

The point at issue was the precise definition of what area of land was meant by the words 'the coast of Labrador', as they appeared in a Commission of 1763 from the British Government to the Governor of Newfoundland. At that time Newfoundland itself had hardly been explored, and its only importance was as a naval base for fishing expeditions to the coast of Labrador, which was therefore claimed by Britain as an integral part of the Newfoundland territory. More recently

---

* *Portrait of My Mother* (1937), originally extracted in *The Times*.

there had been a long-running dispute between Newfoundland, which argued that 'the coast of Labrador' extended to the watershed – which at one point took it some 500 miles from the sea – and Canada, which claimed that Labrador formed part of the province of Quebec. Everything had to be investigated as far as the headwaters of the great Hamilton (now the Churchill) river; and the question depended (among other things) upon the interpretation of various letters patent, acts of Parliament and royal proclamations from 1763 onwards. 'Great volumes of documentary evidence were prepared,' Monckton wrote afterwards.[6]

I did what I could to put as much information as I had into Simon's mind and notebook, but when we got to consultations in October the Newfoundlanders were appalled that he did not seem to have a more complete knowledge of the case, and I well remember their urging Sir Clive Burn, then a partner in the firm of solicitors handling the case, to get an adjournment, because they thought that Simon could not conduct the case. When the case was over and before the decision was made known they were the first to appreciate the magnificence of his performance. Both his opening and closing speeches were masterly.

To Colin Pearson and me, who were the Juniors, he sometimes seemed a very hard taskmaster. It wasn't the work in Court that troubled us, but what we had to do between the rising of the Court at 4 and its meeting the next morning at 10.30. Several times we had scarcely an hour in bed but we often told each other that we really couldn't complain since Simon worked himself equally hard, though of course not for the same hours because he had to be addressing the Court. His opening speech lasted four days. At the end of the first two days in which he had delighted our supporters, he horrified me by saying as he left the rostrum: 'I have come to the end of the bit I know.' But by that time he had more background and resources from which to draw. We had a long night session before he resumed next day, and though I felt a bit anxious, I grew to understand that he must really have meant: 'I have come to the end of the bit I know well enough' . . .

At the end of the case he gave a good example of his apparent inhumanity. The case finished just before lunch and Clive Burn, Barrington-Ward and I, and I think Pearson, decided with relief to go off and celebrate in a joyful lunch. We were debating whether to ask Simon to join us when we heard him say to his clerk: 'What is the next thing, Ronald?' and we were deterred.

The case had lasted fourteen days, after which the Judicial Committee reserved their judgment for over three months. Then, at last, the decision was given in favour of Newfoundland by the Lord Chancellor, Lord Cave, supported by Lords Haldane and Finlay.[7]

The case in which Simon led Monckton in the House of Lords was *Seymour v. Reed* in 1927, which decided that a cricketer should not be taxed on his benefit match. 'It was touch-and-go,' said Walter;[8]

I had won it before Mr Justice Rowlett, but had lost it later in the Court of Appeal. There were obvious difficulties, for the Easter offerings of Rectors of Parishes are liable to tax. I think I had been selected probably more for my interest in Kent cricket, including of course Jim Seymour, the appellant, than for my familiarity with income tax law.

Simon had a prodigious knowledge of cricket statistics and on the morning of the hearing he came to me, not to consider what authorities to cite, but to know how many cricketers had had more than one benefit. I told him (as the fact then was) that I only knew of Hobbs except that there was some talk of a second for Frank Woolley. Simon opened the case by saying that it was a lovely May morning. Their Lordships might have spent it at the Oval watching the only cricketer who in the history of the game had been awarded a second benefit. How different this was from the annual Easter offerings of a parson!

The House of Lords held by a majority of four to one – Lord Chancellor Cave and Lords Dunedin, Phillimore and Carson, with Lord Atkinson dissenting – that the appellant James Seymour 'was not to be assessable in respect of this sum inasmuch as it was a personal gift and not a profit or perquisite arising from his employment'.[9]

The other great advocate besides Simon whom Walter admired, with whom he appeared in one case, and from whom he learned a great deal, was Sir Edward (Lord) Carson, the Irish Unionist leader. The case was a libel action brought by Alexander Lyle-Samuel, a Liberal MP, against one of Odham's newspapers. Carson appeared for the plaintiff in one of his last cases, as a KC; while Patrick Hastings represented the newspaper in one of his first; and Walter Monckton had a watching brief for another journal which might have been implicated. 'Carson's great quality,' Walter wrote of him,[10]

lay in the simplicity and clarity with which he put the points in his cases.

He was not an intellectual giant, like Simon, but with great natural gifts, a fine presence, a magnificent voice, great courage and wide sympathy and understanding, he combined a thoroughness and single-mindedness which made him master of his cases. He selected his cases and was not one of those, of whom there were many in my young days, who took a great number of cases at the same time. It was his practice to be in court throughout the case.

I learned from him that in a jury case one should be in court until the verdict has been given. Not only was he simpler than most advocates, both in his questions and his speeches, but he was much shorter.

Carson and Simon, often pitted against each other, were perhaps the greatest members of the Bar in their time, and Monckton was fortunate in having known them both, although Carson was then past his prime.

2

In 1929 Walter Monckton was led by Norman Birkett in an interesting and important libel action which went up to the House of Lords and became a leading case in the law of defamation. This was the case in which Mr Cyril Tolley, the amateur golf champion, sued J. S. Fry and Sons Ltd, the well-known firm of chocolate manufacturers, in respect of an advertisement inserted by the firm in 64 newspapers, including the *Daily Mail* and the *Daily Sketch*, which Tolley claimed had infringed his amateur status as a golfer.[11]

The advertisement showed the champion swinging his golf club with a packet of Fry's chocolate protruding from his pocket, while the caddy was looking on, and holding up a second packet. Beneath this caricature was the following limerick:

The caddy to Tolley said: 'Oh, Sir!
Good shot, Sir, that ball see it go, Sir.
   My word, how it flies
   Like a Cartet of Fry's
They're handy, they're good, and priced low, Sir.'

Cyril Tolley alleged that the advertisement was libellous, since it gave the clear impression that he had permitted a picture of himself to be used in order to advertise Fry's chocolate, presumably for some financial consideration; and that he had therefore destroyed his reputation as an amateur golfer.

The defendants, for whom Birkett and Monckton appeared, admitted publication, but disputed Tolley's interpretation of the advertisement, and submitted that the words of the limerick could not possibly be held to be libellous. The plaintiff was represented by Rayner Goddard QC (later Lord Goddard, Lord Chief Justice), and H. M. Giveen; and the trial took place in the King's Bench Division of the High Court, before Mr Justice Acton and a common jury.

Questioned by Birkett in cross-examination, Tolley admitted that other well-known people had been caricatured in similar advertisements, including several Cabinet Ministers. 'But they are professionals,' was the amateur champion's comment when their names were put to him.

'You don't complain of the drawing, do you?' asked Birkett.

'It is not a particularly good swing,' the plaintiff answered, 'and I don't think it is a particularly good limerick. The presence of a packet of chocolate in my pocket insinuates that I chew chocolate when I play golf!'

'That is hardly libellous,' Birkett rejoined. 'It has been made quite plain, I hope, that you received no payment, were not consulted, and gave no approval whatever to this cartoon. It is well that that should come from the defendants.'

When the case for Tolley had been concluded, Birkett suggested that the only action which it might have been reasonable to bring against J. S. Fry and Sons would have been for the unauthorised use of Tolley's name. It was wrong, he argued, to pretend that any libel had been perpetrated. Despite Birkett's arguments, the judge ruled that there was a case to answer. The matter was therefore put to the jury, who very rapidly found in favour of Tolley, awarding him £1,000 in damages.

When the defendants appealed to the Court of Appeal, this decision was reversed. All three members of the Court, Lord Justices Greer, Slessor and Scrutton, were agreed that the damages were too great; and two of them (with Lord Justice Scrutton dissenting) declared that the advertisement was not *prima facie* defamatory.

However, Tolley subsequently took the case to the House of Lords, which found for him by a majority of four to one. Lord Dunedin, in the majority, declared:

> I find that the caricature of the plaintiff, innocent in itself as a caricature, is so to speak embedded in an advertisement . . . The inference that is suggested is that his consent was either given gratuitously or for a consideration for its appearance . . . It seems to me that all this is within the province of a jury to determine. The idea of an inference in the circumstances is not so extravagant as to compel a Judge to say it was so beside the mark that no jury ought to be allowed to consider it.

Thus it was held that language or conduct which in its natural or ordinary meaning is innocuous may be rendered defamatory by reason of the special circumstances in which it was published. Accordingly a new trial limited to the assessment of damages was ordered; but rather than undergo further litigation, Cyril Tolley accepted his costs together with a settlement of £500.

Meanwhile Walter Monckton had applied for silk; and this was granted in February 1930 by the Labour Lord Chancellor Lord Sankey; so that by the time the Tolley case reached the House of Lords, Walter was already a King's Counsel. To have taken silk less than 11 years after being called to the Bar was no mean achievement; and this was recognised when 30 of Walter's pupils, past and present, entertained him to dinner in March at the Isola Bella Restaurant.

Walter Monckton's first important case as a silk concerned the role of the police in making arrests.[12] Here, one Fred Russell had used false pretences to extract £150 from an Oldham tradesman. The police mistakenly arrested Fisher, a man who had a number of convictions for obtaining money in a similar manner, and kept him incarcerated for several hours in the local police station. On being released, Fisher reckoned that his treatment amounted to false imprisonment, and he sued the Oldham Corporation for damages, on the grounds that they were the masters of the police who had arrested him, and were legally responsible for anything which their servants had done in the normal pursuance of their duties.

The case was tried before Mr Justice McCardie, with Fisher being represented by Mr Tristram Beresford, then a junior; and the Oldham Corporation by Walter Monckton and by Roland Oliver, who was later a High Court judge. Beresford argued that the Corporation, through its watch committee, not only paid the police, but had so many powers over them, including those of appointment, regulation, and dismissal, that they were clearly master and servants. Walter Monckton and Roland Oliver, on the other hand, argued that in common law police constables were not servants of the local authority in whose area they served, but of the Sovereign. Furthermore, corporations had no legal liability for the mistakes of their constables, who acted on their own authority, usually under warrant or statutory powers.

The judge upheld Monckton's arguments. If the police, in arresting Mr Fisher, had been acting as servants of the Oldham Corporation, then (he observed) it would mean that the Corporation would be in complete control of all arrests and prosecutions. That would involve a serious constitutional change, fraught with danger. Mr Justice McCardie therefore gave judgment for the Oldham Corporation; and this case established the general principle that police constables, though appointed by the watch committee of a borough, are not the servants of that borough; and that the borough cannot therefore be sued in respect of wrongs committed by officers of the borough police force.

Perhaps the most notorious case in which Walter Monckton was involved at this period – certainly the one which attracted the maximum publicity – was the 1932 case in which a bishop prosecuted a clergyman in his diocese for immorality. The bishop was the Right Rev. Bertram Pollack, KCVO, Bishop of Norwich and former headmaster of Wellington College. The cleric was the Rev. Harold Davidson, Rector of Stiffkey in Norfolk. The trial was presided over by Mr K. Keppel North, the Chancellor of the diocese; Mr R. F. Levy and two other juniors appeared for the rector; and the bishop was represented by the same silks as had appeared in the Fisher case, Roland Oliver and Walter Monckton. Instead of being heard in Norfolk, as might have been expected, the case was transferred by mutual consent to London, since 68 out of the 70 witnesses to be called lived in the capital.[13]

Davidson was an eccentric character who for years had been known as the 'Prostitutes' Padre' because of his interest in 'fallen women'. He claimed to have been inspired by Jesus Christ's relationship with the harlot whom he met in Simon the Apostle's house: she was the one who anointed Jesus's feet with oil, and who traditionally (but almost certainly incorrectly) was identified with Mary Magdalen, the woman who had been healed of evil spirits, witnessed the Crucifixion, and later found the empty tomb.

The rector, aged 57, was a married man with five children. Stiffkey, near Blakeney and about a mile from the east coast, was a small parish with not more than 500 parishioners; and Davidson only ministered to them at weekends. The rest of the week he spent in London, a practice he had carried on for many years, apparently after receiving permission from the Archbishop of Canterbury to work there on charitable causes. The Stiffkey living yielded £800 a year, in those days a handsome income; but the rector had been bankrupt since 1925, so that his annual income was now less than £400. Between 1927 and 1931 he received additional income from the Queen Anne's Bounty Fund, some £1,227 in all, but of this £650 went to the Official Receiver.

Before his ordination in 1903, Davidson had been an actor, and among other parts had played the curate in the popular comedy *Charley's Aunt*. During the Great War he had served as a padre in the Navy, and was in the same ship as Commander Oliver Locker-Lampson RN, whom he asked to give evidence on his behalf.

'I have known him for some time and he was in a ship with me in the war as a chaplain,' Locker-Lampson wrote to the Bishop of Norwich. 'If I was to give evidence, he is so far as I know a man of complete sexual morality and no trace of misbehaviour in this connection was evident while I have known him.' However, Locker-Lampson did not wish to give evidence or to be drawn into 'such an unsavoury case' in any way. 'Could I not induce Davidson to give up his living,' Locker-Lampson inquired, 'if the case stopped now and so save money on every side?'

'I am afraid that long ago we made a suggestion to our friend that he should resign his living and submit himself to my judgment,' the Bishop replied. 'This he has refused to do. The future will show whether he was wise or unwise in his decision.'

In the event Davidson was charged with five specific allegations of immorality with women, including prostitutes, under the Clergy Discipline Act of 1892. He denied all the charges completely.

In the case which followed, Roland Oliver conducted most of the prosecution, leaving Walter on the sidelines for much of the time; but it was a fascinating experience. The hub of the case against Davidson was that for many years he had been systematically misbehaving with young women, pursuing, pestering and living with them. As he saw it, his object had been to rescue them from a life of sin and to influence them for good; but according to the prosecution he had in reality been consorting with them for his own self-indulgence.

Evidence was given by a number of girls, by their landladies and by private detectives employed both by the Bishop and by Davidson himself. The issue turned solely upon the credibility of these witnesses, their testimony being largely one of accusation and denial. For instance, Dorothy Burn, an 18-year-old waitress who worked at a Lyons café in the City, swore that Davidson used to visit the café dressed in his clerical clothes and hold her hand, telling her that she was lovely and ought not to be working there 'because I was too good for the job'. He allegedly followed her everywhere, giving her his card and telling her 'Ring me up if you feel lonely. Come out and we will have a good time!' He had also told her that if she wanted to go away for the weekend, she could go to his place at Stiffkey. This led Mr Levy to ask her in cross-examination: 'There could be no harm in going to a clergyman's house where his wife and daughters were living, could there?'

'I don't know,' replied the waitress, raising a laugh. 'I would not like to chance it.'

On the other hand, another witness said that she had known Davidson for 24 years and shared his interest in rescue work, in which she herself had been engaged for over 20 years. He had often kissed her, and also girls in her presence – girls he had brought to her house – but her husband had never objected. Asked about his reputation, she described him as 'a very excellent man, a little eccentric, a little indiscreet, but of the highest moral standing in every possible way'. She added that she had never heard a word said against him, or a breath of scandal.

The rector's sister, Mrs Alice Cox, also spoke on her brother's behalf. 'The whole world,' she declared, 'knows my brother's doings. He never hides anything.' She described how he had often brought girls to her house in the middle of the night and asked her to help them. With one exception, all the girls had been grateful. That exception was Barbara, a loose woman who lived with an Indian. Although Davidson helped her in various ways, she swore that he had tried to seduce her: which according to Davidson was the exact reverse of the truth.

Another girl whom Davidson had helped was Nellie Churchill, who at the time of the trial was in a mental home. However, her landlady told the court that she had found her and Davidson in Nellie's bedroom in the dark. Davidson had excused himself by saying that the gas would not burn, although there was a coin in the slot; but after he had left, the landlady concluded damningly, she had turned the gas on quite easily.

What was to be made of this contradictory evidence? Davidson's counsel said that his client was not an immoral person, but a man who liked to do good and to help his fellow-creatures, befriending girls because they needed more help than boys. And the fact remains that, although Davidson was accused of sexual promiscuity, only one of the 40 girls interviewed by the Bishop's detectives alleged actual immorality, and she afterwards withdrew her statement, swearing an affidavit to that effect. The truth is probably that Davidson was obsessed by sex, but did not indulge in it physically either with any of the girls who were mentioned, or with any of the many others whom he knew. Nevertheless, the Chancellor found him guilty of all five charges and he was sentenced to be defrocked.

The verdict was a terrible shock for Davidson; and before the defrocking ceremony he went to Stiffkey church, despite having promised the bishop to stay away, and struggled with the temporary priest during divine service to the accompaniment of shouts and screams from the congregation. The defrocking ceremony itself took place in Norwich Cathedral; and as the necessary words were intoned by the bishop, who pointed his crozier at Davidson in the nave, the defrocked clergyman declared: 'I am entirely innocent in the sight of God!' Then he knelt in silent prayer.

No longer a cleric, Davidson determined to keep himself in the public eye by whatever means possible, so that he could continue to declare to the public at large that he was innocent. First he exhibited himself on Blackpool pier, where so many spectators paid twopence a time to see him that he was reported to be earning £500 a week. Then he appeared on the stage in various towns, before finally showing himself in a lion's cage at an amusement park in Skegness, preaching and proclaiming his innocence. In his excitement, he trod on a lioness's tail, which caused her mate to maul him before the tamer could rescue him from the cage. Davidson was eventually dragged out bleeding and badly injured, but conscious enough to ask the time. When he was informed that it was 3.30 p.m., he exclaimed characteristically: 'Ah, I'm in time to make the front page in the evening papers!'

He died next day and was buried in Stiffkey churchyard, his funeral being attended by 3,000 mourners. The village blacksmith described him as a good man; while an old fisherman said that he did silly things, but nothing bad. His coffin, surmounted by carnations, bore a card inscribed 'To the memory of our beloved ex-rector'.

3

For some time Walter Monckton had been junior counsel to the Office of Works, the Government department responsible for the maintenance of a vast range of buildings and estates, ranging from the royal palaces and parks – and other official buildings such as the Chequers estate, and embassies and legations abroad – to coastguard stations and Broadmoor lunatic asylum.[14] Then in 1930, the year he took silk, Walter was also appointed Chancellor of the Diocese of Southwell and Recorder of Hythe. 'My congratulations to Hythe,' his ex-pupil D. N. Pritt wrote to him. 'Don't send anybody to prison.'

Being Chancellor considerably increased the strain under which Monckton laboured, involving as it did travelling to out-of-the-way rural parishes to deal with such matters as whether someone should be granted a faculty to set up a gravestone. Walter often travelled by chartered aircraft and was usually accompanied by his private secretary Brian Davidson who was, like himself, an ex-President of the Oxford Union and also a keen fox-hunter. As Davidson later recalled:[15]

Flying then was not the stately business it has since become. We would swoop down on a likely-looking field near to the parish church, circle round to drive the sheep into a corner, and touch down. Then out would step the Chancellor – followed by his private secretary with the tin box containing the full-bottomed wig. The faculty granted or refused, we flew off again. Most times we had the same pilot, a splendid character called Stace. Once we hit an air pocket and lurched violently. It was over a cemetery. Stace turned to his passengers: 'Sways, doesn't she?' he said. 'Just like a woman's hips.' Morale was restored.

No doubt it was Monckton's successful performance of the duties connected with the Office of Works and the Diocese of Southwell, as well as his friendly meeting with the Prince of Wales at Oxford, that facilitated his appointment in 1932 as the latter's Attorney-General. Before vacating his office the previous Attorney-General, Geoffrey Lawrence, who had been made a judge, placed Monckton on a shortlist of possible successors; and, after consultations with the Prince of Wales, Walter was offered the job. 'I need hardly say how gratefully I accept the position,' he replied to the Prince, who had remembered him. 'It is a long time since we were together at Oxford.' The office of Attorney-General to the Prince of Wales was an ancient one which dated back to the middle of the fourteenth century; and it involved giving legal advice to the Duchy of Cornwall, whose Council meetings Walter now began to attend.

Alongside all these tasks the steady flow of Monckton's normal work continued; and it was observed that in his professional life his conduct was consensual rather than antagonistic. Edwin Herbert, later Lord Tangley, a solicitor in the firm of Sydney Morse, first met him in 1928 and, admiring his advocacy, gave him a great many briefs: but not in markedly tough cases. 'Several times at the Parliamentary Bar,' Tangley has recalled, 'I had to tell Walter to go in and start fighting.'[16] It was also recognised that Walter would give up when he realised the judge was against him, preferring not to continue, as other counsel were inclined to do, when he came to regard his client's case as hopeless.

One case which fell into this category was a libel action brought in 1933 by the United Kingdom Advertising Company, which owned an hotel and restaurant called the Thames Riviera on Tagg's Island near Hampton Court, against the printer and publishers of *Reynold's Illustrated News* in respect of an article which had appeared in that journal.[17] The plaintiffs complained of references in the article to 'midnight champagne bathing parties from motor cars' by 'gay mixed parties of men and girls to the more secluded reaches of the Thames'; and to the statement that the 'regular devotees of the all-night parties are those who, still unsatiated in their lust for excitement when

London's West End restaurants close their doors soon after midnight, turn to the Thames Riviera to carry on their amusement'. This article, alleged the plaintiffs, meant that the Thames Riviera was a place frequented by immoral persons where scandalous bathing and dancing scenes took place.

The case was tried in the King's Bench Division of the High Court before Mr Justice Charles and a special jury; and the managing director of the plaintiff company, in giving evidence, strengthened his case by stating that the article had led to a damaging loss of custom.

The defendants, for whom Walter Monckton appeared, admitted that they had published the words complained of, but denied that those words referred to the plaintiffs. Their second line of defence was that if the words did refer to the plaintiffs, then, so far as they consisted of matters of fact, they were true; and so far as they consisted of comment, they were comments on matters of public importance.

However, a police superintendent stationed in the area and called as a witness by the plaintiffs, stated that the Thames Riviera was properly conducted as a pleasure resort, and added that so far as he knew there had been no scandalous parties on the Thames in July 1931.

'If what is in the article were true,' the judge remarked, 'any one of us could have gone down and seen all these things going on.'

'I'm afraid you would have been unlucky, my lord,' replied the witness, raising a laugh.

The defendants were handicapped by the fact that the writer of the article could not give evidence, as he had recently died. *Reynold's News'* news editor attempted to remedy this loss of a key witness by testifying that the writer had gone up and down the river in a motor boat to see things for himself; but he had not known of the hotel, or of such a name.

'But your investigator *must* have known of it,' Mr Justice Charles interjected. 'If he had been up the river, he must have seen the electric signs on both sides of the hotel!'

The witness persisted in his certainty that the investigator had not known of the hotel. Why, he had been proud of the fact that he had coined the phrase 'Thames Riviera', which he did not intend to apply to a particular hotel, but to the area as a whole, as in 'Cornish Riviera'. However, by now it was clear to Walter that the judge was against him; and he felt that the jury was too. He therefore did not press the case further, and his surmise about the jury was correct. The jury found for the plaintiffs and awarded them £1,000 damages, to which the judge added costs, and judgment was entered accordingly.

A curious case in which Walter Monckton was occupied at this period concerned the unlicensed drinking of intoxicating liquor at all hours by members of both Houses of Parliament. The matter was initiated by Walter's Oxford friend A. P. Herbert, not then an MP, who applied for summonses against the Kitchen Committee of the House of Commons on the grounds that they had no legal right to sell alcoholic drinks.[18] Herbert's application was heard by the Chief Metropolitan Magistrate Sir Rollo Graham-Campbell; and Walter (who together with Harry Strauss had agreed to represent Herbert without a fee) spoke for most of one morning: 'a masterly performance', according to Herbert. When Walter sat down, the Chief Magistrate said:

> Mr Monckton, I am very much indebted to you for your interesting and learned argument. Having regard to the fact that in certain circumstances I may have to try this matter, I think it very desirable that I should say no more on this occasion than this, that so far you have not satisfied me that I have jurisdiction to issue the processes for which you ask.

In the event, Sir Rollo did not have to try the case; and when it was finally heard, in December 1934, by Lord Chief Justice Hewart, Mr Justice Avory, and Mr Justice Rigby Swift, Walter was occupied with a railway inquiry which he was unable to leave. In his absence Harry Strauss battled on manfully but unsuccessfully, though he did persuade the court not to award costs against Herbert, whose financial resources were extremely limited. The Lord Chief Justice, permitting himself a smile, hoped that the funds of the Kitchen Committee might be of use; 'and, if not those funds,' he added, 'the matter ultimately may not prove to be beyond the scope of a supplementary estimate'.

Walter often gave professional opinions in cases where he was consulted; and one such opinion from the 1930s should be mentioned, since although it was not officially recorded, he considered if of sufficient importance to mention it in his notes. The case concerned a Mrs Janie Buckley, who lived in a caravan at Bickfield, and who on 14 April 1936 was arrested on a charge of fortune-telling under an old statute, the Vagrancy Act of 1824. She appeared before the magistrates at Cannock, Staffordshire; and since this occurred in the days before the introduction of the modern system of legal aid, she was not represented professionally in court. Her defence was that she was not in Cannock at the time alleged, but was in or about the caravan in Kent; and she asked leave to call a number of local witnesses, including the owner of the land on which her caravan stood, in order to establish her alibi. This was refused, and she was duly convicted and sentenced to three months' imprisonment. She was also refused leave to appeal to the quarter sessions.

Mrs Buckley was a constituent of the Conservative MP Sir Waldron Smithers, who sat for the Chislehurst Division of Kent. He took up her case with a view to her obtaining compensation for false imprisonment, and asked Walter Monckton for his opinion. Walter stated that he was[19]

> unhesitatingly of the opinion that the trial before the magistrates did not dispose of the matter satisfactorily, and had the appeal been heard, it would have succeeded. The misfortune of Mrs Buckley's position is that she has no legal remedy. An action for false imprisonment or malicious prosecution would be bound to fail. Nevertheless I cannot leave the case without expressing frankly my opinion that justice does not appear to have been done to this woman.

The outcome was that an appeal was made to the Home Secretary, then Sir John Simon, and in the circumstances Mrs Buckley was released. Sadly, she had already had to serve more than two months of her prison sentence.

These cases only represent a tiny fraction of the huge volume of work which weighed upon Walter Monckton during these years; a volume which would be substantially increased from the year 1933, when Monckton was to be appointed constitutional adviser to the Indian princes, of whom the foremost was the Nizam of Hyderabad. Monckton's appetite for work continued to be fed by the difficulties of his private life; and to be matched only by his relish for fox-hunting.

The West Kent hunt, to which Walter subscribed, consisted of some 17 square miles of woodland, hill downs and vale country, bounded on the north by the Thames, the south by the Eridge, the east by the Tickham, and the west by the Old Surrey and Burstow hunts. The kennels were at Otford, a picturesque village a few miles north of Sevenoaks. It was an old hunt, partly hunted by the famous John Warde, the so-called Father of Fox-hunting, in the late eighteenth and early nineteenth centuries; and in Walter's time it was enthusiastically supported by farmers, there being 35 couples of hounds. Walter was joint master for the 1932–3 and the 1933–4 seasons, and was later field master for some years.

'I well remember what must have been a unique occasion in February 1935,' he wrote of the time when he had taken up his work as adviser to the Nizam of Hyderabad:[20]

I had been Master of the West Kent Foxhounds in the previous season, and was still Field-Master in 1934–35. A sudden conference was fixed at the India Office at 4 p.m. on a Saturday afternoon . . . at which I and my Junior and instructing solicitor were to represent the Nizam. I was determined not to miss a complete day's hunting and arrived just in time at the India Office for the conference in scarlet with very dirty breeches and boots. The general feeling was that this had not happened before and was not likely to happen again.

Although he wrote about it lightly, hunting had become much more than a relaxing way of escaping from the tensions of both his professional and his private life. Walter Monckton on his horse (like T. E. Lawrence on his motor-bike) was not above hurling his personal message of defiance at the universe, daring it to do its worst; and each time that he survived, his sense of personal worth was temporarily restored. The result was that Monckton's courage out hunting became legendary; and on his death a sporting paper wrote of him:[21]

As a rider to hounds Walter Monckton was bold to the point of recklessness, going flippantly over a trappy country with apparent disregard for his own neck, the famous monocle screwed firmly into his eye, where it remained all day without benefit of cord. He had cracking falls, and once at least was picked up unconscious, but was back in Chambers next day. He revelled in 'big' places and a fast hunt. On one occasion when hounds were running he pounded the whole field by taking a five-foot park paling fence into a hard road, landing with a sickening slither, but safely. For a long time afterwards the place was known as Monckton's Leap.

When out hunting, then, Monckton was like a different man: not least in the conspicuous absence of that courteous restraint which characterised his normal dealings both in society and in the courts. He swore volubly, for example, at followers who were riding too close to the hounds.

As field master, Walter had many problems to cope with. One of the worst was the electrification of the railway which ran across that particular 'country', and which now threatened any hounds which crossed it with electrocution. Wire was another problem. Along with the solicitor W. C. Crocker, who had become a neighbour living at Seal Chart near Ightham, Walter employed girls to approach the local farmers, inviting them to have the wire removed, and fences laid, at the hunt's expense. Another positive move was to acquire the 'shooting' tenancy of a wood covert near Kemsing: the point was that the covert always held foxes; but Monckton and Crocker sometimes shot a few rabbits and pigeons 'to preserve the fiction'.[22]

From time to time members of the hunt would visit Fishponds at the Master's invitation; but Polly did not care very much either for Walter's hunting or for his hunting friends; and this indifference was transformed into a positive hatred when in 1933 Walter fell in love with a keen huntswoman from another part of the county.

By this time Walter's estrangement from Polly was almost complete. In her way she had been a good wife, looking after the house conscientiously, and bringing up the children well; but she showed him none of the personal warmth which he needed; and, the children apart, they had no shared interests of the kind which might have made mere companionship tolerable. They could not even enjoy a holiday together. Walter could no longer bear being at Polly's side with no work to distract him. In any case, he had never liked travelling. Even in the early days of his marriage, he was inclined to cry off a family holiday at the last moment, pleading the pressure of work. He did once join them for a seaside holiday. Du Parcq came too, and the two men sat on the beach in their suits, collars, ties and hats. Walter declined to bathe; indeed, the most he would do, like some caricature of an Englishman at the seaside, was to paddle in the sea with the trousers of his work-a-day suit rolled up.

Walter's love affair, inevitable though it was in the light of his strong affections and his failing marriage, was the cause of general disillusionment. With all his charm, he had been considered virtuous and devout, taking Holy Communion once or twice a week, becoming a lay reader, and regularly preaching in the Ightham parish church, where his sermons were popular and well attended. Whether or not he broke the Seventh Commandment is unclear; but whatever the nature of this affair, Walter's feelings ran deep. To begin with, he and Polly stayed together largely for the sake of their children; but there came a time when Walter seriously considered marrying the woman he loved, despite his disapproval of divorce. He is said to have been dissuaded from doing so by his daughter Valerie.[23]

4

It was in 1933, the year that he began the love affair with which he scandalised Kent society, that Walter Monckton acquired one of his most prestigious appointments. It happened like this. His Harrow contemporary Sir Donald Somervell had been acting as constitutional adviser to the Indian princes, of whom the richest was the Nizam of

Hyderabad, his Exalted Highness Sir Osman Ali Khan Bahadur Fatah Jung, GCSI, BBE. The Nizam, whose dynasty had been founded by the great Mogul Emperor Akbar in the sixteenth century, was the leading Muslim ruler in India. His territory, which occupied a considerable portion of the eastern plateau of the Deccan, covered an area half the size of France, with a population of sixteen million (largely Hindu) of whom half lived in the capital, Hyderabad, the fourth largest city in the sub-continent.[24]

Since Donald Somervell was now to be appointed Attorney-General, and could not continue to act as constitutional adviser while he was a law officer, he recommended Walter Monckton as his successor. 'I [had] just been appointed Attorney-General to the Prince of Wales,' Monckton wrote afterwards,[25]

> and I gathered that I owed my position as adviser in constitutional affairs to the Nizam not only to Donald's recommendation, but also to the fact that his Exalted Highness thought that if I was good enough for the Prince of Wales, I was suitable for the foremost Indian Prince: it is a fittingly humble reflection that the legal problems involved could hardly have been more different in their nature and importance.

Hyderabad had remained faithful to her British overlords during the Indian Mutiny of 1857, and had contributed substantially to the allied cause in both men and money during the First World War. In recognition of these services King George V had not only given the Nizam the title of 'His Exalted Highness', but had also dubbed him 'Faithful Ally of the British Government'.

After the Mutiny, the territory administered by the old (British) East India Company had been transferred to the Crown, represented by a viceroy; while the territory belonging to the princes (of whom there were more than 700, and whose lands ranged from huge principalities like Hyderabad, Kashmir and Mysore, down to small-holdings of only a few acres) retained its independence under British protection. Then there were successive constitutional changes such as the Montagu-Chelmsford reforms of 1919, which created local legislatures; and the Government of India Act, 1935. Under the latter, there was to be a federation of 11 provinces, each with a governor appointed by the Crown and with ministers drawn from an elected legislature. Accession by the provinces to the federation would be automatic; while accession by the princes, who were to be invited to join, would be voluntary. Pending the establishment of this federation, the Central

Government under the Viceroy would remain under the control of the Secretary of State in London.

Walter Monckton's work as adviser fell into three phases: during the first, between 1933 and 1935, he attempted to influence the drafting of the Government of India bill in favour of the Nizam; during the second phase, from 1935, when the bill became an Act, until the late 1930s, he encouraged the Nizam to enter the new federation; a policy which he continued during the third phase, in the period of post-war independence from 1946 to 1948. Each phase ended in failure, although Walter himself earned much admiration for his efforts. The problem was that the Nizam disdained the chance of making a sensible bargain both when independence for British India seemed imminent, and later when it became a reality. Walter would write sadly that:[26]

> If [the Nizam] had taken the advice which I tendered him in the 1930s with the support of his Finance Minister Sir Akbar Hydari – and still more certainly if he had taken my advice in 1946–1948, supported as I was by his advisers, not only would the Nizam's position have been secured, both in the administration of his territories and in his personal status and position, but, and no less important, the lot of his Muslim subjects would have been more tolerable than it has since become.

In the 1930s many Indian princes as well as the Hyderabad delegation led by Sir Akbar Hydari paid protracted visits to London, and Walter was obliged to attend innumerable conferences with them in the Hyde Park Hotel. Little progress was made; and decisions which Walter as constitutional adviser recommended for adoption were either not taken, or taken too late. There were typically Oriental and seemingly endless philosophical discussions, which sometimes made Walter sleepy. His head would drop forward, and he would then be nudged by Sir Akbar, and asked: 'Well, Mr Monckton, what do you advise?'

With the passing of the 1935 Government of India Act, the princes had to decide whether they desired to join the new federation. The Nizam of Hyderabad wished to be certain of the continuance of British protection; and there were also problems connected with taxation, customs and the railways. In the circumstances Walter was invited to visit the subcontinent, which he reached early in August. Before setting out, he had learned from the India Office that the princes had resented what they considered to be the exorbitant fees of previous British advisers, so that on this occasion Walter decided that he would make the visit a holiday, and charge neither fee nor expenses. 'It turned out a good stroke of business,' he later observed, 'and was, I think, certainly wiser than going out for too small a sum.'

Monckton flew out by Imperial Airways, landing at Karachi, and continuing his journey by rail via Jodphur and Delhi to Simla, then the residence of the Viceroy and the seat of the Government of India during the summer months. At this time the Viceroy was the Earl of Willingdon, then in his late sixties, and Walter was the guest of his Foreign and Political Secretary Sir Bertrand Glancy, later Governor of the Punjab.

Unfortunately no one had warned Walter about the difference in temperature between the sweltering plains and the cool Himalayas. To make matters worse, he had arranged for the bulk of his clothes to come by sea, with the unfortunate result that they were detained by the customs in Bombay, while he suffered dreadfully from the cold in Simla. In the circumstances he dreaded an invitation to the Viceregal Lodge; and when it arrived he still had no underclothes, let alone evening dress, and had to borrow items from wherever he could.

At length Walter set out for dinner in an evening coat with tails far too long which, in the words of the late Lord Birkenhead, 'gave him the air of a seedy waiter in a restaurant of little account'. There were 30 guests in all and when the Viceroy saw Walter he remarked: 'I understand that you have had a little difficulty with your clothes, and I should like to make my contribution.' Thereupon Lord Willingdon, who did not lack a sense of humour, and knew that Walter was an old Harrovian, presented him with an Old Etonian tie.

The Vicereine, a daughter of Lord Brassey, also had a lively personality with a keen sense of humour. This appeared when she questioned Walter closely about the quality of the underclothes which he had borrowed from an official in the viceregal entourage. 'Lace!' Walter replied in a low voice, but loud enough to raise a laugh from the other guests nearby.

Subsequently Walter made his way back to Delhi, from where a special train belonging to the Nizam conveyed him to Hyderabad. When the train pulled in, soon after dawn, Walter descended from his carriage, unshaven and looking distinctly scruffy, to find the whole of the Nizam's executive council lined up on the station platform to welcome him. He was then driven to Rocklands, the Nizam's resplendent guesthouse, a large, white building with Gothic arches and shuttered windows, set in a shady compound. Awaiting him was a liberal supply of caviare and champagne, two cars and a detective to attend to his wants.

His first experience of Hyderabad hospitality was a so-called 'small dinner' given by the Maharajah Sir Kishen Pershad, a dynamic Muslim happily married to a Hindu, although he had some extra-marital associations. The 'small dinner' consisted of 160 guests consuming 14 courses; after which there were speeches, and the performance of a native dancer whom Walter was told would do a 'love dance' in his honour. Later, he recalled how the dancer had

> eventually made it plain with her eyes – she swayed very slightly but hardly moved her body – that she had other attractions available to me. Most of the British colony were present, and all the distinguished Mohammedan and Hindu residents in Hyderabad. I was ridiculously embarrassed.

Much to Walter's relief – not unmixed with admiration, for Sir Kishen was well over 70 – he was assured that there was nothing to worry about, as his host would personally attend to the lady.

5

Some time was to elapse before the Nizam was disposed to receive Walter, who spent the interim sightseeing and being entertained by the Nizam's staff and other local dignitaries. Each morning he would ride to such show places as Gundipet and Golconda, usually with John Graham, who was controller to the heir apparent, the Prince of Berar. He was also made welcome by the British resident Sir Duncan Mackenzie, who occupied one of the finest buildings in the principality (now a women's college). Walter became especially friendly, however, with the Princess of Berar, who was the daughter of the last Ottoman Caliph Abdul Mejid. She was an extraordinarily able and perceptive lady, who would sometimes accompany Walter on his rides. 'I learned from her what everyone must learn who has Muslim friends,' said Walter, 'how unnecessary it is to talk just for the sake of talking, and that there is no unfriendliness and should be no awkwardness or embarrassment in silence.'

Eventually Walter was received by the Nizam in King Khoti, a less ornate palace than some of his others, but the one in which he preferred to live. Sir Akbar Hydari presented the visitor to His Exalted Highness in the middle of a dimly lit room whose principal ornament was a Victorian statue of a mother and child, which seemed to Walter to glow with a sinister green light. Sir Akbar had warned Walter in advance that he would find the Nizam somewhat 'unusual'; and unusual he certainly was. Here was an immensely rich man in the prime of life, whose income alone was said to be £3 million a year; and yet he came in leaning on a walking stick, looking thin and frail, and dressed in clothes which were depressingly old and shabby. Around his neck was a favourite scarf, now full of holes, which he wore summer and winter except when the heat was almost unbearable. On his head there was a dirty fez; and beneath his ancient long coat, or *sherwani*, he wore dirty jodhpurs, sagging yellow socks, and an old pair of yellow slippers. To add to the strangeness of his appearance, the Nizam's teeth were evidently decaying; his otherwise pallid features were dominated by a large straggly brown moustache; and as he gazed at Walter for the first time, it seemed that there was something not merely inquisitive, but hostile in his look. By contrast his hands were extraordinarily elegant, which reminded Walter that the Nizam was also a most cultured and civilised man, a poet, and a generous ruler whose benefactions had restored the famous Ajanta caves to their pristine beauty.

In his political life the Nizam was extraordinarily difficult to deal with, and it seemed to Walter that he had found himself in an essentially mediaeval court, enmeshed in a web of suspicion and intrigue. 'He gives you his full confidence,' Walter remarked,

> but encourages others to attack you lest you should be too sure of yourself or too powerful. To persuade him you must advise directly, and give reasons in simple, emphatic language without equivocation. It would be hopeless to give him the reasons on both sides, and to suggest that on balance one course is better than another.

The Nizam was particularly anxious for a sea port, realising that a political situation might well arise in which being landlocked would jeopardise the independence of his state. Walter therefore promised (without much hope of success) to try to secure the small port of Masulipatam, which had originally been an East India Company settlement, and had later belonged to the native rulers of the Deccan, including the Nizam's forebears. More generally, it became clear during this interview – the only one Walter was granted during his 1935 visit – that the Nizam was in no hurry either to join the proposed federation, or to strengthen his negotiating position by uniting with the lesser princes, of whom he could have become a powerful and effective leader.

During the remainder of Walter's visit, he was much entertained both by other members of the Nizam's family and by the most distinguished of his subjects; and in order to repay their hospitality, he gave a large reception at Rocklands which John Graham and his wife helped him to arrange. Appropriately, music was provided by the Queen's Own West Kent Regiment, which was stationed at Secunderabad near the state capital. However, when he proposed to pay for the cost of the entertainment, he was told that the Nizam was touched by his liberality, and that he was not to pay a penny. Nor did he. When he repeated this to the Prince of Wales on his return home, the Prince's comment on the Nizam's generosity was 'Lead me to him!'

It was impossible for Walter to complete all his business before returning to England; so next year he returned to Hyderabad, bringing with him as Junior his friend John (later Sir John) Foster. In his fragment of autobiography, Walter wrote that this second visit to India[27]

> was even more attractive than the first. I had Foster with me to appreciate better the Neo-Saracenic architecture of Hyderabad and to get the utmost amusement out of the incidents which befell me . . .
>
> On this occasion the Nizam asked us to tea in his palace where we found Arab soldiers lurking round all the corners in addition to the ordinary Mohammedan guards. The Nizam, Sir Akbar, Foster and I sat on both sides of a square in the middle of which was the extremely squat, green statue of a Victorian woman and child.
>
> Foster was hidden from the Nizam by this figure and the palms which surrounded it. In the middle of a lull in what was never a very lively conversation, Foster said, suddenly, 'Walter, I know what it is; it's the Blessed Virgin.'
>
> The Nizam was pardonably astonished and in a harsh voice asked: 'Who is that man there?'
>
> I had considerable difficulty in restoring the even flow of our talk!

Sightseeing, which Walter Monckton and John Foster enjoyed on this visit, included trips to the fabulous deserted city of Fatehpur-Sikri, built by the great Mogul Akbar in the sixteenth century, and perfectly preserved in its red sandstone; and to nearby Agra, where they saw the renowned Taj Mahal by moonlight. 'That night,' Walter recalled,

> we dined with the Maharajah of Dohlpur. He asked me, as though it were a common politeness, whether I would care to shoot in his State before I left. But when I told him I didn't like shooting, his delight was undisguised. He told me he didn't think the King [Edward VIII] liked it either; he had seen him put down his gun in England because the birds came over too low, and had been much impressed.
>
> The Maharajah was a charming and remarkably mild man. I learned that his habit was to drive into the woods near his Palace in a sort of Ford known as a 'Tin Lizzie' and sound the very vulgar horn which those cars

sported, whereupon ganders came up to the car from all sides to be fed by their master. It must have been an incongruous sight.

Walter Monckton's principal achievement during this 1936 visit to Hyderabad was to settle a dispute about the territory of Berar, which had once belonged to the Nizam's forebears, but which had been leased in perpetuity to the British Government of India. Monckton managed to persuade the Nizam that it would do him more harm than good to recover day-to-day control of Berar, since most of those who lived there were Hindu, and strongly sympathetic to the Congress Party, whose leaders were firmly opposed to the continuing independence of the princes. Walter suggested that the Nizam should be awarded nominal sovereignty of Berar, while the state should continue to be administered by the Indian Civil Service. This solution delighted the Nizam, who presented Walter with an illuminated *firman*, or decree, in which his thanks were recorded in gold leaf.

In the meantime, Walter Monckton had come to see more clearly than ever that joining the federation, and persuading his fellow princes to do likewise, would be the only basis upon which the future of the Nizam and his heirs in Hyderabad could be secured. Unfortunately, Walter could not compel, but only advise.

In September 1936, Monckton's visit was cut short by a cry for help from the Prince of Wales, who had now succeeded his father as King Edward VIII of Great Britain, Defender of the Faith, and Emperor of India. It would have been a heavy burden for any man; and Monckton had foreseen a year earlier what difficulties might arise, and had turned down important preferment in order to be able to serve his Prince.

It had been in June 1935, when Stanley Baldwin became Prime Minister for the third time, and was forming his Government, that Walter had received an offer which he considered very seriously. 'I was sent for,' he later recalled,[28]

> and told that Mr Baldwin wanted to make me Solicitor-General. Although I had had no political experience at all, I should have liked this in many ways, but by this time I was aware that I might have critical work to do for the then Prince of Wales.

Although it had not yet become a matter of public knowledge, Walter was aware, from his close association with the Prince, of his friendship with Mrs Ernest Simpson, and of where that friendship might conceivably lead. This had made him 'sufficiently anxious about the Prince of Wales to feel that I ought to keep out of the political battle and continue to confine myself to my legal work'. Hence he had politely refused Baldwin's offer; and now that the call from Edward VIII had come, he rightly sensed that a crisis was looming in the English court, and he promptly obeyed his master's summons. It was to be ten years before he once again set foot in India.

Chapter 3

The Abdication

I

WALTER MONCKTON'S journey home from India brought him back to England early in October 1936. When he met the King, he found that His Majesty was extremely concerned about the stories in American newspapers and magazines of his friendship with Wallis Simpson. These stories were illustrated by unconventional photographs showing the King and his latest inamorata on their recent holiday cruise in the Mediterranean, for which purpose Edward had chartered the luxury yacht *Nahlin* (owned by the millionairess Lady Yule); and had invited not only Mrs Simpson, but also the Duff Coopers and other friends to join him on the cruise.

The photographs showed that the King and Mrs Simpson were constantly together: whether in the midst of cheering crowds, or on secluded beaches on the Dalmatian coast; and in one of the photographs he had his hand on her arm. The Hearst newspapers ran a serialised version of Wallis Simpson's life story, while *Time* magazine openly called her 'Queen Wally'.[1] By contrast – although there was no way of knowing how long their restraint would last – the British papers generally maintained a discreet silence, largely at the instance of the newspaper magnates Lords Beaverbrook and Rothermere.[2]

On his return to England in the middle of September, the King had continued the royal tradition of spending some weeks at that time of the year at Balmoral; but instead of following established custom, and inviting Cabinet ministers, archbishops, admirals and the like to join him, he had filled the castle with his personal friends whose visits, including those of Mrs Simpson, were duly published (at his own wish) in the *Court Circular*. The King was happy in this little community, and seemed careless of the impression which he might be producing in the larger world. For example, he declined to open the new wing of a hospital in Aberdeen, on the pretext that he was still in mourning for his father; delegated the task to his brother the Duke of York (later King George VI) who was presumably also in mourning; and then, at the very hour of the opening ceremony, he was seen meeting Mrs Simpson off the London train at Ballater station. Behaviour of this kind caused considerable offence in local circles, besides being commented upon most unfavourably abroad. A number of these comments began to reach the Prime Minister, Stanley Baldwin, who received some angry letters with the American press cuttings enclosed.

'Before October 1936,' Walter was to write in his account of the Abdication,[3]

> I had been on terms of close friendship with King Edward, and, though I had seldom met her save with the King, I had known Mrs Simpson for some considerable time and liked her well.
>
> I was well aware of the divorce proceedings which led to the *decree nisi* pronounced by Mr Justice Hawke at Ipswich in October. But I did not, before November 1936, think that marriage between the King and Mrs Simpson was contemplated. The King told me that he had often wished to tell me, but refrained for my own sake lest I should be embarrassed. It would have been difficult for me since I always and honestly assumed in conversations with him that such an idea (which was suggested in other quarters) was out of the question.
>
> Mrs Simpson had told me in the summer that she did not want to miss her chance of being free now that she had the chance, and the King constantly said how much he resented the fact that Mrs Simpson's friendship with him brought so much publicity upon her and interfered with her prospects of securing her freedom. I was convinced that it was the King who was really the party anxious for the divorce, and I suspected that he felt some jealousy that there should be a husband in the background.

The story of the Simpson divorce, and the part which Walter Monckton played in it, really begins back in February 1936, shortly after the King's accession. At that time Monckton heard an important piece of news from Sir Maurice Gwyer, First Parliamentary Counsel to the Treasury: news which was later confirmed by Sir Lionel Halsey, a council member of the Duchy of Cornwall. It was to the effect that Mr Ernest Simpson, talking to the Baronet and ex-Lord Mayor of London, Sir Maurice Jenks, claimed to have had an extraordinary conversation with the King. Apparently Edward had told Simpson that he loved his wife, and wished to marry her! Subsequently, Walter was told, Sir Maurice had reported this to the Prime Minister.

Walter, knowing nothing of the real situation, and never having met Mr Simpson, thought it most likely, as he later explained, that there was 'some possibility of blackmail upon an extravagant basis'. He could not bring himself to 'believe that the King had said what was attributed to him . . . nor was I at liberty to pass on the rumour to him'.[4] However, although the King's words had reached Walter at third hand, they were true both in substance and in fact. This emerges from what Jenks told Baldwin at their meeting on 4 February.

Some time before, said Jenks, Mrs Simpson's husband had been put forward for admission to a Masonic lodge of which Jenks was the worshipful master. In spite of the fact that Ernest Simpson's candidature was supported by the Prince of Wales (as the King then was), who belonged to the same lodge, it was rejected. Upon the Prince demanding an explanation from the worshipful master, Jenks told him frankly that without breaching Masonic law they could not possibly admit a candidate whose wife was believed on good grounds to be the mistress of another member of the same lodge. According to Jenks, the Prince had then 'promised that there was nothing between himself and Mrs Simpson', with the result that Ernest Simpson was subsequently admitted. Since then, said Jenks, he had been told by Ernest Simpson that he had found out that the King wished to marry his wife as soon as possible after she had divorced him. Simpson had gone on to say that he would like to leave England, only he felt that this would facilitate the divorce; and what he really wanted was to have his wife back again. 'The *mari complaisant* is now the sorrowing spouse,' Jenks remarked, adding that he had suggested to Simpson that he should see the Prime Minister, and had told him that he would ask Baldwin whether he would receive him.

Baldwin flatly refused to do so, pointing out that he was not Mr Simpson's official ministerial adviser, but the King's. Nevertheless the Prime Minister considered that what he had learned was sufficiently important for him to consult Lord Wigram, at that time the King's principal private secretary. This he did the same evening, accompanied by his Cabinet colleague J. C. C. (later Viscount) Davidson, Chancellor of the Duchy of Lancaster. However, no further action was taken by Baldwin after this meeting, and so evidently they considered that the idea of the King marrying a *divorcee* who would then have two previous husbands still living was unthinkable.[5]

Having failed to move the Prime Minister, Ernest Simpson decided that the only thing for him to do was to have it out with the King in person. Many years later, Walter Monckton learned what had

happened next from Bernard Rickatson-Hatt, editor-in-chief of Reut-
ers. Over lunch at the Guards Club, Rickatson-Hatt told Monckton[6]

> that in February 1936 he had been at York House with the King and Ernest
> Simpson. Rickatson-Hatt got up to go, but Simpson asked him to stop,
> and in Rickatson-Hatt's presence, Simpson told the King that Wallis would
> have to choose between them, and what did the King mean to do about
> it? Did he intend to marry her?
> The King rose from his chair and said: 'Do you really think that I
> would be crowned without Wallis by my side?'

Monckton concluded his account of this incident by stating that it
fitted the date 'when Mr Baldwin was approached – so it was said –
by Sir Maurice Jenks with the story that the King meant to marry Mrs
Simpson, which was alleged to have come from Mr Simpson'.

Several times during the summer of 1936, before Walter left for his
second visit to Hyderabad, the King and Mrs Simpson visited him in
his Chambers in Harcourt Street to talk about her divorce. The King
made it clear both on those occasions, and in the course of other
interviews at York House (which continued to be his residence while
his mother still occupied Buckingham Palace), that he wished Mrs
Simpson to secure her divorce without any fears about the possible
repercussions in his own life; and he asked Walter to suggest whom
she should consult with a view to initiating proceedings.

The result was that Mrs Simpson subsequently came to Walter's
Chambers on her own; and Walter introduced her to Toby Matthews,
a partner in Charles Russell & Co. In answer to a direct question,
she told Walter that 'she wanted to be free of her recent marriage; that
she was getting older, but might well meet someone whom she could
happily marry'. Later, when she and Monckton were walking together
'in the little lane behind the exits of Harcourt Buildings', she told him
that[7]

> it was ridiculous to imagine that she had any idea of marrying the King.
> At that time [recalled Monckton] I thought so too, but I knew that
> the divorce proceedings were likely to cause increased risks of publicity
> damaging the King, and I was not altogether surprised when Toby told
> me that after discussing the matter with his partner Gerald Russell he had
> decided that his firm could not act. It was as a result of this decision that
> I introduced Mrs Simpson to Theodore Goddard who acted for her
> throughout the proceedings.

By this time Ernest Simpson had acquired a mistress, Mary Raffray,
a married woman who had been Wallis's bridesmaid at her wedding

to Win Spencer. Evidence of Ernest Simpson's misconduct first came to Walter's notice during a holiday on Dartmoor, which he spent with his old wartime friend George Allen, the King's solicitor. They were staying at the Duchy of Cornwall hotel in Princetown; and one evening they went a few miles north to Two Bridges, where they had arranged to see one of the Duchy Land Stewards. Outside the hotel, Allen saw Ernest Simpson in a car with a lady who was not Wallis Simpson, and may have been Mary Raffray. On their return to Princetown Allen took steps to trace Simpson and obtain evidence of his misconduct: 'though the evidence was, I think, not used as the basis of the petition,' Monckton recalled, 'because Mr and Mrs Simpson thereafter stayed in their flat together'.[8]

Mary Raffray had been staying with the Simpsons for some weeks. One weekend the three were invited by the King to his country house, Fort Belvedere in Sunningdale, habitually called the Fort. They were invited again for the following weekend, but Ernest protested that Mary had just been to the Fort and might prefer to go somewhere else. Whereupon Wallis shrugged her shoulders and said she would go without them, which she did. As soon as she had left the flat in Bryanston Square, Ernest Simpson apparently said to Mary Raffray: 'I know an hotel in Dover . . .'

Wallis returned to the flat on Sunday night and told the others that the King would be dining with them the following evening. On the Monday, the King arrived a little early, and Wallis, who had not quite finished dressing, asked Mary Raffray to entertain him until she came down. When she entered the living room, Mary found the King sitting on a couch. Naturally she curtsied; and as she rose His Majesty asked abruptly: 'How were the chalk cliffs?' Mary stammered some non-committal reply, and years afterwards she would say: 'That nasty little King put detectives on us!' But it was more likely to have been George Allen's agents.

Mary, who now sensed that her hostess was suspicious, packed her bags and left for the South of France, where she stayed at the Carlton Hotel in Cannes. On her first morning there, she addressed two envelopes, one to Ernest and the other to Wallis. Mary then went to the beach, where in the sunshine she wrote a love letter to Ernest, and a bread-and-butter letter to his wife. By mistake she put the letters in the wrong envelopes. Immediately after posting them she realised her mistake, and cabled frantically to Wallis: 'DO NOT OPEN LETTER ADDRESSED TO YOU AS IT IS NOT FOR YOU'. If Mary Raffray expected that Wallis would obey this injunction, she was grievously mistaken. Wallis read the letter which had been written to her husband; and it contained all the evidence that she needed for her divorce. Ernest, realising that his affair had been discovered, immediately moved out of the flat to the Guards Club.[9]

2

Meanwhile Walter, as the King's legal adviser, was becoming increasingly worried by the manner in which His Majesty was publicising his association with Mrs Simpson, and 'didn't know to whom to turn'. Eventually he decided to consult Winston Churchill, since the King liked him, and Walter knew him slightly. Also Churchill was not in Government or Court circles, which made him more approachable. In the event they met on 7 July in Churchill's flat in Morpeth Mansions, where Walter found him

> extraordinarily sympathetic and ready to help. Up and down his room . . . he walked and talked. I can hear him now: 'Life is a tease. Joy is the shadow of sorrow, sorrow is the shadow of joy.' He told me how he refused to sit at table with people who criticised the King. But he was plainly anxious about what I told him. He was all against divorce proceedings in which he saw no advantage; the presence of Mr Simpson was a safeguard. Moreover he was anxious that I should make plain to the King how important it was that his friendship should not be flaunted in the eyes of the public. He particularly said that Mrs Simpson should not go as a guest to Balmoral.

Three days later Churchill (whose own account of their meeting in Morpeth Mansions tallies with Walter's) was present at a dinner which the King gave in York House. Among the other guests was Wallis Simpson: without her husband. Churchill found some opportunity of mentioning to the King that he had recently talked with Walter about the hostile rumours which had swept the capital. The King had not expected this; and afterwards he asked to see Walter, who told him what Churchill thought. However, Churchill's views had no discernible impact. The King, as Walter later recalled, simply[10]

> made the old answer about the divorce, that he didn't see why Mrs Simpson should stay tied to an unhappy marriage simply because she was his friend. And as to the suggestion of keeping the friendship quiet, he said he thought I should have known him better; he was not ashamed of his friendship, and he was not going to hide it or try to deceive people.

By the time Walter had returned from Hyderabad, the arrangements for the Simpson divorce were already in train. Theodore Goddard, the solicitor acting for Mrs Simpson, had arranged that the case should be heard on 27 October at the Suffolk Assizes in Ipswich. This was not designed to avoid publicity (as was generally supposed) but because the lists in the divorce division of the High Court in London were full for some considerable time ahead. Mrs Simpson's leading counsel (instructed by Goddard) was Walter's friend and colleague Norman Birkett, KC; and of course Birkett *could* have made an application to the High Court that the case should be 'expedited'; but this might have led to complications, and would certainly have attracted unfavourable publicity. Hence the choice of Ipswich; and in order to comply with the residential qualification required by the assize court, Mrs Simpson rented a house some ten miles away at Felixstowe. There, before the hearing came to court, she spent several rather dull weekends. However, she was occasionally visited by the King; and she also had the company of her English friends George and Kitty Hunter, in whose London flat she and the King sometimes spent romantic evenings.

Meanwhile Walter had been fully informed about the current state of affairs; and one of his first actions was to accompany Lord Beaverbrook on a visit to Esmond Harmsworth, Chairman of the Newspaper Proprietors Association. Together the three men arranged how best to secure the discretion of the British press; and it was subsequently agreed by most newspaper editors that the plain facts of the divorce case should be reported without editorial comment. On several occasions Beaverbrook and Harmsworth saw the King at Buckingham Palace when Walter was present; and both magnates, according to Walter, 'gave the impression that they thought that with patience and time the King would have a good chance of marrying Mrs Simpson and keeping the Throne'.

The King invited both Walter Monckton and Norman Birkett to lunch with him at Fort Belvedere on Saturday 24 October, so that they could discuss the best way to manage the divorce proceedings; and Walter noted afterwards that 'Norman was deeply impressed with the King's straightness and kindness and devotion to Mrs Simpson, and was captivated by his charm'.* Three days later Mrs Simpson's

---

* It is possible that this discussion about the divorce took place after lunch, since Mrs Simpson attended, together with George Allen, the King's solicitor, and Walter Frampton, Birkett's junior.

divorce petition was granted, and she was awarded a *decree nisi*. The petition had been undefended, and there had been no particular difficulty, although the judge, Mr Justice Hawke, was intensely irritated by the number of police and press reporters present, the reason for which appears to have escaped him.[11]

About a fortnight later, the King decided that it was time to be utterly frank with Walter, who later recorded how they sat together in the Empire Room at Buckingham Palace, and how the King told him

> that he intended to marry Mrs Simpson when he was free. Although I had not taken the view that his mind was made up in this direction, I cannot say that the news came as a shock to me. When the King told me of his decision I suggested that he might wait before taking any steps to act on a determination which could not in any event be given effect until the end of April 1937 [when Mrs Simpson's *decree nisi* would become absolute]. But I could see at once that he did not agree with this advice because he felt that he could not go forward with the Coronation on 12 May 1937, meaning in his heart to make the marriage whatever happened and, as he felt, deceiving the Government and the people into imagining that he had dropped the association, or at any rate, did not intend to marry.[12]

In response to an urgent request from the King, Walter arranged to meet him the following Sunday, 15 November, in his old rooms on the second floor of the Augusta Tower in Windsor Castle. When they met, the King immediately produced a letter from his principal private secretary Major Alec Hardinge, who had taken over from Lord Wigram. It was a letter which the King greatly resented. In it, Hardinge informed him that the press could not be kept quiet much longer, and that senior members of the Government were already discussing 'the serious situation which [was] developing' over the King's association with Mrs Simpson. Accordingly he urged that Mrs Simpson should be sent abroad *'without further delay'*. He added that the Government might well resign on the issue; and that he had 'reason to know' that His Majesty would find it impossible to form a new one. The tone of the letter was disagreeable; and as Walter read it for the first time, the expression on his face left no doubt that he was as shocked by it as the King.

As usual, Walter counselled patience, in particular advising him not to dismiss Hardinge, 'as this would indicate a breach over Mrs Simpson'. The King reserved his judgment on that matter; but asked Walter in any case to act as his personal adviser, and to liaise between him and the Prime Minister. 'I realised,' the King later recalled, 'that I was asking for a good deal. With a gallantry consistent with his generous spirit, he immediately volunteered to serve me. In the events that followed he played his part with a skill that impressed Mr Baldwin as much as it helped me.'[13]

Walter's part was certainly not an easy one; and his role as adviser began with the King taking exactly the opposite course from the one which had been recommended to him. Immediately after Walter's departure that evening, the King had a conversation with Wallis Simpson, in the course of which he decided to throw caution to the winds, to send for Mr Baldwin as soon as possible, and to tell him that they intended to marry.

Accordingly the Prime Minister received a royal summons to meet the King in Buckingham Palace on the evening of the following day, 16 November 1936. When Baldwin was shown in, the King came straight to the point. 'I understand,' he declared, 'that you and several members of the Cabinet have some fear of a constitutional crisis developing over my friendship with Mrs Simpson.' Baldwin admitted that this was so.

In reports of their subsequent conversation, there is some doubt as to which of them first raised the marriage question;[14] but there is no dispute about the substance of what was said, in a conversation which was carried on with complete frankness on both sides. The King appears to have begun by asking whether the marriage he had in mind would be approved by the country at large; and Mr Baldwin replied emphatically that it would not. 'I believe I know what the people would tolerate and what they would not,' he added. 'Even my enemies grant me that.'[15]

Then, according to the Prime Minister, the King remarked that he would tell him something that he had wished to tell him for a long time. 'I want you to know,' he said, 'that I have made up my mind and that nothing will alter it. I have looked at it from all sides – and I mean to abdicate to marry Mrs Simpson.'

'Sir, this is a very grave decision and I am deeply grieved,' Baldwin replied. 'It is impossible for me to make any comment on it today.'

The King repeated that he had made up his mind: he would abdicate in favour of his brother the Duke of York, and he would tell his mother that evening. This he did over dinner at Marlborough House, into which Queen Mary had moved from the Palace. The Princess Royal was also present, and the two women were both deeply shocked by what the King had to say. In particular they flatly refused to meet Mrs Simpson, when the King asked whether he could bring her to Marlborough House; and their discussion, such as it was, ended in deadlock. 'It was not, I am sure, because they were wanting in understanding,' the King later reflected charitably, 'it was because the iron grip of Royal convention would not release them.'

Walter Monckton soon became aware that the Prime Minister wished to see him; and next day they met in Baldwin's private room in the House of Commons, for the first of a number of such interviews. Baldwin told Monckton 'how gravely anxious he was about the whole situation and how certain that the country and the Dominions would not stand for the marriage'. Monckton conveyed Baldwin's views to the King the same evening. 'From that time,' Walter noted in his account of the Abdication, 'I became the channel between the Prime Minister and the King, and I tried, so far as I could, to prevent the acerbities which might so easily have arisen in a situation of such delicacy and world-wide importance.'[16]

3

Meanwhile the King had departed on a two-day visit to South Wales to meet the unemployed miners. On his return to London on the evening of 19 November, his mail contained a letter from Walter Monckton dated the previous day, in which Walter wrote that he had 'taken pains' to collect the views of a wide range of his contacts, in the House of Commons, the Bar, the Stock Exchange, the press, and 'in other places where this problem is the one topic of discussion'. The consensus of opinion, Walter told the King, was that he could not 'throw up the job without letting the whole side down irretrievably in the eyes of the whole world'. He had also come across a widespread feeling that the divorce suit had been arranged for the King's convenience, and that he was securing advantages denied to the ordinary person. 'Some even say,' added Monckton, 'that the present association is enough to justify an intervention in the suit.' He therefore suggested that in order to avoid risking the successful outcome of the divorce proceedings, it would be wise for the King to arrange

a purely temporary separation for the immediate future in order to secure our real objects. I know it would make the present difficulties even harder for you, but wouldn't it help on the longer view?

The King, however, was not to be persuaded. Walter went to see him on Friday 20 November, and reported that evening to Baldwin that His Majesty appeared to be very glad that the two of them had met to discuss the crisis. 'He trusts us both, I'm sure,' Walter continued. However, Baldwin would find that his decision was[17]

> unchanged on the main question. And he is facing the rest and, considering all that is involved, with a real appreciation of the interests which you would wish him to have in mind. I think he will want to see you about Tuesday or Wednesday. I shall no doubt see him before then and I will let you know anything worth reporting. At present his ideas are a little fluid, but I shall remember what you said to me and do my best. He will not do anything precipitate or selfish, saving *il gran rifiuto*.

In the meantime, public awareness of the King's difficulties continued to grow; and lots of slanderous quips were current, some of which Walter must have heard in the course of his investigations. Here are three typical exmples:[18]

> Seen the new play? *The Unimportance of Being Ernest?*
> Talk about being busted in the service! The King, who was once Admiral of the Fleet, is now third mate on an American tramp.
> There's absolutely nothing between the King and Mrs Simpson – *nothing*, not even a sheet.

The King spent the weekend at Fort Belvedere where Mrs Simpson and her aunt Mrs Merryman were guests. Mrs Simpson remarked that the King looked harassed and exhausted, so that it was with some misgiving that she brought up the idea of a morganatic marriage as a possible solution to their problems. It was an idea which had been suggested to her during the King's absence in Wales, when she was lunching at Claridge's with Lord Rothermere's son Esmond Harmsworth. Morganatic marriage, not uncommon in the European royal families, was a device whereby the wife, though legally married, did not acquire her husband's rank; nor did any issue of the marriage inherit either their father's possessions (apart from his private property) or his hereditary titles. So the suggested compromise, as subsequently reported by Baldwin to the Cabinet and the House of Commons, was that 'the King should marry' and that 'Parliament should pass an Act enabling the lady to be the King's wife without the position of Queen' but with some such title as Duchess of Cornwall.[19]*

* Some members of the British Royal Family, such as the Duke of Cambridge and the Duke of Sussex, who 'married' commoners, are sometimes described as having contracted morganatic marriages. (The Duke of Cambridge married an actress who styled herself Mrs Fitzgeorge, and their children were known as Fitzgeorges.) However, since they had not obtained the consent of the reigning sovereign as required by the Royal Marriage Act of 1877, they were not legally married at all.

The King's immediate reaction was hostile; but on second thoughts he agreed with Mrs Simpson that it might be worth trying, as a means of keeping him on the throne. 'I'll try anything in the spot I'm in now,' he said. Accordingly he sent for Esmond Harmsworth; and, on learning that the idea had originated with his father,* he empowered Harmsworth to go ahead and put it up to the Prime Minister. Harmsworth saw Baldwin in Downing Street on the evening of Monday 23 November, and found him apparently both surprised and interested when the plan was put to him. He even promised to refer the matter to the Cabinet.

However, Baldwin was not really as surprised as he pretended, since he had already been warned what to expect by Davidson, who had been talking to Baldwin when Harmsworth was shown in, and had been 'trying to picture the scene in the House of Commons when S.B. had to explain why Mrs Simpson was good enough to be the King's wife, but not good enough to be Queen'. Davidson, who had left the room after Harmsworth's arrival, returned once Harmsworth had left, and asked Baldwin whether he had been right. According to Davidson, Baldwin replied that he was, and added: 'He wants Mrs Simpson to be a Duchess – not to be royal, but less than royal, but rather better than the ordinary Duchess.'[20]

As Monckton had predicted some days earlier, the King summoned Baldwin for an audience on the evening of Wednesday 25 November. The audience began with the King asking Baldwin whether the Harmsworth proposal had been put to him. He added that he believed he would have the support and sympathy of a very large part of the people. He realised that they might be unwilling to accept Mrs Simpson as Queen, but he felt that they would accept a morganatic marriage, provided that the Government was willing to introduce the necessary legislation.

Baldwin's reply was curious. Slowly and (according to the King) with very careful attention to his words, he replied that he had not considered the question. When the King appeared understandably surprised, the Prime Minister clarified his position. 'I can give you no considered opinion,' he said. But if he were asked informally for his immediate reaction, it would be that Parliament would never pass the necessary legislation. To the Cabinet, he reported the conversation in less courteous language, which conveyed a fundamental hostility. He had told the King, he said, that 'if he thought he

* In fact the idea is said to have come from Colin Brooks, the City editor of Lord Rothermere's newspaper the *Sunday Dispatch*.

was going to get away with it in that way, he was making a huge mistake'.

When the King pressed his point, and asked whether the Prime Minister was certain that Parliament would not pass the necessary bill, Baldwin replied that if the King really wished it, he would examine the proposal formally. 'Yes, please do,' answered the King.

'It will mean putting it formally before the whole Cabinet and communicating with the Prime Ministers of all the Dominions. Do you really wish that, Sir?'

The King replied that he did. Before leaving, Baldwin said that he would try to find out the prospects of such a measure being carried in the House of Commons. He also urged upon the King the advisability of Mrs Simpson leaving the country before any formal decision was reached. Finally, he told the King that he would summon a special meeting of the Cabinet within the next 48 hours.

As the Prime Minister was leaving, the King remarked that he would like to consult some of his own friends, particularly Lord Beaverbrook.

This came as a considerable surprise to Baldwin. Not only was Beaverbrook the Prime Minister's principal political enemy, but hitherto he had not been known to enjoy the King's confidence. Indeed, he had never at any time moved in royal circles; and he had only been to Buckingham Palace once in his life: at the time of the Simpson divorce hearing, when the King had successfully appealed to him to use his influence with the British press to keep that case out of the headlines. Since then, the King had been thinking of asking Beaverbrook to see him again, but had delayed doing so until after Beaverbrook had sailed for America, where he was hoping to find a cure for his asthma in the dry climate of Arizona. He was in mid-Atlantic when he received a cable from Walter Monckton saying that the King urgently wished to see him; and in the event he spent only a few hours in New York, while he waited for his ship, the *Bremen*, to turn round for her homeward voyage.

The story subsequently gained ground that Beaverbrook responded to the King's request solely with the object of overthrowing Baldwin. However, this rests on little more than what A. J. P. Taylor has called 'late-night gossip by Randolph Churchill; not,' as he so rightly says, 'the most reliable of authorities'.* Of course, Beaverbrook always

* In a review, published on 24 April 1966 in the *Sunday Times*, of Lord Beaver-brook's *The Abdication of King Edward VIII*, Randolph Churchill stated: 'It was not until four or five years ago that by chance one day I asked Lord Beaverbrook why, if he was so far from being a monarchist and one who scarcely knew the King, he had put himself to so much trouble on his behalf. He replied ironically: "To bugger Baldwin." So much for charity.'

enjoyed playing the role of a 'fixer'; but to be fair to him, he could seldom resist a call for help. He had shown more than once that he was a true foul-weather friend, not least in his dealings with Randolph's father. Beaverbrook himself later declared that

> I did not enter the struggle to dislodge the Prime Minister. That would be a welcome by-product of my efforts. But I was striving to help the King because I believed he had a right to command support and because his cause was just. My efforts would be primarily directed to helping safeguard the Throne and trying to secure for the King freedom to marry the woman of his choice, a freedom enjoyed by the humblest of his subjects.

Beaverbrook landed at Southampton on the morning after Baldwin's audience and drove straight to Fort Belvedere, where the King was waiting for him. 'You have done a fine thing for me,' the King exclaimed as he grasped his hand, 'and I shall always remember it.' Over luncheon the King brought his guest up-to-date on the situation. But when he heard that the King had asked Baldwin to lay the morganatic marriage proposal before the Cabinet, Beaverbrook's face darkened. Such an idea, he said, would appeal neither to the British Cabinet nor, in his opinion, to the British people. He strongly advised the King to withdraw it at once. The King appeared to be convinced; but the same evening he telephoned Beaverbrook in London to inform him that Mrs Simpson preferred the morganatic marriage to any other solution, and that therefore he intended to pursue that possibility.

There was little or nothing that Beaverbrook could do in the face of this determination. It was clear to him that the Government had only to reply that a morganatic marriage was impossible, for the King to be left with a choice between abandoning Mrs Simpson and abdication. And since the King had made it abundantly clear that the former course of action was out of the question, it now began to look as if there were no alternative to abdication.[21]

4

What of the King's lady-love, Wallis Simpson, who had brought him so far down this dangerous road? She had been born on 19 June 1895, the illegitimate and only child of Teackle Wallis Warfield and Alice Montague. Their home was in Baltimore, the state capital of Maryland. The Warfields and Montagues were both old American families, and both had fought on the Confederate side in the Civil War. Teackle himself was descended from a Governor of Maryland, while Alice was related to a Governor of her home state, Virginia.

Wallis's birth took place not in Baltimore, as might have been supposed, but in Square Cottage, a cabin belonging to the Monterey Inn, Monterey County, in the Blue Ridge Summit mountains of Pennsylvania near the border with Maryland. Teackle and Alice had migrated to this popular summer resort partly because of Alice's pregnancy, but more particularly because Teackle was in an advanced state of tuberculosis, and it was hoped that he would benefit from the mountain air.

Having been born out of wedlock, the infant girl was not baptised. Her parents simply named her Bessie Wallis – the Bessie being later discarded. On 19 November 1896, when Wallis was seventeen months old, Teackle and Alice were married in Baltimore; but no members of the family turned up to support them; and a year later Teackle died at the age of 27, leaving Alice penniless.[22]

In the circumstances, Alice's mother-in-law Mrs Anna Warfield agreed to take in both her daughter-in-law and her grand-daughter. Anna was a despotic creature, and Alice escaped from the household as soon as she could, first living alone, and then marrying John F. Raisin, son of the local Democratic Party leader. But she did not take her daughter with her: Wallis remained with her grandmother for the next five years. By 1902, however, when Wallis was seven years old, her mother's second marriage failed; and mother and daughter were taken in by Anna's widowed sister Bessie whose husband, David R. Merryman, an auctioneer, had died the previous year.

Here Alice and her daughter were made most welcome. Aunt Bessie adored them both, and was to remain a life-long friend of Wallis. In due course, Wallis was sent to Oldfields girls' school, the most expensive of its kind in Maryland, where she was known as something of a tomboy, and where her best friend was a pretty girl called Mary Kirk, later Mrs Jacques Raffray; and later still, curiously enough, Mrs Ernest Simpson.[23]

Mary was also the principal bridesmaid when in November 1916, at the age of 20, Wallis rushed into a disastrous marriage with Lieutenant Earl Winfield (or 'Win') Spencer of the US Navy. Win turned out to be an alcoholic, and a sexual adventurer – both a womaniser and a homosexual. Marked by a number of separations and subsequent reconciliations, the marriage somehow lasted for eight years before ending in the inevitable divorce.[24]

It was towards the end of their association that Win was posted to Chinese waters (known as the Asiatic station), and 1924 found him and Wallis living together in Hong Kong. It was in this British colony that Win allegedly introduced his wife to the luxurious brothels known as 'singing' or 'sing-song' houses. Here, it was rumoured, Wallis became proficient in the technique of various sexual perversions, both heterosexual and lesbian. At this time she certainly visited Canton, Shanghai, Tientsin and Peking, where she became expert at exploiting foot-and-shoe fetishism. This had been a Chinese trait for hundreds of years, was probably responsible for the local custom of compressing women's feet, and meant that in China a female foot carried the same kind of sexual charge as in the West might have been carried by her breasts.[25]

This is important because shortly after Wallis first met the Prince of Wales, she discovered that he had long been a repressed foot-fetishist; and she consequently indulged his perversion to the full. The sight of Wallis skilfully manipulating her shapely legs and feet encased in silk stockings and high-heeled shoes was enough (as she could not help noticing) to bring the Prince to a state of intense physical excitement. This phenomenon, as the sexual psychopathologist Krafft-Ebing was the first to point out, rests upon the basis of a more or less masochistic desire for self-humiliation.[26]

Most previous writers about Wallis Simpson, later Duchess of Windsor, have depicted her as a wronged wife who was sexually innocent. Wronged she undoubtedly had been, by two husbands; but she was far from being sexually innocent.[27] Indeed, she was quite promiscuous at one time; and even before she finally parted from Win she had enjoyed a series of lovers. They included 21-year-old Count Galeazzo Ciano, Mussolini's future son-in-law and Italian Foreign Minister, whom she met in Shanghai. As a result of their cohabitation she became pregnant. According to another US Navy wife, Wallis personally procured an abortion, which destroyed her chances of ever having a child, and caused her severe gynaecological problems for the rest of her life.[28]

Whether or not she became acquainted with lesbianism in Hong Kong, Wallis was undoubtedly intrigued by the power which she could exercise in this direction. In his edition of the *Wallis and Edward Letters*, Michael Bloch observed that 'all her life, Wallis – with her rather masculine appearance, her brittle and self-possessed manner – exercised a great fascination on lesbians'.[29] In July 1931, for example, she enjoyed a holiday in the South of France with a party of women who included three lesbian sisters – Mrs Gloria Vanderbilt, Thelma

Viscountess Furness and Mrs Consuelo (Tamar) Thaw – whose father Harry Hays Morgan was US Consul-General in Buenos Aires.[30] Another notorious lesbian in the Cannes group was Nada Marchioness of Milford Haven, daughter of the Grand Duke Michael Michaelovich of Russia and sister-in-law to Lord Louis Mountbatten, later Earl Mountbatten of Burma. Nada's husband George, 2nd Marquess of Milford Haven, was a noted collector of erotica.

In Cannes, Wallis shared an hotel room with Tamar Thaw, while Gloria Vanderbilt did likewise with Nada Milford Haven. Wallis would eventually drop these friends, particularly after a sensational law case in which Gloria Vanderbilt was involved. Vanderbilt was attempting to recover custody of her daughter, also called Gloria, from her sister-in-law Gertrude Whitney; and it was alleged that Gloria senior was unfit to bring up her daughter on account of her sexual proclivities, her lesbian relationship with Nada Milford Haven being cited against her.

Thelma Furness had been the mistress of the Prince of Wales; and her fatal mistake had been to go off to New York to visit her twin sister, and to tell Wallis to 'look after him while I'm away'. In the event, Wallis looked after him so well that she superseded Thelma as the Prince's favourite companion. Incidentally during her absence Thelma slept with the Ali Khan, a fact which the Prince discovered or at least suspected.

Wallis displayed her new dominance in public. At dinner one night at the Fort, when the guests included both the Simpsons and Thelma Furness, the Prince used his fingers to pick up a lettuce leaf which he proceeded to nibble. Wallis, who was sitting beside him, slapped him hard on the hand and told him to use a knife and fork in the future. The Prince meekly obeyed, while Wallis gave Thelma a cold, haughty glance as she revelled in her victory. It was Thelma's last visit to Fort Belvedere.[31]

Some years later, when Wallis's handwriting was analysed by a male graphologist, he found her[32]

> A woman with a strong male initiative in the sense of activity, vitality . . . She *must* dominate, she *must* have authority, and without sufficient scope for her powers can become disagreeable. In a narrow circle, without big tasks to perform she could be impatient, irritable. She needs a large field of organisation, of influence . . .
>
> She is extremely temperamental, but it is more emotional impulse than real feeling. Her capacity for sacrifice is not great, but in playing her part good might come of it, though primarily all she does comes from her wish

to be important. In the pursuit of her aim, she can be inconsiderate and [can] hurt – but on the whole she is not without some instinct of nobility and generosity. She is ruled by contradictory impulses; there is a certain restlessness in the writing, a sign that the satisfaction she gets is not strong enough to harmonise her life. She is ambitious and demands above all that her undertakings should be noted and valued.

Walter Monckton was once told by Rickatson-Hatt, who had been a good friend to both Ernest and Wallis Simpson, that Wallis was[33]

extremely attractive to men, amusing and kind on most occasions, but capable of hardness. She had often made Simpson extremely unhappy, and then overwhelmed him with kindness and affection in making up the difference.

Rickatson-Hatt says that she likes the good things of the earth and is fundamentally selfish. He thinks her intention was to have her cake and eat it. She was flattered by the advances of the Prince of Wales and the King and enjoyed his generous gifts to her to the full. She thought that she could have them and at the same time keep her home with Simpson.

Long before February 1936 Simpson had tackled her on the matter though he had never up to then, apparently, made a direct approach to the King. She had always told him that he could trust her to look after herself; she enjoyed the attention she received and there was no harm in it. Rickatson-Hatt himself thinks that but for the King's obstinacy and jealousy, the affair would have run its course without breaking up the Simpson marriage.

In his account of the Abdication, Walter recorded Rickatson-Hatt's views 'because he clearly has a considerable knowledge of the parties . . . and a completely objective outlook together with a good memory, and some considerable insight into the characters of Mr and Mrs Simpson'.

On 5 April 1935, Henry (Chips) Channon, the American-born socialite and British MP, remarked in his diary that Wallis now had 'complete power over the Prince of Wales, who is trying to launch her socially'. He added that 'she already has the air of a personage who walks into a room as though she expected to be curtsied to'; although he also admitted that she was witty and charming. On 31 May the same year, Chips arrived at the Covent Garden opera to see Lily Pons in *The Barber of Seville* from Lady Cunard's box, when his hostess was joined by the Prince of Wales and Mrs Simpson. 'I was interested to see what an extraordinary hold Mrs Simpson has over the Prince,' noted Chips. 'In the interval she told him to hurry away as he would be late in joining the Queen at the LCC Ball – and she made him take a cigar from his breast pocket. "It doesn't look very pretty," she said. He went but was back in half-an-hour.'[34]

As time went by Chips Channon became gradually more attached to Wallis. Not only did she mellow somewhat, but he grew to admire her for what he considered to be her beneficial influence on King Edward VIII, as the Prince had now become. At a dinner at the Brownlows, given for the purpose of arranging the King's initial meeting with Lord Beaverbrook, Chips noted that: 'The King's attention to Wallis is very touching. He worships her, and she seems tactful and just right with him, always prefacing her gentle rebukes with "Oh, Sir . . ."' Wallis confessed to Chips Channon's wife that she always kicked him under the table hard, when she wanted him to stop talking; and gently, when she wanted him to go on. But sometimes she was too far away, and then it was difficult.[35]

But at the Fort there was no doubt who was in control. In March 1936, shortly after the Prince became King, his great-uncle the Duke of Connaught and the Duke's friend Lady (Leonie) Leslie came for tea. Years later, Lady Leslie told her grand-daughter Anita that the party, which included Wallis, took a walk in the grounds. It had been raining and it was wet and muddy. When they returned to the house, Wallis commanded the King: 'Take off my dirty shoes and bring me another pair!' Perhaps there was an element of shoe fetishism in her order. At any rate the monarch did as he was bidden, brought a clean pair of shoes from her room, knelt down, removed the muddy shoes and changed them for a clean pair. Both the Duke and Leonie Leslie were stupefied by this performance.[36]

The final word may be left with Walter Monckton. 'No one will ever really understand the King's life during the [Abdication] crisis,' he wrote,[37]

who does not appreciate two factors. The first, which is superficially acknowledged by many of those who were closely concerned in the events of these days, was the intensity and depth of the King's devotion to Mrs Simpson. To him she was the perfect woman. She insisted that he should be at his best and do his best at all times, and he regarded her as his inspiration. It is a great mistake to assume that he was merely in love with her in the ordinary physical sense of the term. There was an intellectual companionship, and there is no doubt that his lonely nature found in her a spiritual companionship.

5

On the morning of Wednesday 2 December 1936, the national news-papers all carried an address which the Bishop of Bradford, the Rt Rev. Dr A. F. W. Blunt, had made to a local Diocesan Conference. In it, he had boldly expressed the hope that the King was aware of his need for God's grace at his Coronation; and, if so, that he would display 'more positive signs of his awareness'. When composing this address, some six weeks previously, the Bishop knew nothing about the King's relationship with Mrs Simpson, and (as he subsequently protested) had meant to refer only to His Majesty's negligence in church-going.

The national press simply printed the substance of the Bishop's address as an ordinary news item, though *The Times* went so far as to extract the significant reference to King Edward VIII for the main page. The provincial papers in the Midlands and the North, however, led by the *Manchester Guardian* and the *Yorkshire Post*, went a great deal further. Assuming that the Bishop had been referring to the King's private life, they ran editorials dealing with the gossip which had been current in certain sections of society; and the London evening papers, which were on the streets while the Cabinet was discussing the 'King's matter' in Downing Street, followed suit. It was evident that the long self-imposed silence of the leading English newspapers could not last much longer; and indeed it was broken within the next 24 hours.[38]

Mrs Simpson was now staying at the Fort since, in Walter's words, 'London had become an unpleasant place for her to be in'. On the morning of Thursday 3 December, she appeared in the King's room with a picture-paper in her hand. 'I had no idea,' she said, 'it would be anything like this.' She added that she had made up her mind to leave England that very afternoon.

The King agreed with her, and arrangements were immediately made for Wallis to stay with two American friends, Mr and Mrs Herman Rogers, at their villa in Cannes. Accordingly she left, escorted by the King's Lord-in-Waiting Lord Brownlow, a most devoted friend. As Wallis later described in her book *The Heart Has Its Reasons*, they were pursued across France by a host of press reporters.[39]

Meanwhile the King had conceived the idea of making a public radio broadcast to appeal directly to his people; and he summoned Walter Monckton and his solicitor George Allen for their help in drafting a speech. What he wanted to tell his subjects was that it had taken him many years to find the woman whom he wished to make his wife, and that, having found her, he was determined to marry her. There was no question of Mrs Simpson becoming Queen, and this was spelled out in a couple of sentences:

> Neither Mrs Simpson nor I have ever sought to insist that she should be Queen. All we desired was that our married happiness should carry with it a proper style and dignity for her, befitting my wife.

The draft broadcast was finished during the afternoon of 3 December. Walter then returned to London with a copy for Baldwin, whom the King had summoned to meet him that evening in Buckingham Palace. Walter was not present at this audience, which the King began by reading out loud the text of his proposed broadcast to Britain and the Empire. When he had finished, he asked the Prime Minister what he thought of it. Baldwin replied that he must consult his colleagues; but speaking for himself, he had no doubt what their answer would be: 'that the proposal was thoroughly unconstitutional'. The King then went to Marlborough House, to dine with Queen Mary, the Princess Royal and the Duke of York. Once again, he made it clear to the three principal members of his family that he intended to marry Mrs Simpson even if it cost him the Throne.[40]

Walter Monckton was waiting in the Palace when the King returned at 11 p.m., and he was invited to drive down with him to the Fort and stay there. Walter did so, and remained there until the King left the country eight days later. Apart from Walter and the servants there was no one else, not even an equerry or a private secretary, while the King remained mostly indoors, afraid that if he left the house he might miss a telephone call from Wallis. 'Those telephone calls,' Walter later recalled,[41]

> with a bad line at a long distance, will never be forgotten by any of us. The house is so shaped that if a voice is raised in any room on the ground floor it can be heard more or less distinctly in the whole house.
>
> I have heard it suggested that the King was, during the days that followed, in no state, because he was drinking too much, to reach any decision. Nothing could be more ridiculous. Life was for all of us disorganised, a series of interruptions with snatches of sleep. I certainly drank more than the King, but among all the great men who saw us constantly throughout those days I never heard one who thought either of us had been drinking! (More half-consumed whiskeys poured out than I have ever seen.)
>
> Between Thursday [the 3rd] and Sunday the 6th [of December] there was a great wave of sympathy for the King and a desire in many quarters

to retain him at all costs. The Cabinet's anxiety was for a speedy decision, and although I thought that Sir John Simon [the Home Secretary] was anxious, if he could, to keep the King and persuade him to give up his intention to marry, I felt that there was at any rate a strong element in the Cabinet who as early as this felt that his immediate abdication upon generous terms was desirable. I think that there is little doubt that due provision would have been made for an income and a title if he had expressed his willingness to go at once.

Towards the end of a further audience at Ford Belvedere on 4 December, the King had asked Baldwin whether he would mind him seeing Winston Churchill, 'as an old friend with whom he could talk freely'. Momentarily off his guard, the Prime Minister agreed, though he regretted it almost at once. 'I have made my first blunder,' he told the Cabinet next day. The result was that Churchill dined at the Fort with the King and Walter Monckton on Friday 4 and Saturday 5 December. 'His advice was that the King should ask for time,' Walter wrote afterwards.[42]

> He said that he could not say that the King would win through if he stood and fought, but that he ought to take time to see what measure of support he received. His presence was a great encouragement to the King who liked him, and mimicked his mannerisms superbly without the slightest malice:
> 'We must have time for the big battalions to mass. We may win; we may not. Who can tell?'

Earlier on 5 December, Walter had lunched privately with two guests in a room at the Windham Club, which had become his headquarters when in London. His guests had been Sir Horace Wilson, a Treasury official who was the Prime Minister's personal adviser; and Sir Thomas Dugdale (later Lord Crathorne), his parliamentary private secretary. Walter had put forward a suggestion to resolve the crisis: two bills should be introduced into Parliament, the first legalising the King's renunciation of the Throne, and the second bringing Mrs Simpson's divorce proceedings to a satisfactory conclusion by making her *decree nisi* absolute. As Monckton later wrote,[43]

> This would finally have cleared up a grave constitutional position affecting the whole world and have left no ragged ends or possibilities for further scandal. It attracted Sir Horace Wilson, and when Mr Baldwin came down later in the day to the Fort with Mr Dugdale, he expressed to the King, at an audience at which I was present, his views that this provided the right way out. At the audience the scheme was not suggested either by the

King or by the Prime Minister, but I asked leave to speak and propounded it as my own, thus avoiding embarrassment to both of them.

Walter added in his account that Baldwin 'said he would resign if he could not carry his colleagues. He would see the possibly awkward ones on Sunday.'

The 'awkward ones', whom Baldwin summoned to meet him in the Cabinet room on Sunday 6 December, were Neville Chamberlain, Ramsay MacDonald, John Simon, Oliver Stanley, Runciman, Inskip, Halifax, Kingsley Wood and Hoare. Walter waited in an anteroom, hoping that an agreement could be reached along the lines which he had proposed. These were acceptable to the King, whose fighting spirit had been roused only briefly by Churchill's suggestion that he should continue to press for a morganatic marriage. Afterwards Monckton wrote:[44]

> On the Sunday morning a meeting of 10 or 11 of the Ministers took place at Downing Street . . . [and] after a long debate in which Mr Baldwin strongly urged that this solution be accepted, the Ministers decided that they must reject it. I was then called into the Cabinet Room and Mr Chamberlain told me the reasons that had compelled them to this decision. They were briefly, that the two bills smacked of a bargain where there ought to be none; that the second bill [the Simpson divorce] would affront the moral sense of the nation and that it would be resisted and debated, and that in the course of the debate unpleasant statements and suggestions would be made.

In view of the general feeling, Baldwin said that he must agree that the proposed measures should be dropped, the decision being confirmed by a meeting of the whole Cabinet at 5.30 that evening.

At the morning meeting, Walter Monckton had been asked what the King's reaction would be to their decision. He replied that His Majesty had hoped that both bills, which the Prime Minister 'had looked upon with favour', would be acceptable. 'This decision will greatly disappoint him,' he added. 'In the light of the present circumstances, he will probably ask for additional time for further thought.'

At this point Ramsay MacDonald spoke up. 'How much time will the King ask for? How many days?'

'Hardly days,' answered Walter. 'I anticipate he will require weeks.' It would be necessary for the King to consult his advisers, Monckton went on, since 'a divergence of view had arisen'.

'This matter must be settled before Christmas,' Baldwin interjected. Some ministers remarked that this was too long to wait, and the matter should be settled immediately. One minister was heard to say that the continued uncertainty was hurting the Christmas trade. According to Walter, this observation emanated from Neville Chamberlain. 'Baldwin was ready to resign,' Walter noted, 'but I told him the King would not wish that.'

Finally Monckton told Baldwin and the other ministers that he would report what had taken place to the King. When he did so, later that day, it was with some feeling: 'It did seem to me,' he would later recall, 'that the Chancellor of the Exchequer [Neville Chamberlain] was being a trifle more mercenary than his office demanded.'

A curious series of incidents now occurred which formed, as it were, a subplot within the main drama whose climax was rapidly approaching. Theodore Goddard, Mrs Simpson's solicitor in her divorce proceedings, learned that an affidavit was about to be served by a private individual on the King's Proctor, with an application to the effect that the individual concerned was in a position to show why the *decree nisi* should not be made absolute. Such an application could only be made 'by reason of material facts not having been brought before the court and/or by reason of the divorce having been obtained by collusion'. Goddard naturally felt that he had a duty towards his client to reveal this intervention, and that he should see Wallis Simpson immediately. He informed Walter, who passed on the news to his master. The uncrowned King thereupon summoned Goddard immediately to Fort Belvedere, and, feeling that news of the intervention would only upset Wallis, explicitly forbade her solicitor to make the journey to Cannes.[45]

It was now the evening of Monday 7 December; and Goddard hastened to Downing Street, where he found the Prime Minister holding a copy of the statement which Mrs Simpson was going to release to the press on Tuesday morning. This was not a plain renunciation of the King but an offer, 'if such action would solve the problem, to withdraw forthwith from a situation that has been rendered both unhappy and untenable'. Baldwin, who was anxious to learn what Mrs Simpson's intentions really were, accordingly pressed Goddard to disobey the King and visit his client, telling him that it was his duty so to do.*

Goddard flew to Cannes the following morning accompanied by his doctor (since he suffered from a heart complaint) as well as by his law

---

* According to Davidson, who later told Hoare, Goddard was also charged by Baldwin with the delicate task of recovering Queen Alexandra's emeralds, which the King had inherited from his grandmother and given to Mrs Simpson.

clerk. However, the doctor also happened to be a gynaecologist; and when this became known to the press, it gave rise to the unfounded rumour that Mrs Simpson was already pregnant, and Goddard's law clerk was incorrectly supposed to be an anaesthetist! On reaching Cannes, the solicitor consulted with his client. Wallis assured him that 'she was, and still is, perfectly willing' to instruct him 'to withdraw her petition for divorce' and was also willing to do anything to prevent the King from abdicating. Having heard what she had to say, Goddard pronounced himself 'satisfied beyond any doubt that this is Mrs Simpson's genuine and honest desire'. By the time Goddard returned to London, however, the intervener had turned out to be an elderly clerk named Francis Stephenson, employed by a London firm of solicitors; and he had decided not to proceed with his application.[46]

In the meantime Mrs Simpson's press release had been read over the telephone to the King, who had approved it, not realising that she was ready to break off their engagement and withdraw her divorce petition. Indeed, several newspapers proclaimed that the crisis was over. However, the King soon cleared up any private misunderstanding by assuring Wallis that if she were forced to throw him over, he would follow her to the ends of the earth and get her back. He insisted in particular that she must not listen to Goddard, or be influenced by anything he said; and eventually Wallis agreed.[47]

For his part, Baldwin was desperately anxious that the crisis should be brought to a speedy end; and when he saw Walter Monckton on the morning of Tuesday 8 December, he suggested that Walter should go down to the Fort and make one last effort to persuade the King to remain. 'He must wrestle with himself in a way he has never done before,' said Baldwin; 'and if he will let me, I will help him. We may even have to see the night through together.'

'Hasn't everything been said that needs to be said?' the King queried, when Walter telephoned with news of the proposed visit. In the light of the rebuffs he had suffered, particularly the rejection of the Simpson divorce bill by the Cabinet, Baldwin's 'sudden solicitude', as he put it, struck the King as 'a trifle odd, if not gratuitous'. However, since 'it would have been ungracious not to receive him', the King said Baldwin and his parliamentary private secretary could come down to the Fort.

Leaving Simon to answer any questions which might be put in the Commons, the Prime Minister set off after lunch, accompanied by Dugdale and Walter Monckton. It was Walter's first experience of motoring with the Prime Minister, and he never forgot it. The journey was made in Baldwin's small black car, into which the driver and his three passengers were tightly squeezed. A recent collision had evidently made Baldwin more nervous than ever about being driven, since the driver had instructions to keep to a steady 25 miles an hour. The inevitable result was that drivers wishing to overtake, and unaware that the car had such distinguished occupants, set up a furious honking in its wake. Meanwhile Baldwin puffed implacably away at his pipe, and indulged in all the irritating little habits which Walter had come to know so well, particularly humming and snapping his fingers; whilst the vehicle became so full of tobacco smoke that the others literally gasped for air. 'I was praying for the journey to end,' Walter later recalled, 'because I was so anxious about what was happening on the telephone with Cannes, and I knew the King must be more tired than ever, and might hate the prospect of the Prime Minister staying the night.'

Indeed, when the King spotted Dugdale in the act of depositing Baldwin's suitcase in the hall, he looked so distressed that Walter persuaded Sir Edward Peacock, who was in attendance, to offer to put Baldwin up at his own house nearby. Baldwin said that in the circumstances he would return to London after dinner; and then he began what was to be his last audience with King Edward VIII.

The audience was held in the drawing room, with its large windows looking out on the gardens and the woods beyond. The King sat in his usual chair by the fire with Baldwin at right angles to him on the sofa, and Walter Monckton in a chair between them.

The more tired Baldwin was, the deafer he became: which on this occasion had a curious result. He had taken up his familiar theme, urging the King not to marry 'for the sake of the country and all that the King stood for'; and the King had replied very wearily 'that his mind was made up', and begged to be spared any more advice on that subject. Baldwin, however, had not heard a word, and much to Walter's astonishment he returned to the attack more vigorously than before. Then, turning to Walter, he asked him if he thought he had done all he could; and Walter had to reply that 'he had done even more, it was plain that he had not heard the King's request to desist'.

The audience at an end, the King appeared so exhausted that Walter suggested that the two of them should have dinner alone in the King's bedroom, leaving Baldwin and the other guests – eight in all, including the King's brothers the Duke of York and the Duke of Kent – to dine by themselves downstairs. However, the King would not give way; and he eventually walked into the panelled dining room dressed in his favourite white kilt, and sat down at the head of the table with Baldwin on his right. He now seemed in excellent spirits, the conversation never flagged, and the topic which had brought them all together was never mentioned. 'Look at him,' the Duke of York whispered to Monckton. 'We simply cannot let him go!' But both of them knew, as did Baldwin and everyone else at the table, that there was no longer any hope of stopping him.[48]

6

On the morning of Wednesday 9 December, Walter Monckton travelled up to London, and reached Downing Street shortly before the usual weekly meeting of the Cabinet. Joined by Peacock, he reported to Baldwin, Chamberlain and Sir John Simon that the King remained absolutely determined to abdicate. Monckton and Peacock then called at 145 Piccadilly, where the Duke of York was then living with his wife, and gave him the same message. They also secured his agreement on two issues of some importance to King Edward: he would be allowed to keep his royal rank in any event; and to live at Fort Belvedere if ever he were given permission to come back to England.

Meanwhile the Cabinet was in session, and formally advised the King to reconsider his decision. 'Ministers are reluctant to believe that Your Majesty's decision is irrevocable,' wrote Baldwin on behalf of the Government, 'and still venture to hope that before Your Majesty pronounces any formal decision Your Majesty may be pleased to reconsider an intention which must deeply distress and so vitally affect all Your Majesty's subjects.' In a second letter, likewise approved by the Cabinet, the Prime Minister reminded the King that, in the event of his abdication he would be obliged as Sovereign, since no higher constitutional authority existed, to provide Parliament with his own Royal Assent to his own Act of Abdication.[49]

Walter rushed both these communications to the Fort. Only one of them required an answer, which the King immediately provided in the form of a brief statement in his own hand:

> The King has received the Prime Minister's letter of 9 December 1936 informing him of the view of the Cabinet.
> His Majesty has given the matter his further consideration, but regrets that he is unable to alter his decision.

During the afternoon, a heavy fog descended on the Thames valley, so that it was not until several hours after he had left the Fort that

Walter reached Downing Street with the King's written reply. The
Cabinet was hastily called together and met, with Walter in attendance,
in Baldwin's room in the House of Commons shortly before 8 p.m.
After receiving the King's statement, and also learning that he intended
to deliver a message to Parliament the following day, the Cabinet
moved rapidly. Baldwin had already told Monckton that everything
must be completed by Friday so that the new monarch, who would
be known as George VI, could hold his Accession Council on the
following day. Now the Cabinet approved the terms of a short Abdication Bill, which had been drafted by the Treasury solicitor; and
they also passed a minute to the effect that after the King's abdication he must be absent from England for a period of at least two
years.

The King had already let Baldwin know, through Walter, that he
intended to leave England on the day that the Abdication Bill became
law, and that before doing so he intended to make a farewell broadcast
to his people. Since he would no longer be King, the Government
would have no authority to seal his lips. 'Some in the Government
looked coldly upon the idea of my supplying an epilogue to a drama
on which the curtain had already descended,' he was to write in his
autobiography *A King's Story*, 'and even my mother tried to dissuade
me. But I was determined to speak. I did not propose to leave my
country like a fugitive in the night.' Apparently some ministers
feared that he would use the opportunity provided by the broadcast
to make an appeal calculated to divide the country. But they need
not have worried. As Baldwin afterwards remarked to his biographer G. H. Young, 'whoever writes about the Abdication
must give the King his due. He could not have behaved better than
he did.'[50]

Wednesday 9 December was developing into one of the most gruel-
ling days of Walter Monckton's life. After the Cabinet meeting he took
the Home Secretary Sir John Simon to dinner at his club, where they
collaborated on drafting the King's message to Parliament. Then at
ten o'clock they returned to Downing Street, where it had been
arranged that Major Hardinge and Alan Lascelles (the King's assistant
private secretary) should join them for a meeting with representatives
of the Dominions Office and the India Office, to coordinate arrangements for the distribution of the Abdication documents throughout
the Empire. Simon was in the chair, and afterwards Walter noted that
he had seen many staff officers, but 'none so competent'. While this
meeting was still in progress, Walter was called to Marlborough House
to show Queen Mary and the Duke of York the text of the Instrument

of Abdication, which was to be signed by the King and his three brothers next morning. 'To give up all that,' commented Queen Mary unhappily, 'for this!'

It was not until one in the morning that Walter arrived back at the Fort with the draft message and the draft Instrument of Abdication. Shortly afterwards he telephoned Dugdale, who had waited up in Downing Street with the Prime Minister, to tell him that the King had approved the documents, and would sign them in the presence of his brothers. Conversation continued between Walter, the King, and Sir Edward Peacock (who was staying for the night) until 2.40 a.m. At that point Peacock told the King that they should all get some sleep. Edward insisted on taking Peacock to his room, where they talked for a while longer; and as the King left, Peacock heard him saying to the exhausted Monckton: 'I just want a word with you'. The next day, Peacock learned that this 'word' had gone on 'until well after three o'clock'.[51]

On Thursday morning, the King's three brothers arrived to witness the signing of the two documents. The Duke of York, who was to become the new King, appeared at 9.30, followed shortly afterwards by the Duke of Gloucester. The Duke of Kent kept them waiting until almost ten o'clock: 'George *would* be late!' commented the King. The signing took place in the Round Room, where Monckton, Peacock, and Ulick Alexander, the Keeper of the Privy Purse, were also present. After the signing, first by the King and then by the three dukes as witnesses, Monckton and Peacock left with the documents – seven copies of the Instrument of Abdication, and eight of the King's message to the British and Imperial Parliaments – and took them straight to Buckingham Palace. There they found that arrangements had been made for sending out cables to each of the Dominions, in such a manner as to ensure their simultaneous arrival.

While he was in London, Walter asked both Baldwin and Chamberlain about what financial provision the King might now expect to receive from Parliament. They made encouraging comments; and Walter then handed the Prime Minister two slips of paper on which the King had scribbled in pencil, in the hope that Baldwin would use the material in his speech in the House of Commons that afternoon. On one of the slips of paper he had referred to his confidence in the Duke of York as his successor; and on the other, he had made it clear that 'the other person most intimately concerned' (in other words, Mrs Simpson) had consistently tried to dissuade him from abdication. This was the only occasion on which, in Walter's opinion, the Prime Minister was less than generous towards his master. He used the first

of the King's two points with 'marked effect', but altogether ignored
the second. 'No doubt,' Walter later reflected,[52]

> it would have been difficult to use it successfully in the House of Commons
> in its then temper, but, to say the least, it was a little hard on Mrs Simpson
> when no reference was made to it. I knew from Mr Baldwin before the
> speech was made that he was anxious to put the King's action in the best
> light, and I realised that he did not welcome the invitation to make the
> desired reference to Mrs Simpson, for this emphasised that it was the King
> and the King alone who accepted responsibility, and was in fact responsible
> for his decision.

Monckton was also annoyed by the Government's decision (communicated to the King on Thursday afternoon by Sir John Simon) to
discontinue giving police protection to Mrs Simpson. The King himself was extremely upset, as there had been several threats to assassinate
Wallis, and it was believed quite possible that there would be an actual
attempt on her life. 'I must say that however correct Simon's attitude
may have been,' Walter commented later, 'I thought he might have
spared the King this [anxiety] by taking the risk of criticism himself.'
No doubt it was due to the strong protest made by Walter at the time
that the decision was reversed within 24 hours.

Before then, on Thursday evening, the King entertained Wallis
Simpson's aunt, Mrs Bessie Merryman, to dinner at the Fort. The
other guests were George Hunter and his wife Kitty: Walter was not
present since he was dining at the Windham Club with his former
pupil Robert Boothby from whom he wished to hear about Baldwin's
speech in the Commons. After dinner Kitty Hunter sent a message to
Sir Edward Peacock asking him to come over to see her at her house;
and when he arrived she burst into tears, protesting that Wallis had
'fooled her to the last, declaring that she would never marry the King'.
Then she provided Peacock with a melancholy account of the dinner
which had just passed. 'The poor King must have had a pretty difficult
time,' he noted later, 'because apparently George and Kitty wept into
their soup and everything else during the meal, in spite of the King's
heroic efforts to carry off the dinner cheerfully.'[53]

In the meantime Walter had been giving Bob Boothby a champagne
dinner at his club. Bob found his host sad but resigned. Walter said
he was quite satisfied that there was no alternative to abdication. Then
he added: 'I wish to God I knew what she does to him!' Evidently he
was ignorant of the nature of their sexual relations. As also was
Boothby. 'She gives him what he needs most, self-confidence,' said
Bob. In his memoirs Boothby would observe that, in retrospect, he

was 'sure that the King was right to do what he did. He had done "enough service to the State"; and could do no more on the throne.'[54]

Next morning, Friday 11 December, Walter called on the Duke of York at his Piccadilly home in order to discuss what title the King should adopt after his abdication. 'I pointed out,' Walter records,[55]

> that the title 'Royal Highness' was one which the Abdication did not take away, and one which would require an Act of Parliament for its removal. The King, for himself and his successors, was renouncing any right to the Throne but not to his Royal Birth which he shared with his brothers. The Duke saw the point and was ready to create his brother Duke of Windsor as the first act of the new reign.

That same day, both Houses of Parliament met in the morning. The Abdication bill was rushed through all its stages, and was granted the Royal Assent by a commission of three peers; after which the Clerk of the Parliaments uttered the traditional words in Norman French: *'Le Roy le veult'*. Thus shortly after 2 p.m. Edward VIII ceased to be King.

Meanwhile Winston Churchill had joined the King and Walter for lunch at the Fort, and had helped to put the finishing touches to the historic broadcast which the ex-King was due to make later that day from Windsor Castle. It became part of the Abdication legend that the speech had been written by Churchill. This was not so, although Churchill did some important work on reshaping the draft. The substance of the message had already been drafted by Walter, with some moving personal additions by Edward, such as his reference to 'the woman I love'. After lunch Churchill was driven back to London with Walter; and, as they left the Fort, tears came into Churchill's eyes, and he recited Andrew Marvell's famous lines on the execution of Charles I:[56]

> He nothing common did or mean
> Upon that memorable scene.

Before the broadcast, Walter returned to the Fort where he dined with Prince Edward (as he now was), along with George Allen, Ulick Alexander, and Godfrey Thomas, who had been Edward's private secretary when he was Prince of Wales, and assistant private secretary when he was King. After dinner, they all drove to Royal Lodge where the Duke of York and Queen Mary were waiting to wish the ex-King well; and from there, Prince Edward and Monckton were driven on alone to Windsor Castle.

Sir John Reith was waiting for them in the room in the Augusta Tower from which the broadcast was to be transmitted. After a few minutes of general talk, the Prince and Monckton were left alone. Edward sat down to try out the microphone, and did a quick run-through of his speech; and then at ten o'clock Reith returned briefly, and announced into the microphone: 'His Royal Highness, Prince Edward.' 'The King began, I thought, a little anxiously,' Walter later recalled;[57]

> but with the sentences his confidence grew, and the strength of his voice, and the final sentence 'God Save the King' was almost a shout. When it was over the King stood up and, putting an arm on my shoulder, said: 'Walter, it is a far better thing that I go to.'

Together they returned to Royal Lodge where Queen Mary and the three royal Dukes were waiting to bid farewell to the Duke of Windsor, as he was about to become. 'The Queen was magnificently brave throughout and took leave of [her son] cheerfully,' Walter noted. 'I shall always remember the car starting and [Edward's] bow to his mother when she left.' Walter waited with the others for most of the next hour, until it was time for him to leave with Edward for Portsmouth, from where the ex-King was to sail for France. The conversation touched on everything but the topic which was uppermost in their minds. 'This is quite mad!' exclaimed the Duke of Kent. At last the moment came for Edward to say goodbye to his brothers. When he came to George, his successor as King, he bowed over his hand, kissing him and parting as Freemasons.

Shortly before their departure, Edward's cousin Lord Louis Mountbatten had arrived with two cars: a Rolls, in which he proposed to drive Edward to Portsmouth; and his estate car, with a driver, for the luggage. 'Thanks, but no,' said Edward. 'Walter Monckton is going with me. We have unfinished business to attend to. Why don't you follow with my bags?'

When they arrived at Portsmouth Docks they were late; and by mistake they entered by the wrong gate. When they found themselves driving past the *Victory*, Edward asked for the car to be stopped, and he and Walter got out of the car to look. 'There's *Victory*!' he exclaimed, pointing at Nelson's flagship. 'I think Nelson would have understood what I am doing. He too loved – loved *deeply*!' Then they walked about, and Edward pointed out various other vessels which he recognised. Meanwhile Admiral Sir William Fisher, the Commander-in-Chief, had sent someone to look for them; and in due course they

were escorted to the destroyer HMS *Furious*, which was to take
Edward to Boulogne. He went aboard with Walter carrying Wallis's
dog Slipper under his arm. Edward insisted that they should have a
last drink together, which they did in the wardroom. 'Goodbye, Sir,'
said the Admiral, his eyes filling with tears. 'Not from me alone, but
from the Royal Navy.'[58]

It was two o'clock in the morning when the destroyer set sail. Walter
immediately returned to the Windham Club in London, where he
settled down at once to write as follows to Queen Mary:[59]

> Your Majesty,
>
> I hope that You will not think me impertinent in writing this letter and
> that You will forgive it if it lapses from the proper form with which I am
> unfamiliar.
>
> Your Majesty knows that I went down to Portsmouth last night with
> your son. During the journey he talked quietly of old times and places well
> remembered by both of us, but above all he talked of You – how grand
> You were, how sweet to him and especially at the last when he wanted it
> most. (You will recognise the words as his.) I left him on the destroyer;
> he was still full of the same gay courage and spirit which have amazed us
> all this week . . .
>
> There is still and there always will be a greatness and glory about him.
> Even the faults and follies are great. And he will, I feel sure, never lend
> himself to any such dangerous courses as some, not unreasonably, fear.
> He has shown that he cares for unity: and he felt deeply the unity of the
> Family with him last night.
>
> My heart is very heavy and I can understand at least the fringe of Your
> Majesty's sorrow.
>
> I will go on trying to help him when he needs me.

Queen Mary answered this communication with characteristic kindness, and with the audience she gave him that same day, Walter
considered that 'this chapter closes for me'. However, there was an
unfortunate aftermath which he had not anticipated.

Next day, Sunday 13 December, His Grace Cosmo Gordon Lang,
Archbishop of Canterbury, delivered a most cruel and public rebuke.
In a wireless broadcast, he recalled that the date of Edward's departure
was also the date upon which King James II had run away from
Whitehall. Speaking of Edward, he went on: 'In darkness he fled these
shores . . . It was a craving for private happiness. Strange and sad it
must be that for such a motive . . . he should have disappointed hopes
so high and abandoned a trust so great.'

The Archbishop went on to describe the ex-King's inner circle as a group 'whose standards and ways of life are alien to all the best instincts and traditions of his people. Let those who belong to this circle know that today they stand rebuked by the judgment of the nation which had loved King Edward.' These words were deeply offensive to such friends as the Brownlows, the Duff Coopers, the Channons, the Mountbattens and Lady Cunard, not to mention Walter Monckton. When Lord Brownlow called at Lambeth Palace and civilly demanded an apology for the false construction which had been placed upon his loyalty to his Sovereign, the Archbishop could only reply that 'The innocent must suffer with the guilty.' Pressed by Brownlow to name the members of the ex-King's allegedly disreputable circle, the Primate was at a loss for words. The fact was that he did not know.[60]

The Archbishop's broadcast attracted a large and overwhelmingly hostile mail addressed to him. One correspondent, widely believed to be the writer Gerald Bullett, was moved to communicate with His Grace in verse. His composition achieved a wide currency, and a copy reached Walter. It read:

My Lord Archbishop, what a scold you are!
And when your man is down, how bold you are!
Of Christian charity how scant you are!
And, auld Lang swine, how full of cant you are!*

---

* As Archbishop of Canterbury, His Grace signed himself Cosmo Cantuar.

Chapter 4

Royal Affairs and Other Duties

I

B
EFORE the Duke of Windsor's departure, the new monarch
asked Walter Monckton to serve him in the same manner as he
had his brother. Consequently Walter retained his office of
Attorney-General to the Duchy of Cornwall. King George VI also
granted Walter the first knighthood of his reign, when he created him
a Knight Commander of the Victorian Order. A KCVO is very much
a personal order of the Sovereign, having been initiated by Queen
Victoria to reward British subjects who had rendered extraordinary
or important services to the monarch personally. The award was
announced with others in the New Year Honours list on 1 February
1937; but since Walter was already in royal service it was unnecessary
for him to attend a formal investiture. Instead the King sent for him
on the day of the announcement, and Walter went along to 145
Piccadilly where the King was still living. George received him in a
little room on the first floor, and Walter had no idea that he was to be
knighted then and there.

After ten minutes' conversation, however, the King pointed to a
yellow footstool in the background and said: 'We shall be needing
that.' Walter pulled it out, and the King told him to kneel on it. When
he did so, the King produced a sword and tapped him lightly on the
shoulder. Walter then started to get up, but the King restrained him,
saying, 'No, I haven't done yet'. His Majesty then tapped Walter on
the other shoulder. When he eventually rose to his feet, the King
remarked: 'Well, Walter, we did not manage that very well, but neither
of us had done it before!'[1]

Shortly after Walter had received his knighthood, some difficulties
arose between the new King and his older brother who (as Monckton

tells the story) 'was troubling him a good deal on the telephone, and I was told to go out and persuade him to discontinue this'. The Duke of Windsor was then staying in Schloss Enzesfeld, Baron Eugene de Rothschild's retreat on a tree-covered slope above a little village some 18 miles from Vienna.

Accordingly, Walter set off in an aircraft of the King's Flight piloted by Wing-Commander Edward (Mouse) Fielden, the Captain of the Flight. They left early one morning. Walter had been dining out the previous evening and did not feel at all like flying. The weather was so appalling that he was sick; and after one very rough bout they were forced down at Cologne instead of reaching their destination, Vienna. 'It was urgent that I should get on and see the Duke as soon as I could,' Walter wrote of his mission, 'and eventually Mouse and I decided that I had better catch a train from Cologne to Vienna which left about 3 a.m. It was a horrible journey and I reached Vienna at about 9 a.m.' Imagine his surprise when he arrived at Schloss Enzesfeld only to discover Mouse Fielden waiting for him with a drink! After saying goodbye to Walter at Cologne station, and then enjoying a good night's sleep, Fielden had woken to fine weather and, helped by a strong tail wind, had been able to fly all the way down to Vienna in just a few hours.[2]

Walter found the Duke looking extremely fit, having been spending his time mostly skiing in the Semmering or sightseeing in Vienna. The matter of the King's disinclination to talk to him on the telephone had to be handled carefully. The point, as Monckton later recalled, was that the Duke of Windsor had kept[3]

> in close and constant touch with his brother by telephone, and gave him firm advice as to the line he ought to take in the questions which came up for his decision. This advice often ran counter to the advice which the King was getting from his responsible Ministers in the Government. This caused him trouble, which no one would understand who did not know the extent to which before the Abdication the Duke of Windsor's brothers admired and looked up to him.
>
> Moreover telephone conversations, especially when they ranged into questions affecting Mrs Simpson, were especially hard for the new King. The Duke of Windsor was particularly quick in understanding and decision, whereas George VI had not the same quickness and was troubled by the impediment in his speech. I was able to dissuade the Duke from continuing these conversations by pointing out to him the disadvantage at which the new King found himself in conducting them.

Before this, there had been another and rather more serious matter to be discussed: namely, the financial arrangements which had been made between the two brothers.

At the time of the Abdication, the Government had promised that they would recommend Edward's inclusion in the 'Civil List': that is, the parliamentary resolution granting pensions to members of the Royal Family which takes place early in each reign. In the event of the House of Commons refusing to vote anything to the Duke, in spite of the Government's recommendation, George VI had undertaken to make his brother an annual allowance of £25,000. In return, the Duke had agreed that George VI could purchase his interest in Sandringham and Balmoral 'at fair value'; that the King should also retain a life interest in the proceeds of the 'sale', and should be given the contents of both those properties; and that any heirlooms the Duke of Windsor had owned should also pass to the new monarch. All these arrangements were contingent upon the Duke undertaking not to see Mrs Simpson until the Civil List became law, or before her divorce decree became absolute.

The Duke's first action on seeing Walter had been to show him a letter, dated 10 February 1937, which he had received from George Allen informing him that the Government 'could not support your inclusion on the Civil List. Nor could they countenance Your Royal Highness receiving an annual payment from the King.' This had been followed by a letter from George VI effectively repudiating his agreement to pay the Duke a pension, and blaming the mood of Parliament who were said to be still 'a little sore with you for having given up being King'. To which the Duke had replied: 'I must tell you frankly that I am relying on you to honour your promise.' As Michael Bloch says, 'what distressed the Duke in February 1937 was not so much that the promised financial help was being withheld from him (for he knew that it would take the new Sovereign time to organise his finances), but that both King and Parliament, in a striking demonstration of unfriendly feeling towards him, appeared to have broken their word'.[4]

Walter somehow managed to maintain communications between the King and the Duke over this very difficult matter, which took many months to settle, and caused the Duke in particular a great deal of worry.

At least there was no difficulty over the divorce! Once the law clerk had withdrawn his objection, Sir Donald Somervell, the Attorney-General acting on behalf of the King's Proctor, was able to declare in the divorce division that there was no longer any reason for complaint; and so the *decree nisi* automatically became absolute on 27 April.[5] At the same time Wallis changed her name by deed poll back to Warfield, and she would describe herself on her marriage certificate as 'single'.

A more difficult set of questions related to Wallis's style and status after her marriage. To his dismay Walter heard of an impending Order in Council which would confer the title and dignity of His Royal Highness upon the Duke of Windsor, but would deliberately exclude both his wife and their descendants, if any. 'If the King had been left to himself,' Walter commented, 'I feel confident that he would not have assented to this course because he knew the effect it would have on his brother.' Monckton warned the Home Secretary not to underestimate the bitterness that this would cause in the Duke. Had the decision been entirely up to the British Cabinet, Monckton's advice might have prevailed, and on becoming Duchess of Windsor, Wallis might also have begun to be styled 'Her Royal Highness'; but apparently there was strong opposition to her receiving a royal title from the Dominions, especially Canada and Australia.

It fell to Sir Walter Monckton to pass on this disagreeable news to the Duke, which he did on the evening of 27 May 1937, together with an apologetic letter from the King, and a copy of the Letters Patent dated the same day embodying the decision as formally published in the *London Gazette*. In his letter the King observed that to have to write about it made him 'unhappy and sad'; he was 'sorry'; he hoped the Duke 'would understand' and would not regard the move as 'an insult', or let it affect their relations 'in any way'.

'This is a nice wedding-present!' the Duke remarked to Walter when he had read both the Letters Patent and his brother's personal letter. 'I know Bertie – I know he couldn't have written this letter on his own.' The Duke's immediate reaction was to declare his intention of giving up the royal title for himself rather than use a style different from that of his future wife. With Wallis's help, however, Walter dissuaded him from this course, pointing out not only that it would have been openly offensive to the King, but also that it would have meant giving up something of substance, and getting very little in return. 'But I did sympathise with him over this,' Walter wrote later.[6]

When he had been King he had been told he could not marry Mrs Simpson because she would have to take his status and become Queen, so he gave up his Kingdom and Empire to make her his wife. He could not give up his royal birth, or his right to be called 'His Royal Highness' which flowed from it. It was a little hard to be told, when he did marry her, that she would not have the same status as himself.

According to Wallis, nothing in the aftermath of the Abdication hurt the Duke of Windsor more than his brother's action in this matter. In Edward's eyes it was a terrible slur upon his wife and, therefore, upon himself. He could not bring himself wholly to blame his brother who had evidently been subject to strong pressures: Baldwin, for example, must have been partly responsible, since it was he who had presided over the Cabinet which had ratified the King's decision; but it made for a coolness between them thereafter.[7] Thirty years later the incident still rankled; and he wrote in a New York newspaper that 'this cold-blooded act, in its uprush, represented a kind of Berlin wall alienating us from my family'.[8]

The Duke and Wallis were now staying together near Tours at the Château de Candé (lent to Wallis's friends the Rogerses by the American industrialist Charles Bedaux*), where they were to be married just over a week later. Monckton left the day after his arrival, but promised to return for the wedding which had coincidentally been fixed for 3 June, the birthday of Edward's father, the late King George V.

The Duke did not send Monckton back to London with a written reply to his brother's letter, but he gave him two oral messages which he delivered in writing immediately after his return. First, the Duke wished the King to know that he had it on the best legal advice – that of Sir William Jowitt, KC – that no Letters Patent were necessary to create him a Royal Highness but that, on the contrary, he had been entitled to that style from the moment of his birth.† Futhermore the Duke wished for an opportunity to be given to Jowitt to discuss the matter with those (presumably lawyers) who had advised the Government. Second, the Duke stated that he could only regard the action which had been taken as an insult to the lady who was shortly to become his wife; and, therefore, as an insult to himself. The Duke followed this up with a formal letter to his brother informing him that he did not deem himself bound by the Letters Patent of 27 May, and

* Bedaux had devised a controversial efficiency system for factory work.

† Jowitt's opinion, endorsed by Patrick (later Lord) Devlin is given in full in Appendix II of *The Secret File of the Duke of Windsor*, ed. Michael Bloch (1988). After the war, when Jowitt became Lord Chancellor in the first post-war Labour Government, the Duke reminded him of his opinion that the act depriving the Duchess of Windsor of the style of HRH was illegal. But Jowitt did nothing and the matter was finally dropped, though not forgotten by the Duke who was intensely disappointed. The arguments questioning the validity of the Letters Patent of 27 May 1937 have been persuasively advanced by Philip M. Thomas in the 1967 edition of *Burke's Peerage*. For the contrary argument see a letter by the present author in *The Times*, 20 September 1972.

pointing out that in George's accession speech of 12 December 1936 he had been happy to refer to him as 'His Royal Highness'. In the event, however, no further action was taken at that time.[9]

Walter returned to the Château de Candé on the eve of the wedding; and along with his fellow-guests, George Allen and Randolph Churchill, he stayed at the Hôtel de l'Univers, the best of its kind in Tours. Besides Baron Eugene and Kitty de Rothschild (who had accommodated the Duke at Enzesfeld), Charles and Fern Bedaux, and Herman and Katharine Rogers, the other guests included the Duke's equerry Major Edward (Fruity) Metcalfe (who was to be best man), and his wife Lady Alexandra;* Dudley Forwood, another equerry; Hugh Lloyd Thomas, Minister in the British Embassy in Paris, who had been assistant private secretary to the Duke when he was Prince of Wales;† Lady Selby, wife of the British Ambassador in Lisbon; Mr Thomas Carter of the Privy Purse Office in Buckingham Palace; and Wallis's aunt Bessie Merryman.

No member of the royal family was present, and only the Dukes of Kent and Gloucester sent presents, although King George VI, Queen Elizabeth and Queen Mary all sent what Lady Alexandra Metcalfe described as 'nice telegrams'.

Cecil Beaton was there to take photographs; and Constance Spry, the London florist, to arrange the floral decorations. The weather was perfect and masses of reporters surrounded the Château: Dudley Forwood had considerable difficulty in coping with them.

The Duke was anxious to have a religious service in addition to the civil ceremony, but there was considerable difficulty in finding an Anglican priest, since the Church of England at that time officially banned the marriage of divorced persons. However, there were a few clergymen prepared to defy the ban; and eventually the service was performed by the Rev. R. A. Jardine, vicar of St Paul's, Darlington. He had proposed himself and, once he had been vetted by George Allen, his offer was gratefully accepted. Walter later described Jardine as[10]

rather a rebellious priest from the Durham diocese, but he seemed a simple man, and genuinely anxious to serve, and to help the Duke. Later on he turned out to have, in spite of the warnings which Allen and I gave him,

---

* Lady Alexandra (Baba) Metcalfe was the youngest daughter of the Marquess Curzon of Keddleston by his first wife. She was aged 33 at this time, good-looking and attractive. Her marriage, which took place in 1925, was dissolved by divorce in 1965. Queen Alexandra, after whom she was named, was her godmother.

† Sadly, Lloyd Thomas was soon to be killed steeple-chasing.

a marked weakness for self-advertisement. On at least one occasion he toured the United States on the strength of having married the Duke and Mrs Simpson.*

Walter Monckton was at dinner with Edward and Wallis on the night before their wedding, together with the Rothschilds, Randolph Churchill, and the Metcalfes. 'I sat on HRH's right,' wrote Lady Alexandra, 'with Monckton on the other side. I couldn't like him more. He is devoted to [the Duke].' And the next morning, she found it strange that only 'seven English people (Fruity, Monckton, Allen, Randolph Churchill and Hugh Thomas, Lady Selby and myself) [were] present at the wedding of the man who six months ago was King of England'.[11]

The civil ceremony was attended only by Fruity Metcalfe, Herman Rogers (who was to give Wallis away) and four journalists; and the religious service took place in the adjacent drawing room, where a wooden chest covered by a silk cloth and surmounted by a Cross and candles, served for an altar. The organist played Handel's Wedding March from *Judas Maccabaeus* and the hymn 'O Perfect Love' during the benediction. The Duke wore striped trousers and a morning coat with a white carnation in his buttonhole; while Wallis appeared in a fetching blue outfit by Mainbocher. During the service Fruity Metcalfe held for the bridegroom the prayer book which Queen Mary had given him for his tenth birthday, inscribed 'To darling David from his loving Mother'.

After the service, which took place about midday, there was a reception followed by a wedding-breakfast of lobster, salad, chicken-à-la-king and strawberries. At the reception the guests were received one at a time by the bridal pair; and immediately they faced the problem of how to treat the new Duchess. Walter gave her a most deferential bow; but then, as he said, his head bowed easily. Meanwhile the French housekeeper took a bottle of champagne and ritually broke it against the château gate, a local tradition, after which she cleared up the broken glass with a broom.

---

* Bishop Hensley Henson of Durham said that if it had been arranged for the marriage to take place within his diocese, he would have prevented any clergyman from officiating. However, he could not control the Rev. Jardine on the Continent. Northern and Eastern Europe was in the jurisdiction of the Bishop of Fulham, and Bishop Henson presumed that he had given his permission. However, the Bishop of Fulham declared that if an Anglican clergyman had officiated at the wedding of the Duke of Windsor, he wished it to be known that this action had been taken without his knowledge or consent.

Later on, Walter managed to engage the Duchess in a private conversation in the grounds, where he 'took the chance to tell her how much I sympathised with her in the difficulty of the task which had now fallen to her, and how much I would always try to help them both'. He went on to warn her very frankly that 'most people in England disliked her very much, because the Duke had married her and given up his throne, but that if she made him, and kept him, happy all her days, all that would change; but that if he were unhappy nothing would be too bad for her'.[12]

The Duchess took his admonitions seriously, saying: 'Walter, don't you think I have thought of all that? I think I can make him happy.' And in this, at least, she appears to have succeeded.

Walter was a passenger in one of the long convoy of cars which went to the station to bid farewell to the Duke and Duchess. They were taking the Orient Express as far as Austria, where they were to spend a prolonged honeymoon in the Schloss Wasserleonburg, generously placed at their disposal by Count and Countess Paul Munster. The bridal couple took with them 266 pieces of luggage, besides the two cairn terriers who had replaced the adored Slipper – sadly killed by a viper's bite. They were also accompanied by Dudley Forwood as equerry, and by two Scotland Yard detectives.

The Munsters were absent when the Duke and Duchess arrived at the Schloss; but they were given a warm welcome by the housekeeper who remarked when the Duke carried the Duchess without stumbling over the threshold into the hall where 30 servants were waiting, that this was a good sign, and meant that they would be very happy together. Wallis was soon scolding her third husband for having abdicated, and denied her the role of royal mistress;* but he was still wholly in love with her, and would remain so.[13]

---

* The Duchess later wrote in her autobiography: 'Only one thing marred our happiness: after the first burst of joy in rediscovering each other and being together we found our minds turning back in interminable post-mortems concerning the events leading up to the Abdication . . . This endless rehash of the lost past became almost an obsession with us until one evening David said despairingly, "Darling, if we keep this up we are never going to agree, so let's drop it for good." Then and there we vowed we would never discuss the Abdication again, and to this day we never have.' *The Heart Has Its Reasons*, pp.299–300.

2

During and after the abdication crisis, Walter Monckton endeavoured to continue his practice at the Bar, besides acting both as adviser to the Nizam of Hyderabad, and as Attorney-General to the Duchy of Cornwall. The interruptions of his various extra-mural obligations inevitably limited his activities; but he had three particularly interesting cases to deal with in the mid- to late 1930s, including one in which the Royal Family were interested, since it concerned an illegitimate daughter of one of Queen Victoria's grandsons.

The first of these cases began at Bow Street magistrates' court on 13 December 1935 when Henry John Cole, a guide in Westminster Abbey, preferred an information against Police Constable 443A, for having unlawfully assaulted him on the previous day. What had happened was this: Cole's permit as a guide in the Abbey had expired as long ago as May 1932. When he had applied for a new permit, the Dean and Chapter of Westminster Abbey had refused his application, and the Dean had given instructions that Cole was to be excluded from the Abbey. Then on 12 December 1935, when a service was in progress, Cole was seen in the Abbey wearing a badge with the words 'Cole's Sightseeing Tours Guide'; and the Dean ordered PC 443A and another constable to eject him from the Abbey.

Cole's case was that the Abbey was a public building which was open for public services; that as a member of the public he had a right to be there; that the Dean had no authority to order his exclusion from the Abbey; and that the constables, by ejecting him, had therefore committed an assault. The case for PC 443A was that the Dean and Chapter had enjoyed complete authority to control whatever happened in the Abbey since it had been handed over to their predecessors in the sixteenth century under Letters Patent granted by Queen Elizabeth I; and that he and his fellow constable had therefore acted quite properly in obeying the Dean's orders and ejecting the plaintiff.

The magistrate found in favour of PC 443A, arguing that the right to attend a church service was limited to those parishioners who had a statutory duty to attend; and that anyone such as Cole who was not a parishioner could be excluded at any time at the discretion of the Dean and Chapter. The constable had acted properly in obeying the Dean; and the information was therefore dismissed.

Cole would not let the matter rest; and his appeal to the King's Bench Divisional Court was heard in mid-October 1936 by Lord Hewart (the Lord Chief Justice), Mr Justice du Parcq, and Mr Justice Goddard. Mr Basil Blagden (later a county-court judge) appeared for Cole; and Walter Monckton and G. G. Raphael represented PC 443A.[14]

Blagden argued that since a service was in progress at the time of Cole's eviction, it must be presumed that he was not there in order to ply for business, but to attend the service like other worshippers. His badge merely showed his occupation and did not remove his right to be there. Nor did the Abbey have parishioners in the traditional sense of the word, as it had no parish: so its services could only be attended by members of the public at large.

In reply, Walter Monckton for PC 443A submitted that the police officer had ejected Cole from the Abbey pursuant to a lawful order of the Dean and without unnecessary force. His action was therefore justified, and he could not be convicted of an assault. It was not true, Monckton added, that the Abbey had no parish attached to it. The close, or precincts of the Abbey, constituted its parish, and all who resided there, such as masters of Westminster School, were its parishioners.

In giving judgment the Lord Chief Justice declared that:

> At no time did this appellant [Cole] say, or say in effect, that though he went into the Abbey wearing a badge, he desired to remain there as a devout worshipper. What he did say by way of argument was that it was true that the authorities exclude him because he was offering his services as a guide, although a permit to do so had been refused to him, but that they could not properly exclude him at all, because in theory at any rate he might have been taking part in public worship.
>
> That argument is in my opinion an afterthought designed to cover what the appellant was really doing . . . The appellant was complaining not that the Dean had interfered with his devotional exercises, but that he had interrupted the flow of half-crowns from sightseers to the appellant as a guide. He never said until recently that his real object in being in the Abbey was to worship. In these circumstances, when one remembers that on the application for his case it was stated with engaging frankness that what was being interfered with was the appellant's livelihood – not his immortal soul but his livelihood – it seems to me that the excursions into ecclesiastical law and constitutional history to which we have listened, however edifying and ably conducted, are here irrelevant.

The Lord Chief Justice, with the agreement of his two judicial brethren, accordingly held that the Dean had the authority to make the order excluding the appellant; that on the appellant's refusal to leave when requested, the respondent was justified in ejecting him; and therefore that the magistrate had been right to dismiss the information.

The second of these cases concerned an alarming but short-lived epidemic of typhoid fever which had occurred in the borough of Croydon in October and November 1937. There had been a public inquiry, at which Walter Monckton had represented Croydon corporation, and at which it was revealed that during the epidemic there had been 322 primary and 19 secondary cases of typhoid, with 43 deaths. Subsequently a Croydon ratepayer, Alfred Read, together with his 15-year-old daughter Patricia, who had contracted typhoid as a result of drinking water supplied by the Croydon corporation, brought an action against the corporation for breach of statutory duty. Walter, who was briefed to represent the corporation, was aware of the importance of his task: it was a test case, whose findings would be regarded as decisive of other similar claims. The case was tried by Mr Justice Stable, with Mr Hubert Wallington KC appearing for Read and his daughter.[15]

Wallington argued for the plaintiffs that the failure of the defendant corporation to appreciate the need for adequate chlorination and filtration, coupled with the failure to provide either suitable sanitary accommodation or proper medical checks at the principal well supplying water to the reservoir for the workmen (one of whom turned out to be a typhoid carrier), constituted negligence. Not only was there a statutory duty to provide 'pure and wholesome water', but there was a contract between Alfred Read and the corporation for the supply of water, and that contract was for the sale of goods, with an implied warranty that the water should be fit for the purpose for which it was supplied.

In his reply, Monckton stressed that the corporation had been most cooperative in its dealings on this difficult matter, and he also pointed out that chlorination was a recent policy, of which there was much disapproval in some quarters. On the question of negligence, the main thrust of his argument was that the court should judge the actions of the corporation not with hindsight, but in the light of whatever knowledge was actually available to them at the time of the outbreak. He added that, in his view, there was no formal contract between the corporation and the plaintiffs. As for the corporation having breached its statutory duty, the relevant acts only provided for a penalty to be imposed upon those failing in their duty, and specifically excluded any right to bring a civil action; and if such an action were possible, it could only be taken by a ratepayer – not, in other words, as in this case, by an affected relative. Finally, he concluded that the obligation to supply pure water was not an absolute one, and that no action could lie unless it could be proved that there had been a lack of reasonable care on the part of the Croydon corporation.

After weighing up the arguments, Mr Justice Stable concluded that Croydon corporation was guilty of negligence at common law for having lacked the care and skill which should be an attribute of any corporation which supplies water to the public. The epidemic had almost certainly been caused by a typhoid carrier bringing an infection into the well; and there would have been no danger to the public had there been a continuous use of chlorine to keep the water pure. However, he emphasised that such negligence did not amount to a deliberate dereliction of duty, and he paid special tribute to Walter Monckton's arguments on the subject, and to his comment that it was easy to be wise after the event. He also agreed with Monckton that where one person is by statute bound to supply water and another to receive it, there is no contractual relationship between those two parties. He added that the corporation was definitely in breach of its statutory duty under the Waterworks Causes Act of 1847. However, Monckton was correct that this breach conferred a right of action on a ratepayer only, and not on the persons resident in the household, so that the remedy was confined to the adult plaintiff Mr Read. He further stated that although the act of 1847 provided a penalty for a breach of statutory duty, this was not an exclusive remedy, and an action for damages could also be brought in respect of a breach of that duty. Accordingly Alfred Read had a right of action to recover any out-of-pocket expenses resulting from his daughter's illness; while Patricia herself could claim negligence, for which damages were assessed at £100.

Monckton was so interested in the third dispute, the one involving the Royal Family, that it was one of the relatively few cases which he noted for the autobiography which he planned, but of which only a few fragments were actually written.[16] His clients were Queen Victoria's granddaughters, Her Highness Princess Helena Victoria, known as Thora; and Her Highness Princess Marie Louise. The matter concerned their niece Valerie Marie, the illegitimate daughter of their elder brother Prince Albert. The latter had inherited the Prussian Dukedom of Schleswig-Holstein from his cousin Ernest in 1921; and ten years later, on the eve of his death and still unmarried, he had signed a document admitting that Valerie was his daughter by an unnamed lady of 'high noble birth': possibly, since Valerie was born in Hungary, one of the Hungarian nobility.

Valerie had been brought up in Hungary by Jewish foster-parents called Schwalb, whose surname she had adopted as her own. As a young woman she had married Ernest Emmanuel Wagner of Budapest; but that relationship broke down, and in 1938, when she obtained a divorce, Valerie was already planning a second marriage. However, difficulties arose. So far as the authorities of Nazi Germany were concerned, her prospective husband's credentials were impeccable: Prince Engelbert Arensberg was descended from Counts of the Holy Roman Empire, and was in possession of Schloss Nordkirchen, an imposing family seat at Ludinghausen in Westphalia. All the documents about Valerie, however, showed that her maiden name was undeniably Jewish; and she would therefore be unable to marry the man with whom she was in love.

Valerie therefore appealed for help to the British diplomatic representatives in Berlin and Budapest. When they passed on her appeal to Marshal Goering, stressing her royal connections, he is said to have declared firmly: 'It is I who decides who is royal and who is not.' It was at this stage that Walter Monckton was brought into the case by Valerie's aunts; before long a certificate had been obtained declaring that the bride and groom were free to marry; and Walter met them in the Hôtel Bristol in Paris to give them his personal reassurance that all would be well. In the event they were married at Charlottenburg, Berlin, on 15 June 1939, shortly before the outbreak of the Second World War. Sir Neville Henderson, the British Ambassador in Berlin, was present; and the bride was given away by the only remaining male member of her family, her uncle Prince Frederick Leopold of Prussia. The whole affair was kept very secret, and no mention of it appeared in any newspaper.*

Afterwards Princess Helena Victoria wrote to Walter Monckton, thanking him for all the work he had done 'to bring the happy event about for the young couple' – not that they were particularly young: the Prince being 40 and Valerie only a year younger at the time of their marriage. Later on they would occupy Walter from time to time with further problems; and Walter's second wife Biddy would eventually call them 'a very tiresome couple'.[17]

---

* The *Almanac de Gotha* (1941) describes Princess Valerie Arensberg as being 'of Schleswig-Holstein' and as having been born at Liptovsky Svati Mikulas, Hungary. Her putative father Prince Albert of Schleswig-Holstein, being heir to vast estates in Silesia, which he duly inherited from his cousin together with the Dukedom, lived mostly in Germany where he served as an officer in the Prussian army, although he was born in England and educated at Charterhouse. During the First World War he had held an army staff appointment in Berlin.

3

Walter Monckton continued to give valuable service to the Duke and Duchess of Windsor. Within three months of their wedding, in August 1937, he flew once again to Austria where he met them at Schloss Wasserleonburg in Carinthia. There he found that although their financial worries had subsided, the Duke's bitterness over the question of his wife's title, or rather lack of it, was unabated. The Duke was also bored by his lack of occupation, and they were both fretting about when they would be allowed to return to England. The Duchess, in Walter's words, appeared to be 'in some sense beating against the bars. She wanted [the Duke] to eat his cake and have it. She could not easily reconcile herself to the fact that by marrying her he had become a less important person.'[18]

It was shortly after this, in October 1937, that the Windsors visited Germany, where they were entertained by Goering, Goebbels, Hess and Ribbentrop, and even had tea at Berchtesgaden with Hitler – who kept them waiting for an hour. Churchill was worried that this possibly ill-advised visit would attract unfavourable comment in England; but in fact it aroused little interest, since well-known politicians such as Lloyd George and Halifax had also had interviews with the Führer.

After leaving Schloss Wasserleonburg, which had only been lent to them, the Windsors had some difficulty in deciding where to live. For one thing they were still hoping to return to England in the near future; for another, the Duke preferred the country, while the Duchess liked the town. In the event they spent the winter of 1937–8 in Paris, where they stayed partly in the Hôtel Maurice, and partly in the Château de la Maye, a furnished villa in Versailles. Then in the spring of 1937 they leased the Château La Croe, a villa in Antibes; and later that year they moved back to Paris, where they leased a house at 24 Boulevard Suchet, near the Bois du Boulogne. Walter Monckton visited them in all these places; and as a close friend he began to feel very anxious that the Duke was being deprived of the kind of advice from Government ministers and other responsible people to which he had been accustomed. 'Kings not only live in glass houses,' as Walter put it,[19]

but have constant access to the best advice in every sphere. It was hard to convince people at home how much more difficult it was for the Duke, because of the position he had held and the advice which had been available to him, to keep an even and temperate judgement when responsible Ministers never went near him, and instead he was surrounded by friends who, for one reason or another, lived abroad largely divorced from English society and interests. With someone so quick to take a point, and so impressionable as the Duke, this was a constant anxiety to me. Ministers were anxious lest, if they called upon the Duke, they might be misunderstood by the royal circle at home. I am satisfied that there was never any solid foundation for that fear. I persuaded the Prime Minister Mr Chamberlain, Lord Halifax, Mr Churchill and Mr Duff Cooper to call upon the Duke. Their visits were welcomed and improved the atmosphere.

In February 1938, soon after they had settled in Versailles, the Duke and Duchess learned from the newspapers that the King and Queen were to make a State Visit to Paris in June. George Allen happened to be with them at the time, concluding various financial arrangements; and the Duke asked him to write to Walter on the subject. In his letter Allen spoke of the Duke's hopes that Their Majesties' stay in Paris would be a great success, and that it would include both paying a call on the Duke and his wife, and arranging for them to be invited to one of the official receptions. 'He feels that such a reception would serve the general interest,' wrote Allen, 'since it would become known to everyone that the estrangement which has existed in the past has now ended.'

Complicated negotiations then took place between the Duke and the King, with Walter acting as intermediary. The result was that the Duke and Duchess decided to be away from Paris during the state visit to avoid any possible embarrassment to the King. In writing to the Duke, Walter had made it clear that King George and Queen Elizabeth hoped to see the Duke and Duchess 'later on'; and Walter added that the King had given instructions that they were to be *'treated with proper attention and respect'*.

Subsequently the Duke wrote to the King to tell him that:

> Some proper recognition of our position as your brother and sister-in-law would seem to be in accord with your stated instructions. We have, as yet, I regret to say, detected no evidence that your instructions are being carried out, and we frankly feel that a formal reception given for us by your diplomatic representatives in Paris is distinctly overdue, to say the least.

One reason for the Duke's desire to be received at the British Embassy was that, in advance of the royal state visit, he and the Duchess were finding themselves shunned by French society. The Duke's letter had its effect: in May the Windsors accepted an invitation to dine at the embassy; and the following month they left for Antibes. In the event their departure was somewhat premature, since following the death of

Lady Strathmore, the Queen's mother, the state visit was postponed until the end of July.

Then in August 1938 (the month before the fatal Munich agreement), Walter was at La Croe with the Windsors for a few days, and found the Duke obsessed both by his remoteness from political events, and by a longing to return to England with his Duchess. 'By withdrawing from the great position which my birth had destined me to fill,' he was to write many years later, 'I had become something alien, something apart.'[20] Walter was shortly due to visit Balmoral, and so was able to tell the Duke that he would speak to the King about his brother's wishes. In fact, he went to Balmoral immediately after he had flown back to England; but before talking to the King he had a word with one of his fellow-guests, the Prime Minister Neville Chamberlain. Afterwards, Walter wrote:

> The Prime Minister thought that the right course was for the Duke of Windsor to be treated as soon as possible as a younger brother of the King who could take some of the royal functions off his brother's hands. The King himself, though he was not anxious for the Duke to return as early as November 1938 (which was what the Duke wanted) was not fundamentally against the Prime Minister's view. But I think the Queen felt quite plainly that it was undesirable to give the Duke any effective sphere of work. I felt then, as always, that she naturally thought that she must be on her guard because the Duke of Windsor, to whom the other brothers had always looked up, was an attractive, vital creature who might be the rallying-point for any who might be critical of the new King who was less superficially endowed with the arts and graces that please.

The result of Walter's visit to Balmoral was that he was given the difficult task of postponing the Duke's return from November into the New Year. 'The Prime Minister,' recalled Walter, 'would not have minded a return in November but the King, and particularly the Queen, thought it inadvisable so soon. Therefore I paid a number of visits to the Duke and Duchess in Paris, and their return was put off until the outbreak of war.'[21]

In August 1939, when war was imminent (though neither Walter nor the Duke realised this), Walter frequently spoke on the telephone to Antibes. However, by this time telephone conversations through a French exchange were only permitted in French, a language in which Walter's lack of proficiency meant that his discussions with the Duke were of limited value. The best that he could do was to assure the Duke that the position, though serious, was *'pas sans espoir'*. Walter later wrote that:

The Duke was strongly against the waste and horror of war, and felt it ought somehow to be avoided. Neither of us saw that it was inevitable. Almost on the last day the Duke sent a telegram to Hitler which I have never seen mentioned, in which, as a citizen of the world, he asked him not to plunge the world into war. Hitler replied that he never wanted a war with England, and that if it took place it would not be his fault. During the last day or two before war was declared I had a troublesome time speaking constantly to the Duke from 10 Downing Street and urging him to come back, making elaborate arrangements for the purpose.

At the very last moment, when Walter had already instructed Mouse Fielden to fly the King's plane to Antibes and bring the Duke and Duchess back to England, the Duke sent a telegram refusing to make the journey unless he were promised accommodation at Windsor or in one of the other royal palaces. The result was that after a midnight conversation with Alec Hardinge, Walter was compelled to cancel the flight, and war was declared with the Duke and Duchess still at Antibes.[22]

The Prime Minister then decided that the Duke should not be allowed to return to England unless he agreed to accept either the post of Deputy Regional Commissioner to Sir William Portal in Wales, or that of Liaison Officer with the British Military Mission headed by General Howard Vyse, to the Commander-in-Chief of the Allied Armies in France, General Gamelin. Feeling that his brother should be interviewed about his preference, the King told Walter Monckton to fly to Antibes and talk to the Duke in person. It was also decided that Walter should travel in an aircraft which the Windsors would be bound to think unsuitable for their own use, since if there was a shortage of space Walter might be left behind on the Riviera. Walter was therefore sent out, as he later recalled,

in a small Leopard Moth sitting beside the pilot. As the Duke afterwards said, it looked to him as though the tyres were flat and the plane tied up with string. It was when the King told me at Buckingham Palace to make this journey that he suggested I should write a book on 'Odd Jobs I Have Done', and it turned out an odder job than he or I anticipated.[23]

The pilot was a flying officer in the RAF to whom the route was entirely new. They arrived at Le Bourget without any difficulty, and took off again for Lyons; but failing light and uncertainty as to the route persuaded them to come down at a little aerodrome at Paray-le-Monial in Burgundy. After a perfect landing they were directed by a rather suspicious couple to the town. There they found an inn, where they were enjoying a pleasant meal when they were suddenly taken away to the Mairie as probable spies. At first it seemed impossible to explain themselves: the pilot spoke no French at all; and Walter's French was not recognised as such until the local curé arrived, and Walter and he had an animated conversation about the validity of Anglican Orders; after which the curé threw up his hands and remarked that no one but an Englishman could talk such French, and the two suspects were released. Apparently what had aroused suspicion was the sight of a man in civilian clothes descending from a Royal Air Force machine.

Next morning, a thick fog held them up until midday; but at length they reached Antibes, where they were met by the Duke's equerry Fruity Metcalfe, who seemed very upset by the Duke's earlier refusal to make the journey back to England.

In discussing his future with Monckton, the Duke told him that he would prefer the post in England; and since both the Duke and Duchess heartily disliked flying, Walter thought that it could easily be arranged by Winston Churchill, now First Lord of the Admiralty, for them to be picked up by a destroyer. This was indeed possible; and in mid-September the Duke and Duchess motored to Cherbourg, from where Lord Louis Mountbatten transported them in HMS *Kelly* to Portsmouth. There they disembarked on the same quay from which Edward had left after his abdication; and Walter, who had been there to bid his master farewell, was there with Lady Alexandra Metcalfe to welcome them home.

Earlier, Walter had telephoned Buckingham Palace to ask for a royal car to be sent down for the returning exiles, but this had been refused. Lady Alexandra Metcalfe therefore drove Walter in her own car to Portsmouth where, before meeting the Windsors, she took the precaution of booking rooms for them in the best hotel in Southsea. As it turned out, Churchill had given instructions that they should spend their first night back in England at Admiralty House, Portsmouth, as guests of the Commander-in-Chief, Admiral Sir William James. Next day, since the King had made no arrangements for their accommodation, Lady Alexandra conveyed the Windsors to her country house, South Hartfield Manor in Sussex.

From Hartfield they made frequent visits to the Metcalfes' town house in Wilton Place, which became their office, and where the Duke, helped by Walter Monckton and by Walter's son Gilbert, coped with a stream of visitors, and a flood of correspondence.[24]

Walter felt that his principal task was to improve the relationship between the Windsors and the remainder of the Royal Family and, as he later wrote:

Long and rather boring discussions took place in order to bring about a meeting between the King and his brother which I finally achieved by excluding women, as I explained to Alex Hardinge that it would save trouble if it was a stag party. I motored up with the Duke to Buckingham Palace. Commander Campbell met him at the Royal Entrance, and took him up to his brother's room. I went into the Equerry's room, and waited for an anxious hour. Then the brothers came down together; the King came over to me and said: 'I think it went all right.' The Duke watched him with a wary eye, and asked me afterwards what he had said. I told him, and he said that it had been all right because, on my advice, he had kept off contentious subjects.[25]

Afterwards, however, both Edward and Wallis felt more deeply than ever that they had been deliberately isolated, and they communicated this feeling to their friends, who were sympathetic. 'I do think the royal family might have done something,' noted Baba Metcalfe.

He [the Duke] might not even exist but for one short visit to the King. Wallis said they realised there was no place ever for him in this country and she saw no reason ever to return. I didn't deny it or do any pressing. They are incapable of trusting anybody, therefore one feels one's loyalty is misplaced.

These feelings of isolation were intensified when the post which the Duke had preferred was suddenly cancelled; and so on 20 September the Duke and his Duchess left England once again, this time to take up the post with the British Mission to General Gamelin. Walter Monckton saw them off, and this sad farewell brought to an end the period of his close friendship with the Duke, although a year later they were to meet again in dramatic circumstances. In Walter's service to the Duke, as his biographer Lord Birkenhead remarks, 'it would be difficult to find a better example of selfless devotion'.[26]

4

On the outbreak of the Second World War in September 1939, Walter Monckton agreed with his friend Stafford Cripps that they must both give up the Bar and engage in war work for the duration. Walter, who once told Churchill that he had been making £60,000 a year in his profession, was still only 48, and hoped to rejoin the army. Memories of his days as a major in the West Kents flooded back; and Walter resurrected his old uniform, adding to it the KCVO ribbon.

In the meantime he went on with some work which he had begun before the outbreak of war: that is, examining IRA internees who had been detained on charges of committing acts of violence and sabotage in England and Wales. At the request of the Home Secretary Sir James Anderson (later Lord Waverley) Monckton had been appointed first Chairman of the Advisory Committee on Internment and Repatriation of Enemy Aliens, a position which gave him little pleasure. 'I am busy at Internees at Burlington Gardens (tarts' parade – I need a special guard),' he wrote to his daughter Valerie. 'The Home Secretary has asked me to go on for a week or two.'

A few days before war was declared, Valerie had married Sir Basil Goulding, an Irish baronet and a successful industrialist in Eire. Both were to serve in the war, Valerie in the FANYs and Basil in the RAF. Their union pleased Walter, besides bringing about a reconciliation with Polly. However, it was only a short while before he and Polly had once again drifted apart, and eventually Walter obtained a legal separation, although they were not divorced until 1947, the year in which Walter was to marry as his second wife Bridget (Biddy), former Countess of Carlisle. Incidentally, Polly performed courageous ambulance work in Chelsea during the London air raids; while their son Gilbert joined the 5th Royal Inniskilling Dragoon Guards in which he served with distinction and rose to the rank of major-general.[27] Meanwhile Walter sold the family home in Cadogan Place (bought only two years previously) and moved into the Windham Club, later finding living quarters in the Ministry of Information, to which he had become officially attached.

For in October 1939 Monckton's hopes of rejoining the army were dashed when the Prime Minister offered him the civil post of Director-General of the Press and Censorship Bureau. Walter accepted, though he realised that his duties would be difficult and complex. Although his office was in that part of the Ministry of Information located in the Senate House of London University in Malet Street, he would be responsible to the Home Secretary in Whitehall. Each of the armed services would have its own prior censorship, which Walter must respect; nor could he either initiate or edit news items: his duty was merely to provide an apparatus for their simultaneous issue to the BBC and the press.

Duff Cooper, a future Minister of Information, would remark that the trouble about the Ministry was that there were too few ordinary civil servants in it and too many brilliant amateurs: ex-ambassadors, distinguished men of letters, members of the Bar, retired Indian civil servants and the like, who continually complained of being 'frustrated'.[28] In the circumstances, however, this was hardly surprising; and Walter soon found that he was frequently at odds both with the Foreign Office and with the representatives of the three armed forces. The most problematic area in his view was the censorship of opinion as opposed to news. Walter felt certain that the varying policies of the different departments who operated censorship should be brought into line, and that the final decision and responsibility should be vested in himself, as the civilian head of the Bureau; but this desire remained unfulfilled.

In January 1940 Sir John Reith, former head of the BBC, was appointed Minister of Information in succession to that able judge but singularly inept politician Lord Macmillan; and when, a month later, Reith was elected MP for Southampton, it was suggested to Walter Monckton that he too should enter the House, where he could become parliamentary secretary to the new minister. However, he turned this down. 'We are still in the middle of the journey towards a reasonable code of conduct accepted by all,' he wrote to Reith. 'Until the end of the journey is in sight I think it would be far too soon for me to give up personal direction of the frail little bark.'[29]

There was indeed much to be done. Foreign correspondents were particularly annoyed by the treatment of the stories which they filed. 'During the first years of the war nothing was so absurd as the British censorship,' wrote the American journalist Quentin Reynolds who represented *Collier's Weekly*. 'It was stupid, infuriating and without any basis.' In *Only The Stars Are Neutral*, his book of wartime experiences, Reynolds gave some telling examples. A reporter in the London office of the *New York Times* discovered that army and RAF doctors were treating open wounds with sulfathiozole. The reporter checked with several doctors who told him that the drug was amazingly successful. However, the censor had never heard of it, would not believe that it was a drug, and flatly refused to allow the reporter's story, on the grounds that sulfathiozole must be a code word. Again, the traitor William Joyce, known as 'Lord Haw Haw', gleefully announced in one of his broadcasts on German radio, that the reason why Nazi bomber pilots found it so easy to locate London was that the River Thames pointed the way. Another *New York Times* reporter wrote an article in which he repeated this well-known piece of information; but he was sternly informed by the censor that he could not mention the Thames, as 'It would give the enemy important information.' Reynolds himself submitted a script containing a few slighting remarks about Germany for a BBC broadcast on a Sunday night. 'Many of our Sunday night listeners are churchgoers,' he was told. 'It is all right to hate the Germans on weekdays but not on Sundays.' Winston Churchill was Prime Minister at the time; and it was only after Churchill had described Hitler as 'that guttersnipe' in a Sunday broadcast, which breathed hatred of the Nazis, that Reynolds was allowed to do his broadcast on the following Sunday.[30]

On 6 January 1940, the day after the announcement of Reith's appointment, Walter lunched with Robert Bruce-Lockhart, who was shortly to become Director General of the Political Warfare Executive, and who found Walter 'nice and pleasant, but *not* a big man'. Walter repeated that he had no wish to go into the House of Commons; and the two men discussed Chamberlain's recent ministerial changes, and the Hore-Belisha affair. The Prime Minister had offered Hore-Belisha (at that time War Minister) the Ministry of Information; but this appointment had been blocked by Lord Halifax, the Foreign Secretary, on the grounds that 'it would have a bad effect on the neutrals because Hore-Belisha was a Jew and because his methods would let down British prestige'. The result was that Hore-Belisha had resigned as Minister of War, and his resignation had been built up into a big story by the press. Walter, sympathising with Hore-Belisha, thoroughly approved of this; while Bruce-Lockhart believed that the value of 'the man who democratised the Army' had been somewhat exaggerated.[31]

Then in April 1940 the Prime Minister Neville Chamberlain declared that both the Press and Censorship Bureau, and the Postal and Telegraph Censorship (energetically directed by Edwin Herbert, later Lord Tangley) were to be brought under the control of the Ministry of Information. At the same time Walter Monckton was appointed deputy director of the Ministry; and, in order to strengthen the ties between the Ministry and the Foreign Office, Monckton was also made an additional Under Secretary of State for Foreign Affairs. Administratively, this was a considerable improvement, although the difficulty of working with the armed services remained.

The following month, when Churchill became Prime Minister, Reith was replaced as Minister of Information by Duff Cooper, and there was a crisis when the services refused to release news to the Ministry. Bruce-Lockhart wrote of Monckton's efforts to put things on a proper footing:[32]

All agree that Monckton has done much lobbying of politicians and newspaper men . . . Monckton really wants unification of all forms of news and propaganda under one minister (himself) but is wise enough to put crisis to public as news crisis. Sympathy of public is with him. This is only good piece of propaganda he has done! His joke: 'Give us the straw and we'll drop the bricks!'

This was not quite fair to Monckton, who had no wish to be Minister of Information, whose proper role he defined at about this time in the following memorandum:[33]

> . . . A Ministry of Information cannot function without:
> (a) Unity of Command over the whole field of propaganda.
> (b) Command (not necessarily, of course, for publication) of all information available to Heads of the Services and to the Foreign Office.
> (c) Authority to handle the issue of official news by direction and controlling its form, timing and treatment.
> Not one of these conditions is fulfilled at present.

For example, the Minister had no control over covert or 'black' propaganda, which purported to come from inside Germany but was actually transmitted from secret stations in the United Kingdom. These secret stations were controlled by Bruce-Lockhart and his Political Warfare Executive, and he was very jealous of any outside interference. The only broadcasting stations which Walter officially controlled were those of the BBC for the transmission of overt as distinct from covert propaganda; and even in this area control was ineffective, as responsibility for this work within the BBC had been shared out between various quite independent divisional commanders.

The function of overt propaganda, as Walter explained in a BBC broadcast, was:

> . . . to tell the world what we are fighting for.
> We explain what is involved in the struggle for freedom; the right to think, to speak and worship according to our consciences. And we show what would inevitably happen to us if we lost the war. Here's a recent quotation from one of Hitler's newspapers which shows what he would like to do to us: 'We will bring to Britain a revolution of blood and tears which as a punishment will reduce the British people to degradation.'
> In the darkest hour we know that in the end we shall feel on our faces the breath of morning. When that day comes it will have been worth the agony of waiting and watching to be able to bring you the good tidings of victory.*

The press (with the exception of foreign correspondents) remained

* 25 April 1941.

independent; and the Ministry, compelled to act on the assumption that its role was merely to disseminate whatever information it had officially received, could do no more than advise or request. Walter believed that it should have a far more substantial role, with unquestioned access to whatever information was available, however confidential. Then, as Walter's memorandum concluded, it should be the task of 'some one person' within the Ministry,[34]

> on his own responsibility and at his own risk, to decide what news should be issued and when. The present system, as has been demonstrated over and over again, results in news being held up while the question of its release is considered by one or more other Departments whose primary function is not the handling of news . . .
>
> From time to time there has been widespread dissatisfaction with our news and propaganda. There is great dissatisfaction at the moment: and it is largely justified.

Although Walter was appointed Director-General of the Ministry of Information in December 1940, this unhappy state of affairs continued until July 1941 when Brendan Bracken replaced Duff Cooper as Minister of Information. Under Bracken's flamboyant personality, the Ministry functioned for the first time as it should.

In the meantime another politician, Lord Beaverbrook, had been unsuccessfully pressing Monckton to enter Parliament. 'I entirely agree with you,' Walter had explained to him in May 1940,[35]

> that the work I am doing here is likely to be detrimental to my personal interests, and that on purely selfish grounds I might be wise to give it up and go into the House of Commons, but I could not bring myself to do that at this moment. Indeed I feel that the only alternative to continuing here is to get back a commission in the army, and this I should greatly like to do as I think an older man could undertake my duties as well as I can.

Monckton's wish for active service remained unfulfilled; but fortunately the frustration of his work at the Ministry was to some extent relieved by a number of interesting journeys abroad.

The first of these was to Paris in February 1940, for discussions with the French censorship authorities. While Walter was over there, he called briefly on the Duke and Duchess of Windsor at their home in the Boulevard Suchet;* and he also travelled to Lille where his son

---

* The Duchess lived there full-time, as she was working in Paris for the French Red Cross; while the Duke joined her there when he was not required at Vincennes by the British Mission to General Gamelin.

Gilbert was stationed. Only 16 weeks later, on 2 June 1940, Gilbert
was reported missing. He had already been awarded the Military Cross
for his bravery on the retreat to Dunkirk; and had then volunteered
to stay behind with another squadron to cover the last stages of the
evacuation. Fear for Gilbert's safety once again drew Walter and Polly
together for a short while; and when, against all the odds, Gilbert
arrived safely in London, the two of them met him to welcome him
home.

5

Walter Monckton's second foreign visit, towards the end of July 1940,
took him to Lisbon, to which the Duke and Duchess of Windsor had
escaped after the fall of France. Walter had been sent there by
Churchill to hasten their departure to the Bahamas, of which colony
the Duke had recently been appointed Governor and Commander-in-
Chief. As Walter later explained, 'There was some doubt in the minds
of the Government whether he would go in the end, and in what frame
of mind. So I was sent out on what turned out to be another very odd
job.'

After reaching Lisbon in a flying-boat, Walter arrived on the evening
of Sunday 28 July in Cascais, where the Windsors were the guests of
a Portuguese banker, Dr Ricardo Espirito Santo Silva, who had lent
them Boca do Inferno, his seaside villa. Walter had brought with him
a letter in which the Prime Minister warned the Duke against expressing in his new post any views which were out of harmony with those
of the Government. 'Even while you have been staying at Lisbon,'
Churchill continued,

> conversations have been reported by telegraph through various channels
> which have been used to your Royal Highness' disadvantage. In particular,
> there is danger of use being made of anything you say in the United States
> to do injury, and to suggest divergence between you and the British
> Government. I am anxious that mischief should not be made which might
> mar the success which I feel sure will attend your mission. We are all
> passing through times of immense stress and dire peril and every step has
> to be watched with care.

In his letter the Prime Minister also told the Duke that Walter
Monckton would 'talk over certain matters of which you should be

verbally informed'. The most important of these was the news of a German plot against the Duke and his wife.

The organisation of this plot had apparently been entrusted to a senior Nazi police officer, Walter Schellenberg, who had been accompanied to Lisbon by two assistants. According to Schellenberg's own later account, he had been instructed to use whatever means were necessary to lure the Duke to Spain; and he claimed that shortly before Walter's arrival he received a telegram from Ribbentrop telling him that 'the Führer orders that an abduction is to be organised at once'.[36] There is some doubt about the truth of this, as no copy of any such document has ever been discovered in the captured German archives; but such a plot was certainly feared by the British Secret Service (represented in Lisbon by David Eccles); and the pro-British Portuguese authorities consequently increased their security measures. The Duchess of Windsor later recounted how she and the Duke (always 'David' to her) received news of the plot from Walter:[37]

> British Intelligence had picked up information that German secret agents were plotting to kidnap us.
>
> 'But how could we possibly be of any use to them?' David asked, incredulously.
>
> Walter was very serious. 'Winston is convinced that Hitler is crazy enough to be tempted, in the event of a successful invasion of Britain, to try to put the Duke back on the throne in the belief that this would divide and confuse the people and weaken their will to resist further.'
>
> David was flabbergasted. 'Winston couldn't possibly think of that,' he replied.
>
> 'Sir,' Walter said, 'in war Winston is always ingenious and imaginative. He overlooks no possibilities – however unlikely.'
>
> If plot there was, David and I were afterwards to decide that it must have been a pretty simple piece of intrigue. One day we received a call from a distinguished Spaniard. Our visitor said he had come on a confidential mission on behalf of the Spanish Government to offer us a house in Spain. David thanked him, saying, 'I have accepted a post under the British Colonial Service, I intend to serve my country.'

The 'distinguished Spaniard' was Don Miguel Primo de Rivera, Marqués de Estella, Civil Governor of Madrid, son of the man who had been dictator in the 1920s, and a founder member of the Spanish Fascist Party, the Falange. His first visit to the Windsors had come in mid-July, after the Duke had accepted the Governorship of the Bahamas. As the Duchess correctly surmised, the Germans were behind Don Miguel's offer, and had the Windsors gone to Spain they would have been detained there, pending a successful outcome to Hitler's plans for invading Britain.

After Don Miguel's departure, the German Ambassador in Lisbon, Baron von Stohrer, telegraphed the Foreign Minister in Berlin, von Ribbentrop, with a full report, in which he made it clear that the Duke had

> expressed himself most freely. He felt almost a prisoner and surrounded by spies etc. Politically the Duke has moved further and further away from the King and the present English Government. The Duke and Duchess do not fear the King, who is utterly stupid, as much as the clever Queen, who is constantly intriguing against the Duke and particularly against the Duchess.

Although this telegram was not officially published until after the war, as part of the captured German archives, it may well have been one of the telegrams intercepted by British Intelligence and decoded by them at Bletchley Park. If so, they would have been reassured by its contents. Baron von Stohrer had to admit to Ribbentrop that when Don Miguel, pretending to 'know . . . nothing of any German interest in the matter, asked "on his own account" whether the Duke "might yet be destined" to play a large part in English politics and even to ascend the English throne, both the Duke and Duchess seemed astonished. Both seemed completely enmeshed in conventional ways of thinking, for they replied that under the English constitution this would not be possible after the Abdication.'[38]

Don Miguel made a second flight to Lisbon, arriving at Cascais while Walter was staying with the Windsors. On this occasion he tried to persuade the Duke not to go to the Bahamas 'on the ground', according to Walter, 'that he had information of a plot by the British Government to have him killed there. It sounds fantastic, but he managed to impress the Duke and Duchess.'

The Duke informed Walter, and Walter took Don Miguel out to the garden, where in the course of a lengthy conversation he explained to him that without some concrete evidence he could not advise the Windsors to remain in Lisbon. Indeed, plans were already in hand for their departure on 1 August aboard the American Export Lines *Excalibur*, which was bound for New York, but was to be specially diverted to Bermuda.

Faced with Walter's demand for evidence, Don Miguel could only beg for time: could not the Windsors be kept in Lisbon for another ten days while he assembled the necessary proof? Walter remained firm. 'I told him that I could not do as he wished,' he wrote later.[39]

> The Duke would go by the American ship which was about to start next day, but I would stop him in Bermuda, if by the time he was due to leave that island evidence was forthcoming to justify such a step, and [in those circumstances] I would fly back to Lisbon at a day's notice. This did not satisfy [Don Miguel], but neither was the Duke satisfied until I had secured by telegram the attendance of a detective from Scotland Yard to accompany them and look after them.

Meanwhile Schellenberg could do nothing in the face of Portuguese security measures for the protection of the Duke and Duchess on board the *Excalibur*. 'The ship was searched several times from top to bottom,' he later explained. 'Security measures were doubled, then redoubled; everything helped to confirm my reports to Berlin on the impossibility of carrying out the abduction.' The German Embassy in Lisbon overlooked the docks and the River Tagus; and, as Schellenberg wrote in his memoirs,[40]

> On the day of the Duke's departure I was in the tower room of the German Embassy watching the [*Excalibur*] through field-glasses. It appeared so close that I seemed almost able to touch it. The Duke and Duchess went on board punctually, and I recognised Monckton too. There was some excitement about the hand luggage. The Portuguese in their zeal insisted upon searching that too. Finally the ship cast off, and moved away down the broad mouth of the Tagus. Slowly I returned to my house. The chapter was closed.

The Duke and Duchess had been a little late in embarking, as before leaving Portugal the Duke had wanted to thank the Portuguese Premier, the dictator Dr Salazar, for his hospitality and assistance. A brief meeting was arranged; after which the Duke and Duchess were once again seen on their way by Walter Monckton, who escorted them on board the *Excalibur*, and went ashore shortly before 6.40 p.m. when she weighed anchor at the start of her long voyage across the Atlantic.

On his return to London, Walter made a full report to the Prime Minister, adding that he had mentioned the matter of the possible attempt on the Duke's life both to the Colonial Secretary Lord Lloyd and to the Metropolitan Police Commissioner Sir Philip Game. Sir Philip had pointed out that[41]

> the only possible danger might be that the Germans might make an attempt on the Duke's life and say it was done by the British. He did not suggest

that this was probable, but if it is a danger to be guarded against he would need to send a second detective to the Bahamas. I understand the Duke is likely to arrive today or tomorrow. I have no more news from Spain about the alleged plot.

In fact the *Excalibur* reached Bermuda on 9 August. The Duke immediately telegraphed Walter from Government House as follows: 'Have arrived. Impossible to continue until we hear from you.' Walter replied the following day: 'After enquiries here am satisfied no foundations for allegations which reached us in Lisbon. Accordingly do not think any need to delay continuance of your journey.' The Duke therefore sailed with his Duchess to the Bahamas, arriving in Nassau on 17 August to take up his governorship.[42]

Meanwhile Churchill had written from Downing Street to thank Walter 'for the trouble you took and the service you rendered', adding that: 'It was very lucky you were on the spot to dissipate strange suspicions.'[43]

Chapter 5

The Ministry of Information

I

AFTER separating from Polly, Walter found a congenial female
companion in 31 year-old Leonora Corbett, an intelligent and
glamorous actress with whom he had a passionate affair. On
her departure for New York, where Leonora was to play Elvira in
Noël Coward's play *Blithe Spirit*,* the affair died a natural death; but
they remained very close friends: she addressed him in her letters as
'MDDDW', or 'My Darling, Darling, Darling Walter'; while for his
part he made her the repository of confidential matters which his
biographer Lord Birkenhead has suggested that he would have done
better to keep to himself. One of these was his account of the Abdication, for which he refused a publisher £100,000, not wishing it to
appear during his lifetime.[1]

Another theatrical figure who succumbed to Walter's charm was the
French actress and singer Alice Delysia. Not so youthful as Leonora
(Alice was actually two years older than Walter) she shared Leonora's
beauty, loyalty and good nature. From humble beginnings as a
midinette in a Paris dress shop, she had embarked upon a stage career
at the old Moulin Rouge before progressing to the Folies Bergère. In
1914, at the age of 25, Alice had moved to London where she appeared
in many plays and revues under Charles Cochrane's management;
and while Walter was attached to the Ministry of Information she
starred as Hortense in a successful revival of a comedy by Marguerite
Steen and Derek Patmore, *The French for Love*. Walter would later

* Leonora Corbett had an immense success with *Blithe Spirit*, which ran for two
years. Afterwards she settled in New York where she died in 1960, aged 52.

enjoy her favours when he was working for the Ministry in Cairo, while she was touring the Middle East entertaining troops for ENSA* under the direction of Basil Dean.†[2]

After so many loveless years, these love affairs renewed Walter's spirit; though there were still times when, as he wrote to Leonora on 27 March 1941, he became[3]

> horribly depressed from time to time with the burden of this Ministry. There is so much to do, and with all his great and good qualities my Master [Duff Cooper] is very hard to get to the point of drastic action or to take great interest in a concrete form. Still I cannot expect everything and it is something that he does not worry me or interfere with me. I am desperately anxious to get our work in the USA in a reasonable condition. At present I feel that the Ministry is flopping badly in foreign propaganda, and that big changes in personnel must take place to improve the thing, but it is just in this direction that I find my Master unready to move.
>
> The annoying thing is that I have served over twelve months and a bit here and would very much like to be transferred to other work, preferably back into [army] Service, but I do not think they will let me go.

The changes in personnel which Walter advocated followed immediately on Brendan Bracken's appointment in July 1941. His first day in office, Bracken went through the list of staff with a fine toothcomb, and had soon decided to sack people right and left. Once he was clear about who should go and who should stay, he followed up his decisions in person. Entering one office, he would introduce himself and say quite bluntly: 'Ah, yes, you're Mr So-and-so. Well, you're out. The letter terminating your employment is on its way.' In another office, occupied by a more fortunate individual, he would say: 'I know what you do, Mr X. I want you to stay and really put your back into it.'[4]

It was on this first day that Bracken received a letter which made him cry out in astonishment: 'Here's someone anxious, for a change, to sack himself. Walter Monckton of all the unlikely people!'[5] Walter had written to his new master explaining that:[6]

> During the last few months in particular, as Duff would tell you, I have longed to go. I have no more heart for the job, as I fundamentally disagree with the scheme under which the Ministry has to work. Since the Ministry has had, all too little power and authority, I have had to do my work depending solely on the maintenance of good relations with other Departments of State and with the Press. I have no stomach for a battle without

---

* Entertainments National Service Association.

† Alice Delysia (née Lapize) died in 1979, aged 90.

the necessary weapons under a Government which has no real faith in
the Ministry or its work.

It was true that the Prime Minister did not then believe in 'killing
Hitler with your mouth', or in the RAF dropping leaflets composed
by the Ministry of Information. However, Bracken was living in
10 Downing Street; and his intimacy with Winston Churchill (so great
that it was incorrectly rumoured that he was Churchill's illegitimate
son) placed him in a uniquely powerful position. Churchill was content
to leave his protégé to get on with the job, which Bracken, who was
himself the proprietor of several journals, and knew Fleet Street well,
managed with conspicuous success. In time he converted Churchill to
his belief not only in 'white' but also in so-called 'black' propaganda,
including the dropping of leaflets; and before long he had virtually
incorporated Bruce-Lockhart and his Political Warfare Executive into
the Information Ministry, besides dismissing Dr Dalton as Minister
of Economic Warfare, finding in Lord Selborne a more cooperative
Minister responsible for 'special operations', sacking the top executives
of the BBC, and thoroughly overhauling that institution with regard
to both foreign and home broadcasts.[7]

Walter Monckton was glad to be removed from the turmoil caused
by these changes, since Bracken had persuaded him not to resign, but
instead to go on a propaganda mission to Soviet Russia, which had
become our ally after being attacked by Hitler and his Nazi hordes in
June 1941. Walter was excited by the prospect of this mission, not
least because it would give him a chance of seeing his old friend and
Bar colleague Stafford Cripps, who was now the British Ambassador
to Russia. On 2 October 1941 he wrote to Leonora Corbett telling her
that he had been[8]

in a frightful whirl during the past week over the Moscow project. I feel
that there is a piece of work to be done and that it is the right gesture. I
am not going out simply to get something or to make a bargain, and there
is some virtue in talking over things with friends; and when two of you are
fighting the same dragon and the lives of all are at stake it is just as well to
be friends. My idea is not to go out and say smooth things but to be quite
candid about differences of ideology, and at the same time to let them see
that we on this side realise how desperately each needs the other's help,
and that in the last analysis we *are* on the same side.

Walter left a few days later from Plymouth in a Sunderland flying
boat. His destination in the Soviet Union turned out not to be

Moscow, as he had thought, but Kuibyshev,* a drab and muddy town on the middle Volga over six hundred miles to the east. It was to Kuibyshev, since Moscow was gravely threatened by the German advance, that Stalin had evacuated both the diplomatic corps and most of his Government departments.[9]

Among Walter's fellow passengers on the flight from Plymouth was Oliver Lyttelton (later Lord Chandos), a Minister of State and a member of the War Cabinet, who was returning to his post in Cairo from where his jurisdiction extended throughout the Middle East. In Gibraltar, their first stop, they stayed with the Governor, Lord Gort (popularly known as 'Fat Boy'), who considered that he had been treated less well than he deserved after his work in France with the British Expeditionary Force, of which he had been Commander-in-Chief. 'He feels deeply the way he is passed over,' wrote Walter, 'and says the Germans (as he heard from Madrid) appreciate what a good show he put up with very little to do it with.' While he was in Gibraltar, Walter found that he was able to do useful work with those in charge of propaganda. 'How important these personal talks are,' he wrote in his diary. 'They want help with their paper and with their broadcasting station, and I think we have managed, by cabling Brendan, to assure a move.'[10]

Their next stop was Malta where the Governor, General Sir William Dobbie, was a religious fanatic: 'half Cromwell and half Stonewall Jackson', as Walter described him, 'a Bible in one hand and a sword in the other'. Walter had useful discussions with Dobbie over various Ministry of Information problems in Malta; but he soon realised that Dobbie needed to be relieved, since he was worn out by the persistent enemy bombing of the island; and he told Churchill so, which led to an angry exchange of views. While he was staying in Malta, incidentally, Walter was asked by Dobbie to see his 'Morning Glory'; but being no gardener, he declined, fearing that some weird religious rite was about to take place![11]

Walter Monckton and Oliver Lyttelton reached Cairo on 10 October; and Walter spent a week in Lyttelton's attractive villa near the Pyramids: lent to him by Chester Beatty, it was known from the colour of its tiles as Beit-al-Azrak, or The Blue House. Walter also did some information work in Lyttelton's office at 10 Sharia Tolumbat, near GHQ in Cairo; and before he left, Lyttelton told him that on his

---

* Kuibyshev, formerly Samara, was named after Valerian Kuibyshev, a senior Bolshevik, who organised the revolutionary seizure of power in Samara. He held a number of important posts, siding with Stalin in the inter-party struggle after Lenin's death. Samara was renamed when Kuibyshev died in 1935.

return from Russia he would like him to become his Director of Propaganda in the Middle East, and a member of his War Council.

And so on, alone, to Teheran, where Walter had a memorable audience with the Shah, drinking tea with him in the water-garden of a many-pillared summer palace. However, Walter was held up in Persia for more than two weeks, since although the Russians were now officially our allies, they still refused to allow a British aeroplane to fly in their air space. Eventually Stafford Cripps made a personal appeal to Molotov, the Soviet Foreign Minister, who was persuaded to send a Russian aeroplane down to Teheran to collect Monckton. After a further infuriating delay caused by engine trouble, followed by stops at Baku and Astrakhan, Walter finally reached Kuibyshev in the afternoon of 4 November. Waiting to welcome him was Stafford Cripps, in whose enormous embassy building, previously the headquarters of the local Soviet Boy Scouts, Walter would stay for the next three weeks.

2

Two journalist friends of Walter Monckton's were also staying in Kuibyshev: the British Philip Jordan and the American Quentin Reynolds.[12] They celebrated Walter's arrival as well as Guy Fawkes Day by sending out these invitations:

PHILIP JORDAN AND QUENTIN REYNOLDS
INVITE YOU TO A COCKTAIL PARTY
IN HONOUR OF
SIR WALTER MONCKTON AND THE LATE GUY
FAWKES
HOTEL GRAND, KUIBYSHEV
(*Everything free*)

The party was an immense success, since the hosts had managed to lay in a large stock of vodka, whisky and brandy; and they also offered what was then an unusual delicacy in Kuibyshev – fried potatoes!

The American Ambassador Lawrence Steinhardt came with the rest of the diplomatic corps, excepting only the teetotaller Stafford Cripps. Another guest was the Polish General Anders, who had been released from the dreaded Lubyanka prison to create a new army. There were also numerous journalists, among whom was an American correspondent called Chollerton, who had been in Russia for 15 years, and who made a great impression upon Walter. 'He's amazing,' Walter told Reynolds. 'Do you know what he just did? He poured a drink of Scotch while he was talking to me. He reached for a bottle of water that was on the table and filled his glass with it. He took a drink and said calmly, "My, my, I made a mistake! That wasn't a bottle of water. Ah, well, we can't waste it. That wouldn't be fair to Philip or Quent." It was vodka, and so help me, Reynolds, he calmly drank the whole thing – half whisky, half vodka. He's a wonderful man.'

'He is indeed,' said Quentin Reynolds solemnly. 'We're trying to persuade him to get out of Russia for a while . . . And incidentally, Walter, I want to leave with you.'

'I expected you would,' said Walter drily. 'In fact, I was going to suggest it. I'm going directly to Cairo, and that's the place for you now.'

'I want to get back to London,' said Quentin. 'I don't care about Cairo.'

'Take my word for it,' said Walter looking at Quentin in a way which the journalist thought odd. 'You won't regret it. You'll be glad to be in Cairo.'

In the meantime Walter had numerous conferences with S. A. Lozovsky, the Russian official in charge of the Information Bureau. However, when he emerged he could only tell Reynolds and Jordan that 'Lozovsky was very affable, very pleasant. His French is excellent.' From comments like these it soon became clear that Walter had made no progress whatever. Later Reynolds would write sympathetically that Monckton had[13]

> run up against the same wall of evasiveness that we had met. We could not have had a better advocate than Walter, but the same old censorship remained unchanged. There would not be any additions or better 'co-operation between British and Russian sources of information'. It was such a pity, too. We were all anxious to go on operational trips as we had done in Britain, anxious to glorify the Red heroes at the front, anxious to get under the skin of those magnificent people, anxious to get behind the scenes so we could get the feel of the whole wonderful battle the Red Army was putting up. But no. Not even Walter's persuasiveness could break down the distrust which Soviet officialdom felt for the American and British press.

The 24th anniversary of the Russian Revolution on 7 November (25 October Old Style) was celebrated by a military review, followed by speeches, a concert, the ballet *Don Quixote*, and finally a reception given by the Deputy Minister of Foreign Affairs Andrei Vychinsky, the bloodthirsty lawyer who was infamous for his conduct during the purge trials of the 1930s. Meeting him must have been disagreeable for Walter, who prudently confined himself to talking about present difficulties. The high spot for him, as he wrote later, had been[14]

> the prima ballerina from Moscow – Lepeshinskaya – she took one's breath away, a miracle of assured balance and poise like a porcelain feather, and alive with charm and enchantment and well aware of it. I sat between the Ambassador and Admiral Myles, head of the Naval Mission, and they felt equally lyrical while the junior staff round me could hardly keep in their seats.

Not even a diversion of this kind could make up for the evident failure of his mission, which left Walter not only disappointed, but a little angry. 'These Russians are amazing,' he said at the time. 'They say smooth things, and do damn all when a question of organisation, large or small arises.' Stafford Cripps had suffered for some time from this kind of bitter disappointment, since finding, much to his surprise, that his left-wing views were not at all popular with the Soviet authorities.

In mid-November Walter finally left Kuibyshev aboard an RAF aeroplane, a roomy DC3, which also carried Litvinov (recently appointed Soviet Ambassador to the USA), Litvinov's wife and secretary, Lawrence Steinhardt, Quentin Reynolds, and the Persian Ambassador. It was a slow and tedious journey, which involved unexpectedly prolonged stops at Astrakhan, Baku, Pahlevi and Teheran. In Baku, for example, they were held up by a blizzard; and when the weather cleared Litvinov prevented them from continuing until his wife had recovered from a bout of ill-health. Walter chafed at the delay, since he had heard his new appointment being announced on the British radio, and was longing to get to Cairo and start some serious work. In the meantime it was believed in England and America that their aircraft must have crashed and that they had perished, since (unknown to them) Litvinov had callously broken his promise to send messages on behalf of Monckton and Steinhardt to their respective Governments.

As it turned out, a few days later there very nearly *was* a fatal crash. Taking off in appallingly muddy conditions at Pahlevi, Quentin Reynolds noticed a clump of trees at the end of the runway; and as the machine very slowly gained height he was horrified to see the tops of the trees passing only a few feet below them. He looked around. Steinhardt was cleaning his nails; Walter was wrapping a blanket round his legs; the Persian Ambassador was eating an apple, and Litvinov was reading a detective story. Then Reynolds met the eyes of Group-Captain Hallowell, the air attaché in Kuibyshev, who was also on board. Large beads of perspiration stood out on his forehead, and his hands trembled as he lit a cigarette. 'I've been flying all my life,' he told Reynolds, 'and this is the closest I've been to it.'

Reynolds talked to the others later, but none of them, including Walter, believed him. It had been a nice ordinary take-off, and Reynolds was silly to dramatise it. Reynolds told them to ask Hallowell. He said it was nothing. 'Nothing at all,' he added cheerfully. 'We missed those trees by at least four feet!'[15]

At Teheran airport there was quite a delegation to meet them. It included the British Minister who rushed up to Monckton, calling out 'Thank God, you're safe, Sir Walter!' A United Press man called Peters shook hands with Reynolds, whom he knew, and told him: 'We never expected to see any of you alive.'

'What the hell is all this about?' asked Reynolds.

'My God, you've all been missing for five days,' said Peters. 'There have been no reports of your airplane since it left Kuibyshev. We got one report that you'd crashed in a snowstorm and had been picked up by a boat on the Caspian, but we couldn't verify it . . . The BBC announced that you were all missing, and hope was gradually going.'

Walter, who had been hearing the same story from the Minister, turned to Reynolds. 'You're a fine reporter, you are,' he declared. 'Here we've been missing for five days and none of us knew it. You, at least, should have known it!'

'Nobody ever tells me anything,' replied the unhappy Reynolds.[16]

Walter spent the night in the British Legation; and before he left next morning he was delighted to receive this message from the Prime Minister, which showed that although Churchill had not forgotten their recent difference of opinion, he was genuinely pleased that Monckton was still alive: 'So glad to hear you are safe as we cannot spare you – yet.'[17]

Since there were no flare paths at Cairo airport, aircraft could not land there at night, so the flight from Teheran to Cairo had to be completed in a single day, and Walter's plane took off at six in the morning. Before leaving Teheran, he had tried to persuade Litvinov to accompany him; but the Russian declined, saying that he wanted a rest and would come on later. This was misleadingly reported by someone who claimed that the Soviet Ambassador had been refused passage on an RAF machine, and the result was that questions were asked in Parliament about the so-called 'Litvinov incident'. 'All sorts of apologies were made to Litvinov,' noted Quentin Reynolds, who had accompanied Walter on the flight to Cairo. 'I'll bet Litvinov himself wondered what it was all about . . . Monckton is constitutionally incapable of being discourteous to any of his fellow men.'

When Monckton and Reynolds arrived in Cairo, they found waiting for them Bob Low, an American journalist who worked for *Liberty Magazine*. Reynolds immediately announced that he was now going to take a week off: 'I'm going to be a tourist here,' he told Low. 'I want to see the Pyramids and the Sphinx. I want to ride a camel and wallow in the sun.'

'You'll wallow in the sun all right,' Low replied. 'You're leaving for the desert at six in the morning. I've fixed your credentials; you're accredited to the British Army. In case you don't know it, the big British push started yesterday. It's going to be the hell of a story.'

Reynolds turned to look shrewdly at Walter Monckton. 'So that's what you meant?'

Walter nodded. 'I knew it was coming,' he said. 'But it was so confidential I couldn't do more than hint.' Earlier that day he had written in his diary: 'And now for Cairo and the new job – am I in time to be useful still? How long will it take, and then what in England? I feel as if I were coming out of a dream.'

3

After the squalor of Kuibyshev, Cairo was pleasantly luxurious. Once again, Walter had been invited to stay with Oliver Lyttelton in Beit-el-Azrak, his peaceful villa at Mena near the Pyramids. As Director-General of British Propaganda and Information Services, Walter found himself head of a department which was already functioning well. Its task was to coordinate the activities of the various propaganda groups which were carrying on political warfare in the Middle East, with the particular aim of countering anti-British German propaganda. Much of this was directed at frightening the Arab states into believing that their independence was at stake, and that if Britain won the war, her aim would either be to place them under some kind of tutelage, or to annex them outright.

The territory for which Walter had now assumed responsibility extended from Iraq and the Levant states of Syria and the Lebanon in the north, to Ethiopia and Italian Somaliland in the south; from Libya in the west, to the Persian Gulf in the east. Within this enormous theatre of war, as Walter soon realised, Lyttelton had already been highly successful in coordinating propaganda and information work. It was clear that he had managed this largely thanks to his diplomatic skills, since although he was the only person in the Middle East of Cabinet rank, he had limited executive powers. Monckton admired Lyttelton for his achievements; and Lyttelton in turn considered that Walter had 'added greatly' to their small British society. 'Few people that I have known,' wrote Lyttelton in his memoirs, 'have been more persuasive, and his flexible mind and musical voice, so often used to advantage in the courts, were now turned either to the public business of propaganda or to embellishing the gaiety and conversations at Headquarters.'[18]

Walter's new position involved membership of the Middle East War Council, over which Oliver Lyttelton presided as Minister of State, and which contained (besides a number of ambassadors and civil servants) the three service chiefs. Writing of these remarkable men, Walter Monckton commented that they were[19]

> an oddly assorted trio.* Tedder, I think, has the most subtle and supple mind of the three. But the other two are more attractive personalities. I have seen more of the Auk than of the Admiral. The Auk gives a great feeling of resolution and courage. I shall not forget one conversation between him and Oliver just about the time of Sidi Rezegh and the change in command of the 8th Army.† Oliver was asking whether he could confidently assume that Sidi Rezegh would be captured. The General replied, almost with passion, eagerly searching his mind for the right phrase: 'Oliver – you don't mind if I call you Oliver? – If I don't take Sidi Rezegh' – a long pause, and then – 'You can kiss my _____.' To which Oliver replied with a smile: 'General, you place me in an embarrassing position. I greatly hope that your troops will succeed.' This story, which has the merit of truth, reveals the two types perfectly.

It only remains to add that in November 1941 Sidi Rezegh, a post in the Western Desert about 25 miles south-east of Tobruk, was captured by Auchinleck. It was then recaptured by Rommel, but was finally

---

* Air Marshal Sir Arthur Tedder; Lieutenant-General Sir Claude Auchinleck ('the Auk'); and Admiral Sir Andrew Cunningham.

† General Alan Cunningham had commanded the 8th Army in the Western Desert since August 1941. In the offensive three months later against Rommel's Afrika Korps, British tank losses were severe and Cunningham proposed to disengage and go on the defensive. Auchinleck did not agree and replaced Cunningham with his Deputy Commander General Neil Ritchie, which resulted in the eventual relief of Tobruk. Auchinleck's action was supported both by Churchill and by Lyttelton.

captured a second time by the Auk, thus opening the way for the temporary relief of Tobruk (after a siege of ten months), and the recovery of other lost territory.

Walter established a friendly intimacy with Auchinleck, and visited him at his headquarters in the desert. 'During the last few weeks,' he wrote in December 1941 to his daughter Valerie, 'I feel that I have made a really good friend in Auchinleck. We share each other's anxieties and difficulties, and if he had his way I know that I should be succeeding Oliver, though that would not be an unmixed blessing for me.' In the desert Walter mixed with the soldiers, 'talking to them, finding out what was worrying them', as he recorded in his diary, 'not preaching to them, but learning from them'. His hope was that on returning to Cairo he would be 'able to put something new into the Information Services for the troops'. When he went up the line, where he talked to the troops in advanced positions, Monckton wore old grey flannel trousers and an old check riding coat which, in Lord Birkenhead's words, 'made the troops think that he was an MFH having a day off'.[20]

When he was not travelling, Walter would wake up at 6 a.m. in his bedroom at Beit-el-Azrak and go through the papers he had taken back overnight. Breakfast was at 8.45, and shortly after nine o'clock he would motor with Lyttelton the eight miles from Mena to their office in Cairo. 'This,' he wrote to Valerie, 'is one of the most interesting half-hours of the day in which we discuss the major problems that trouble him.' Work in the office, as one might expect, involved a busy round of meetings with officials, visitors and committees. Then there would be a visit to Auchinleck in his headquarters (when he was not commanding in the desert), followed by a one o'clock press conference. After lunch at 1.30, Walter would take a walk or a ride, returning to the office between 4 and 5 in the afternoon. Then there would be 'More interviews, more papers, more meetings until somewhere between 7.00 and 8.00 when I would motor out to the villa with Oliver. Dinner with Oliver and Moira* and their household and often a few guests. More talk and bed about 12.00.'

Besides the desert, Walter's visits took him to Beirut (where he broadcast to the British soldiers), Damascus, Baghdad and Jerusalem. In Damascus he unexpectedly met his old flame Alice Delysia ('ripe but still alluring'), who was entertaining the forces with ENSA; while at the King David Hotel in Jerusalem he met Mrs Keith Newall,

---

* Lady Moira Lyttelton, whom Oliver had married in 1920, was a daughter of the 10th Duke of Leeds.

Commandant of the 11th Company of the Mechanical Transport Corps in the Middle East Forces. Mary Newall was an extremely good-looking woman, intelligent and self-assured. Women tended to dislike her, and those under her command felt that her only real interest lay in attracting attention to herself; but men fell for her,[21] and Walter was bewitched both by her beauty and by the way she seemed to 'add to the gaiety of life'. The inevitable affair followed.

Early in 1942, Walter's former chief Duff Cooper put in a brief appearance on his journey home from Singapore, staying while he was in Cairo with the British Ambassador Sir Miles Lampson, later Lord Killearn. Duff Cooper's visit coincided with a constitutional crisis caused by the behaviour of the young King Farouk, who had appointed a Fascist and pro-German Government, and who refused to find any room for Nahas Pasha, the popular pro-British politician and ex-premier whom he had dismissed on his accession to the throne. The result was that the British authorities decided to depose Farouk, and Walter was asked to draft an Instrument of Abdication. 'It really is a singular thing', Walter noted,[22]

> though it should not be spread beyond the readers of this diary, that for the second time in my life I had to draft an Instrument of Abdication though on this occasion the King did not go. Still my Instrument of Abdication was duly presented to him by the Ambassador. He thought it quite all right. His only complaint was that the paper on which it was written was not good enough. For that I was not responsible, but it did remind me of the occasion when I presented the Instrument of Abdication for the other King's signature and he observed that there was no ink in the pot.

It was in the evening that the Ambassador and Oliver Lyttelton, accompanied by a strong military escort, drove to the royal palace where they were shown into the King's presence. Farouk took up his pen to sign, but before he could do so his chamberlain intervened with a few words of Arabic in which he begged him to reconsider his position. The King then looked up at the Ambassador and said: 'Sir Miles, will you give me another chance. I am only 21.' The Ambassador, supported by the Minister of State, relented; and it was agreed that Farouk could stay on his throne provided that he sent for Nahas Pasha, and asked him to form a new Government. This Farouk did*,

* Farouk, who led a dissolute private life, was finally deposed as the result of a military *coup d'état* in July 1952 by General Mohammed Neguib and the political leader Gamal Nasser. Farouk continued his sybaritic existence first in Italy and later in Monaco.

thus averting severe difficulties in Egypt at a critical stage of the war, and ensuring that the Suez Canal remained securely in British hands.[23]

Mark Chapman-Walker, then a close friend of Walter's, and a major on General ('Jumbo') Wilson's staff, later wrote to Lord Birkenhead giving a vivid picture of Cairo high society in those days:[24]

> Cairo was not a town at war; it had been declared an Open City by Farouk and therefore could not be bombed. The pre-war Pasha-based society was highly sophisticated and French educated. The Copt women were renowned for their beauty, and the high society in Cairo had now been swollen by diplomats of many Embassies as well as rich *emigrés* from Greece and France. Most of the soldiers were of the aristocratic regiments, and the top English diplomats and Generals had not been in England since the [outbreak of] war. Consequently the previous social habits and times of work were continued. For instance, polo was played every afternoon at Gezira, and at the Mohammed Ali Club the library and sitting rooms were exactly like the Carlton Club, and on the roof gardens at night one not only had impeccable food but saw some of the finest jewellery and prettiest women I have ever seen in my life.

Chapman-Walker particularly remembered one evening when, with Captain (later General) Douglas Darling of the Rifle Brigade, he entertained in L'Auberge des Pyramides, an open-air nightclub, no fewer than three monarchs: the Kings of Egypt, Greece, and Yugoslavia. Walter, who happened to be there, could not resist commenting, as he walked past their table, that with three kings and two knaves, they made up a full house![25]

In February 1942, when Oliver Lyttelton was recalled to London to become Minister of Production, Walter took his place as Acting Minister of State. Although he was sorry to see Lyttelton go, since they had liked each other and found it easy to work together, Walter did not wish to continue under a new chief without, as he wrote in his diary,

> a new and more certain charter. I feel that there is more that I could do, and I do not want to go, but under a new master I should want a wider task with more power and authority. Otherwise I must reluctantly come back to England with the feeling that though propaganda has improved there is a good deal more that I could manage but have not had the chance.

One of the things which irked him was the feeling that people were working far below their full capacity. 'It ought to be possible now to galvanise them with greater enthusiasm and to inform them with a

Walter Monckton at Harrow where he was head of his house and developed a life-long enthusiasm for cricket.

Walter Monckton at Ightham in Kent with his childhood sweetheart Mary (known as 'Polly') Colyer-Fergusson, to whom he was unofficially engaged while still at Harrow.

(*bove*) Walter
onckton with
lly and their
ildren Valerie
d Gilbert on
rseback at their
me Fishponds
ar Ightham in
about 1927.

(*Left*) Gilbert
and Valerie at
Fishponds in the
mid 1930s, when
their parents'
marriage was
failing.

The Duke and Duchess of Windsor after their wedding at the Château de Candé on 3 June 1937. Sir Walter Monckton was present, and warned the Duchess that she must keep the Duke happy all his days, or 'nothing would be too bad for her'.

(*Left*) Harold Davidson, the 'Prostitutes' Padre', in the lions' cage where he was not long afterwards fatally mauled. He had been protesting himself innocent of the charges of immorality successfully brought against him in 1932 by the Bishop of Norwich, represented by Roland Oliver and Walter Monckton.

(*Right*) Sir Walter Monckton at the Ministry of Information in 1939. On the outbreak of the Second World War he had hoped to re-in the army; but instead was appointed Director-General of the Press and Censorship Bureau.

(*Left*) Sir Walter Monckton with Anthony Hawke, after the celebrated 'Chalk Pit Murder' trial of 1947 in which Hawke had prosecuted Monckton's client, Thomas John Ley. Ley was found guilty, but instead of being hanged was sent to Broadmoor as a criminal lunatic.

Lord Monckton with his second wife Biddy (formerly Lady Carlisle) departing for Livingstone in February 1960 at the start of his work as Chairman of the Monckton Commission into the future of the Federation of Rhodesia and Nyasaland.

Members of the Monckton Commission at work in the field. Lord Monckton frequently carried the debate beyond the conference chamber by sending the members of the commission out into the country, so that any preconceived ideas and prejudices could be tempered by personal experience.

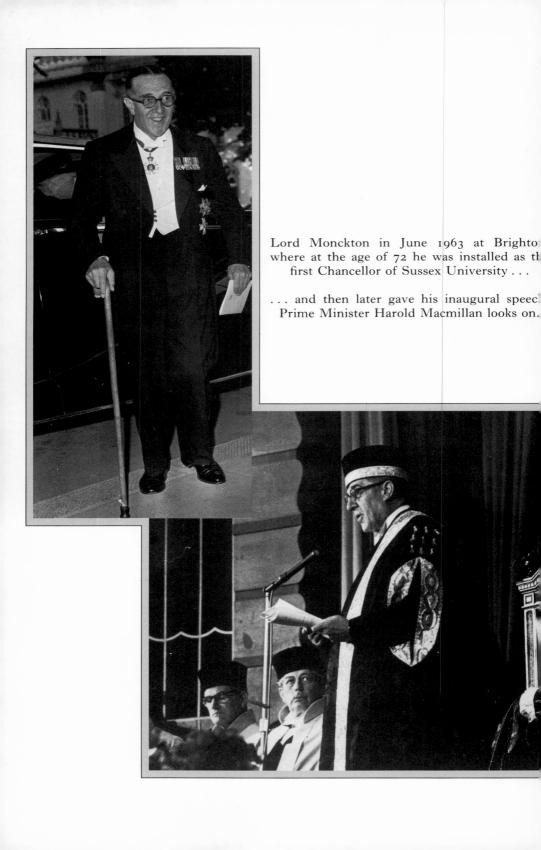

Lord Monckton in June 1963 at Brighton
where at the age of 72 he was installed as the
first Chancellor of Sussex University . . .

. . . and then later gave his inaugural speech.
Prime Minister Harold Macmillan looks on.

greater spirit,' he wrote, 'but perhaps that is not what the new master will attempt to accomplish.'

The 'new master' turned out to be the fifty-one-year-old Australian politician and diplomat Richard (later Lord) Casey, whose work as Australian Minister to the United States had impressed Churchill. Since Casey did not arrive in Cairo until May 1942, Walter Monckton was for three months at the summit of British affairs in the Middle East. There were no serious crises during this period; and Walter particularly enjoyed presiding over the Defence Committee, which he described as 'the heart and soul of the fighting machine in the Middle East', and which contained not only Auchinleck, now a firm friend; but also Tedder: 'a little man who has fire in his belly'; and Admiral Cunningham: 'a sea dog if ever there was one'.[26]

Walter had obtained permission to continue living in Beit-el-Azrak; and in due course Mary Newall quite openly moved in with him. This caused something of a scandal; and when he took her into his office there was soon so much bad feeling from the rest of the staff that the normally mild-mannered *chef de cabinet* Arthur Rucker had to threaten to resign if she were not removed. Walter declared that Mary was 'just a friend'; but nevertheless he did as Rucker asked. Many men would have felt profoundly humiliated by this climb-down; but Walter took it in his stride, and treated Rucker just as before.

When Casey finally arrived to take up his appointment, he asked Walter to stay on as his deputy, but Walter (after obtaining Bracken's agreement) declined; and returned to an uncertain future in England.

4

In mid-May, shortly before leaving Cairo, Walter had received a telegram from his former colleague at the Bar Sir Norman Birkett, who was now a judge, and who had invited him on behalf of the American and Canadian Bar Associations to attend their next annual meeting and to deliver an address. 'This invitation is the most coveted honour of any given to Bench or Bar,' cabled Birkett, 'but at this time America and Canada need an outstanding figure to present Britain's case, remove misunderstandings and cement friendship. You are their unanimous choice, and I urge you to accept as a high patriotic duty.'

Walter decided to accept, and began making preparations for a journey which would take him first to Canada, and then to America. He also decided that on returning to England he would resume his work at the Bar, and for this purpose he took a new set of chambers at 3 Paper Buildings in the Temple. In the meantime he was successively offered two prestigious appointments by Leo Amery, the Secretary of State for India. The first of these, that of Political Adviser to the Viceroy, had little appeal. The second, that of Chief Justice of the Federal Court of India, was more tempting, but again he refused. 'I need hardly say that such a position, following an old friend like Maurice Gwyer, is attractive,' he explained to Amery. 'But I still feel young enough to want more active and executive work. I have always feared the Bench in England as a shelf, and I think this appointment in India might well prove no exception.'[27]

After flying across the Atlantic on 10 August 1942, Walter had a most successful time both in Canada, where he stayed with the Governor-General Lord Athlone; and in the United States, where his address to the American and Canadian Bar Associations, given in Detroit, was well received. His subject was 'Liberty and the Common Law', and he pleased his listeners by his reference to 'the lamp of liberty and learning, the lamp of law and life, kindled by the light which lighteth every man that cometh into the world'.[28]

Walter also spent a few days with the Duke and Duchess of Windsor in the Bahamas. 'How glad we will be to see him and get the low-down,' wrote the Duchess when she heard he was coming. 'I'll bet it's low all right!' She and the Duke were both delighted to see him again. 'He is in excellent form and is *in love*,' wrote Wallis to her Aunt Bessie, 'but still has to be divorced etc.'[29] Presumably he had confessed to his affair with Mary Newall in Cairo. He also gave them their first reliable news for some time from informed circles in London. 'He did not seem gloomy about the war,' the Duchess continued, 'but says [it will last] at least 3 years': a forecast which turned out to be highly accurate.

On returning to London, Walter was engaged in only one legal case of any consequence before he was once again sent abroad by the Government on a special mission. The case, in October 1942, involved him leading for the 13-year-old Lord Furness in a probate suit to determine the validity of certain codicils in the will of the first Viscount. The mission, in January 1943, was to Sweden.

In Stockholm he stayed at the British Embassy, where the Ambassador was his old friend from Oxford days, Victor Mallet. 'Walter came over ostensibly on "Information" business,' Mallet wrote afterwards, 'but this was a put-up affair to bring leading Swedes into contact with an Englishman of persuasion and charm.' Although their country was neutral, the Swedes were not free to travel except on official business, and much of their information about the war came from

German sources. As Walter toured the country making speeches, they listened eagerly to what he had to say. For his part, he was dismayed to find that although most ordinary people were in favour of the Allies, the Swedish authorities displayed considerable pro-German sympathies. 'Most of the leaders, political and service,' Walter wrote in a secret report,

> were moved, so far as I could judge, more by the course of events than by political principle. Many of them were those who have sat on the fence so long that the iron has entered into their soul. The Commander-in-Chief of the Army was sufficiently naive to suggest that we had not fully explored the possibility of communications with Hitler. The Commander-in-Chief of the Navy also gave me the impression that he was well-disposed towards the Germans.

Needless to add, Walter's mission was strongly attacked by the Germans, who described him both as 'the Minister of Agitation' and as 'British Secret Agent No. 1'. However, his mission was regarded at home as a success, and he certainly put the Allied point of view most effectively. He discovered that while Sweden persevered in her neutrality, she kept a wary eye on both the swastika and the hammer and sickle. Indeed, the main anxiety of the Swedes appeared to be that the destruction of German power might 'leave Sweden and, at one remove, Great Britain and the whole of Western Europe open to Bolshevism'. Walter also encountered opposition to the declared Allied policy of demanding an unconditional surrender, which some Swedish critics believed to be foolish, since it offered no hope, and would therefore encourage the German people to fight on to the bitter end. 'I have no doubt from my visits and conferences,' Walter concluded, 'that the vast majority of Swedes – say ninety per cent – are with us in sympathy, but a great many would still desire to see Germany left strong after the overthrow of the Nazis.'[30]

Before long, Walter's work at the Bar was again interrupted, this time by a request from John Simon, now Lord Chancellor, to act that July as a Commissioner of Assize at Warwick and Birmingham. When Walter accepted this responsibility, he was much congratulated by his friends, who believed that it would lead to his being appointed a High Court Judge. Such, however, was not Walter's ambition. 'I am very glad to have this experience,' he explained to a friend, 'but it is only a matter of a few weeks and it does not mean that I am leaving the Bar or aiming at the Bench. It is just that there is a shortage of judges at the moment, and a chance accordingly to undertake some public work which I am gladly taking.'

At Warwick, where he stayed in the judge's lodgings, 13 accused were brought before him at the Assizes, which opened on 3 July. They were charged with offences of murder, rape and the like, and he had no difficulty in disposing of them. At Birmingham, on the other hand, Walter had to try a case of conspiracy in charging for the repair of bomb-damaged property which lasted for three weeks, thus establishing a new local record for length; while there were so many divorce petitions that Walter could not cope with them in a reasonable space of time, and Lord Goddard, then a Lord Justice of Appeal, was brought in to help.

Walter had remained out of favour with Churchill ever since their disagreement about General Sir William Dobbie's fitness to remain Governor of Malta; but their differences were eventually resolved in 1944 when they were both guests at a luncheon party given in her house at Iver in Buckinghamshire by Marina, Duchess of Kent. 'After lunch,' as Monckton later recalled,[31]

> Mr Churchill took me for a stroll in the garden. After some general conversation he said: 'You must think me a very hard man.' I knew at once that he was referring to our difference about Malta and the fact that I had not been in Government service since. I said, 'No, I don't at all. I knew one of us had to go, and I did not think it would be you.' He then turned to me abruptly and said: 'It has been our only difference; you were right and I was wrong.'*
>
> A little later he said that he would like me to come back into public affairs, and to join his Government. I said I was not a Conservative, and I should feel difficulty about that. He said he knew that, and did not think it made any difference. It was a Coalition Government and he could find me a seat. No definite decision was made, and I heard nothing more of it until the time [in May 1945] for a Caretaker Government. He invited me to join this as Solicitor-General on the understanding that I was not committed to any political party.
>
> I was not considered or adopted for a constituency because before nomination day I had been sent to Moscow and later to Potsdam as Chief United Kingdom representative on the Inter-Allied Reparation Commission. I returned on the day of the declaration of the poll (26 July 1945) which Labour won and therefore did not have to consider finding a seat.

Thus Walter began his political career as a minister without a constituency. Later he doubted whether any other Law Officer had held the appointment for so short a time and done so little legal work

---

* Churchill eventually agreed to the relief of Dobbie, who was replaced by the Governor of Gibraltar, Lord Gort. Dobbie died in 1964, aged 85.

(in his case, two Prize Cases and one Opinion); and whether anyone else had been a Law Officer without having been a parliamentary candidate. At first he had thought of standing for Oxford, a two-member constituency; but one of those members, Arthur Salter, was already in the Government; while the other, A. P. Herbert, was 'too old a friend for me to stand against him'. In any case on 29 May, only three days after Walter's appointment, the Prime Minister had announced in the House of Commons that Monckton was to be sent to Moscow to serve as chief United Kingdom delegate on the Reparations Commission.

5

Having spent some weeks briefing himself on the reparations question, Walter flew to Moscow on 16 June 1945. The delegation which he led was some 25 strong, and included able civil servants such as Sir David Waley of the Treasury and Mark Turner of the Foreign Office. The United States delegation was led by Edwin W. Pauley, a Texas oil magnate who was also a great friend of the new American President Harry Truman. However, Walter considered Pauley to be intellectually inferior to the chief Soviet delegate Ivan Maisky, well-known to Walter from his days as Soviet Ambassador to London.

The task of the Reparations Commission was to formulate agreed plans for German reparations, which could be considered by the Big Three – Churchill, Truman and Stalin – when they met in July at Potsdam. The difficulty of this task was increased by the incompetence of the American delegate. On arriving in Moscow, Monckton found that Pauley's chief aim appeared to be to conclude the work of the Commission as rapidly as possible, since he hated Russia and was anxious to return home. The Russians countered with delaying tactics, not realising how agreeable these were to Walter. 'They suited my book very well,' he noted afterwards, 'since I had no power to take any decided stand on the main issues. An election campaign was taking place in England, and one could not expect the Government to form or take a clear-cut policy line.'

In the meantime the British delegation was comfortably, even luxuriously housed in the Savoy Hotel, where its members were amply supplied with eggs, butter, meat, caviare, vodka and champagne; while their hosts supplied them not merely with free transport but with generous hospitality. On 25 June, for example, Walter told his daughter

Valerie that Maisky had given a banquet for the British delegation: 'I should think twenty courses,' Walter wrote, 'and eight wines including vodka. Only one of my lot was the worse for wear.'[32]

Despite Russian prevarication, Monckton gradually learned their intentions. Their chief aim was to further the reconstruction of the Soviet Union by extracting from the British zone, which included the Ruhr, a huge amount of plant and machinery. They were also thinking in terms of exacting from Germany some 20 billion dollars' worth of reparations, of which they would receive half. Pauley, trying to hurry things along, favoured giving the Russians, as soon as possible, anything in the western zone which they wanted, provided that it was evidently surplus to requirements.

Monckton, however, opposed him strongly. 'I had to resist this,' he explained later,[33]

> without making the Soviets think we were hostile, and as far as possible to encourage Pauley to take the same line. There were many things about reparations and about Russia's behaviour in her zone about which we wanted agreement, and our only card or bargaining lever was that we had in the Ruhr something the Russians wanted. If we once opened the door to interim removals the Soviets would gradually get all they wanted without any inducement to agree to the terms we wanted.

Another factor was that the Russians had more or less stripped their zone of anything useful, but had classified such material as booty rather than as reparations. This, as Monckton observed, was

> a serious matter because we all agreed that Russia was entitled to keep half of what might be available as reparations by reason of the sacrifices and losses she had suffered in the war. In particular, whereas we and the Americans between us had lost no more than half a million dead, the Soviets had lost five million. If therefore no reparations were to be had from the area allotted to the Russians they would claim a large proportion of what was in the Western Zone which we had not similarly stripped.

The British delegation estimated that it had been possible at the end of the war to find within the Soviet zone approximately a quarter of Germany's arable land, two-fifths of her moveable plant and machinery, and half her capacity for wealth-production. Since then Russian looting meant that little or nothing was left for reparations; nor was there any coal to be had from the Silesian mines, seized by the Nazis in 1939, but now firmly under Soviet control. 'In these circumstances,' Walter wrote, our general line was to decline to allow the Russians to take anything away from the Western Zones unless and until the general outline at least of a reparation plan had been agreed, and to devise some means by which we could either claim as booty in the Western Zones something corresponding to what the Russians claimed in the East, or get credit in some other way for what the Russians had taken.

Pauley's American delegation at length suggested that the Western powers of Britain, France and the United States should keep whatever was in their zones, 'taking care of other Allied nations except Poland for which the Soviets would be responsible'. (Poland, with Russian encouragement, would soon seize large parts of East Germany, expelling millions of Germans and fixing her western frontier on the line of the rivers Oder and Neisse, pending the peace treaty (which would not materialise for another 45 years).) Pauley felt that this was acceptable; but that if it were agreed by the Big Three, then Poland would have gained more than her fair share of reparations, and to make up for this it would be necessary to give the Soviets something from the western zones. Meanwhile the Soviet Union seized and later annexed the former capital of East Prussia, the port of Koenigsberg, which they renamed Kaliningrad.

In the middle of July the Reparations Commission moved to join the Big Three in Potsdam, where a new series of meetings took place in the Cecilienhof, the old German Crown Prince's Palace near Berlin. Walter's opinions of the Big Three are worth recording. Truman was a disappointment: a respectable businessman, who had been well briefed, but contributed little except an affirmation of United States policy. Churchill was 'good but patchy', and 'perhaps too ready to indulge in long dissertations which were evidently not to President Truman's taste'. Stalin he thought the most effective of the three leaders:

Stalin . . . spoke quietly, shortly, in little staccato sentences which Pavlov, his young interpreter, translated immediately into forceful English. In the discussions Stalin was often humorous, never offensive; direct and uncompromising. His hair was greyer than I expected, and was thinning. He wore it *en brosse*. His eyes looked to me humorous, and often showed as mere slits, but he had a trick of looking up when he was thinking or speaking, to the ceiling to the right, and much of the time he would be pulling at a Russian cigarette.

Churchill's flowing phrases, on the other hand, did not come out so well in translation. For instance, Stalin's 'gracious and generous gesture' was translated by the interpreter as his 'kindness'; while a description of Bulgaria as 'crouching and fawning' was altogether omitted.

The Allied leaders held their final meetings in Potsdam between 17 July and 2 August, Attlee taking Churchill's place half way through when the result of the elections in Britain was announced, and Labour gained power. A general agreement was reached over reparations and the extent to which Germany should be deindustrialised. On 3 August Walter Monckton, who had returned to London, noted in his diary that it was now a week since he had left Potsdam, and that it was

> interesting to see from the morning papers that the decisions for which I hoped for approval were in fact reached before the Big Three finished their conferences. The Russians are to get more out of our zone than I had contemplated – 25 per cent of the removables instead of the 15 per cent which I had in mind – but I have little doubt that the concession was wise on balance. It means that the big decisions are out of the way, and it is hardly likely that I shall be asked by the new Government in these circumstances to remain on as head of the UK delegation.

Walter was not so asked, and consequently returned to his chambers in the Temple to resume practice at the Bar.

Chapter 6

The Fate of Hyderabad

I

WALTER MONCKTON was still constitutional adviser to the Nizam of Hyderabad, but his wartime duties had prevented him from visiting the state. Thus it was a decade after his last visit that in January 1946 he once again travelled to Hyderabad. The capital was architecturally much the same apart from the beautiful new guesthouse in which Walter was luxuriously installed; but India as a whole had undergone some profound political changes.

The plans for an All-India Federation, buried during the war, were never subsequently disinterred. Instead it was proposed by the post-war Labour Government to confer Dominion status on the whole country, which would probably be divided between Hindu India and Muslim Pakistan. What would happen to the Indian states was unclear. Before Walter's arrival, the Viceroy Lord Wavell had told the native princes that their relations with the Crown would not be altered without their consent, but at the same time he had let them know that they should not withhold their consent to any changes that might appear necessary. Meanwhile the Nizam lived on in Hyderabad in his customary isolation, never leaving the capital, and seeing none of his ministers except for Sir Ahmed Said Khan, who was the Nawab of Chhatari and had succeeded Hydari as President of the Executive Council.

Walter soon discovered that the Nizam was resolutely opposed to entering any sort of Indian Union that might be formed; that he still wished for the return of the districts like Berar that had long ago been ceded to the Crown; and that he was still anxious for a sea-port. Walter considered none of the Nizam's desires to be realistic; and indeed he had an uneasy feeling that the Crown would eventually cease to honour its agreements with the princes. 'I have told [the Nizam's ministers],' he wrote in his diary,[1]

> that, although the UK Government is unlikely to admit it, the old treaty obligations for the protection of the State and Dynasty cannot now be relied on. I do not believe that the British will be prepared to send their sons to fight, to preserve the Nizam against democratic India.

As for the Nizam's advisers: they accepted much of this, and could only hope that Walter would be able to persuade the Nizam to modify his views. This had not proved possible before Walter returned to England in February 1946; but two months later he was back in India to represent the Nizam's interests in Delhi, as a member of the Hyderabad Delegation headed by the Nawab of Chhatari.

For in the meantime, a small Labour Cabinet Mission had been sent out from England to discuss the framing of a new Constitution. It consisted of Lord Pethick-Lawrence (Secretary of State for India), Sir Stafford Cripps (President of the Board of Trade) and A. V. Alexander (First Lord of the Admiralty and later Earl Alexander of Hillsborough). Cripps was the directing force; but although he did his best to persuade both Congress and the Muslim League to agree to his plans for giving Dominion status to India, those plans failed when the Congress Party withdrew their initial acceptance. Walter was disturbed by the way in which the Mission treated the problem of the Indian states as a matter of subsidiary importance; and on 6 May 1946 he wrote to Churchill expressing his feelings, and referring to the many treaties whereby the British Government had guaranteed the protection of Hyderabad and the Nizam's dynasty against both internal disorder and external aggression. 'Those treaty obligations,' he pointed out,[2]

> have been constantly reaffirmed in recent years, notably by Cripps himself in 1942. Now it seems to be suggested that we can denounce or forget the treaties – walk out and leave the states to make the best terms they can with the politicians of British India. What a hope we should have with Congress! I must say it sticks in my gizzard when I think of our complacently letting the Nizam and the Princes down in favour of Congress. When one thinks of the attitude of the Princes in both World Wars, and that of Congress in 1942, one wonders if we must always be driven to let down our friends and appease our enemies.

What Walter had in mind was the behaviour of Congress in exploiting the war situation to Britain's disadvantage, abstaining from all participation in the war effort, and even promoting revolution at a time when British fortunes in the Far East were at their nadir.

Churchill was present in the House of Commons when the Labour Prime Minister Clement Attlee announced the Government's intentions with regard to India. In place of Dominion status, upon which the Indian leaders had failed to agree, machinery would be set up whereby the Indians could decide for themselves how they should be governed. 'It will, I hope, be common ground between us,' Churchill told the House on this occasion, 'that we cannot enforce by British arms a British-made Constitution upon India against the wishes of any of the main elements in Indian life.'[3] Walter was delighted by reports of this speech, and subsequently wrote to Churchill from New Delhi telling him that:[4]

Your speech on the Government Statement on India gave great satisfaction to such of the Princes and the Muslim Leaguers as I came across yesterday . . . To my mind the most important point is that we should do all we can to persuade and encourage the principal elements in India to remain attached to the British Empire.

This was to prove a vain hope, since although Walter met the respective Hindu and Muslim leaders Nehru and Jinnah, he could not convince them of the desirability of an India without partition, and with guaranteed independence for the princely states.

At this time there were no fewer than 565 such states ranging from Hyderabad, which had more inhabitants than Canada, and a larger territory than the United Kingdom, to petty principalities smaller than the estates of a Duke of Sutherland or a Marquess of Londonderry. By and large these states had remained loyal to the British Crown not only during the Indian Mutiny, but also during two world wars. It now seemed that with the independence of British India, they would be deprived of British protection and left to deal with the new central Government as best they could. This was not an attractive prospect since Mahatma Gandhi, the Hindu nationalist leader and apostle of 'civil disobedience', regarded native princes like the Nizam as puppets of the British, whose sole purpose was to weaken resistance to the Raj.[5]

Although Walter had been cast down by these developments, he was very much invigorated at this time by a happy personal experience. At an evening party given for the Cabinet Mission in Delhi by the Commander-in-Chief Sir Claude (later Lord) Auchinleck, he met Lady Carlisle, known familiarly as Biddy, the Director of the Women's

Auxiliary Corps in India. Walter invited her to dine with him a few days later, explaining that the short notice was due to the fact that he must return to England for an arbitration. She accepted. They met for dinner in the garden of one of the Nizam's smaller guesthouses; and when a storm drove them indoors Walter proposed to Biddy, saying that he had been determined to marry her from the moment of their first meeting. She agreed, despite the difficulties. Each was married, though separated from their respective spouses; and the necessary divorce petitions might well prejudice Walter's future career. But Walter had made up his mind, certain that his liaisons with Leonora Corbett and Mary Newall had only been passing fancies, and that now, at last, he had found the woman with whom he wanted to share the rest of his life.[6]

Walter set out for England on 1 June 1946 with a sense of renewed strength and purpose in pursuing the Nizam's cause. However, soon after his departure, the Nawab of Chhatari also left Hyderabad, resigning his post in understandable despair. Two months later he would write to Walter condemning Britain's folly in ignoring the wishes of the Muslims and the princes, her friends, while attempting to win the support of Congress, her natural enemy. Chhatari (who had been succeeded as President of the Executive Council by the able but conceited Sir Mirza Ismail from Tranvacore) was so disgusted by the manner in which the British Raj was being brought to an end, that he also surrendered all his British honours and insignia.

An interim Indian Government was established under Pandit Nehru in September 1946, and this was later joined by members of the Muslim League, which had conspicuously refused to take any part in the deliberations of the Constituent Assembly set up to determine how India should be governed. At the same time, negotiating committees were established with the task of deciding how the princely states should be represented in the Constituent Assembly; but Hyderabad would have nothing to do with this process.

However, it was at the Nizam's request that Walter returned to Delhi in November 1946 to take part in further discussions about the future of Hyderabad with the Viceroy Lord Wavell. Once again there was talk about the possible return of Berar, and about the provision of a seaport. 'I have always felt that access to a port is essential to the survival of the State in its integrity and strength,' Walter wrote at this time, 'and that His Majesty's Government, if they are to denounce the treaties, are under an obligation to see that Hyderabad has a reasonable prospect of survival.'[7]

Not surprisingly, however, it seemed impossible to come to any agreement on these matters. Meanwhile Sir Arthur Lothian, the British Resident in Delhi, was succeeded by Charles Herbert; and on 3 December 1946 Walter wrote to his daughter Valerie describing Delhi as[8]

> a hotbed of intrigue and things are naturally insecure. It wouldn't take much of a match to set British India alight, and, if so, the States might soon follow. But Hyderabad, with its huge population in South India, which is predominantly Hindu, has its special dangers for the Nizam and the Muslim ruling clique. They have been slow to see it, and slower still to disarm it by some measure of liberalising policy, and by attempting to avoid the ill-will of the rest of India. But they might last longer than Congress. There is no certainty: it is anyone's guess.

A fortnight later Walter went back to England; and in January 1947 he wrote to Sir Conrad Corfield, the Political Secretary responsible for the princely states:[9]

> If the Princes could be told straight out what is intended with regard to Paramountcy [of the United Kingdom] and the implementation of treaties, and if they could, in consequence, be permitted, even at this late stage, to do what they can for the purposes of political and economic defence, then our position of letting down our friends in order to appease our Congress enemies would be more tolerable. Even now, I cannot persuade some of the Princes that we are going to leave them entirely to their own resources. They cannot speak of the Cabinet Mission, and in particular of Stafford Cripps, without a rush of blood to the head, and for this I cannot blame them.

From day to day the situation grew more alarming. Violence was threatened throughout British India, and Congress added to the uncertainty within the princely states both by sending out secret agents to foment agitation within them, and by demanding that the new Indian Government should inherit Paramountcy over them. Fears of outright revolution prompted the British Prime Minister, Clement Attlee, to make a statement to the House of Commons on 20 February 1947 in which he declared that power would be transferred to the Indian Government not later than June 1948. At the same time he announced Wavell's 'resignation' – in reality he was sacked – and the appointment of Lord Mountbatten as the new and last Viceroy. Finally, to try to calm down the princely states, Attlee announced that Paramountcy would not be terminated until the final transfer of power, while in the intervening period 'the relations of the Crown with individual States may be adjusted by agreement'.[10]

In the light of these new developments, Walter Monckton wrote in

February 1947 to the President of the Executive Council of Hyderabad, asking whether Hyderabad should not now 'be free in respect of increasing its army and starting munitions factories, if it wishes to do so? It is difficult to see how the British Government can, after saying that Paramountcy will end in June 1948, tie His Exalted Highness down in these respects?' At the same time Walter made some reassuring comments both about the new Viceroy and about his two principal advisers, General Ismay, who had been Churchill's Chief of Staff during the war, and Sir Eric Mieville, for long the Viceroy's private secretary, and now recruited to serve as principal secretary. 'It so happens,' Walter wrote,[11]

> that all three have been friends of mine for many years past. I have been keeping in close touch with Lord Mountbatten, and he is anxious for me to go out to India to help so far as I can . . . I shall do all I can to see that the new Viceroy understands that vital part that Indian India [i.e. the parts of India ruled by the princes] must continue to play.

However, Walter was unduly optimistic about the influence that he could exert on behalf of the states. The new Viceroy's inclination was to bring about Indian independence on a unified basis with the utmost rapidity, while endeavouring to persuade the princes to throw in their lot with the Central Government before the transfer of power was effected.

2

Mountbatten and his wife arrived in New Delhi on 2 March 1947; and on the following day Mountbatten took over from Wavell, and was installed in the Viceroy's House, that palatial red-walled building designed by Sir Edwin Lutyens and completed as recently as 1930. The new Viceroy had arrived with a directive from the India Office in London which stated that he should endeavour to implement the recommendations of the Cripps Cabinet Mission and bring a united India to independence. However, he very soon realised that this was impracticable, owing to the intransigence of the Muslim leader Mahomed Ali Jinnah. Partition was therefore inevitable, with the country having to be divided between Hindustan, led by Nehru; and Pakistan, led by Jinnah.[12]

Walter Monckton returned to Delhi in April, with the task of examining a number of questions on the Nizam's behalf. Should he, for example, join the Constituent Assembly? And should he continue to press for the return of districts which had been ceded to the Crown?

At first Mountbatten attached little importance to the future of the princes and their deputies; but when he became aware that it was a problem, he used every trick he knew to get them to agree to accession. Soon it had become clear to many of them that the writing was on the wall. Baroda, Bikaner, Jaipur, Jodphur, Patiala and Udaipur joined the Constituent Assembly; and the Muslim Nawab of Bhopal, Chancellor of the Chamber of Princes, resigned from a body whose members he now considered to be doomed as independent rulers.

Mountbatten's initial plan for independence ran into trouble from Nehru, who objected that it gave the provinces too much leeway in opting for individual independence, which would result in a potentially disastrous 'Balkanisation' of the sub-continent. A new plan was hastily drafted, providing for India's membership of the Commonwealth, and placing less emphasis upon the freedom of the individual components of British India to opt out of Hindustan (India) or Pakistan, and become independent. This revised plan was accepted by all parties: Hindus, Muslims and Sikhs; and on 4 June Mountbatten announced at a press conference that power would be transferred in nine weeks' time on 15 August 1947. This was ten months earlier than the date originally proposed by the Attlee Government, but the Viceroy was convinced that any further delay would endanger the prospects of national harmony. In the event, partition would take place in only two provinces, the Punjab and Bengal; and in one princely state, Kashmir.

The right of the princely states to independence was effectively destroyed at a meeting on 13 June which was attended by Nehru and Vallabhbhai Patel for the Hindus, Jinnah for the Muslim League, Sardar Baldev Singh for the Sikhs, and Sir Conrad Corfield for the Political Department of the Government of India. Nehru angrily denied that the states had any right to independence; while Corfield took the opposite view, in which he was supported by Jinnah, who declared that every Indian state was sovereign in all respects other than as set out in their treaties with the Crown; and that therefore the princely states were at liberty to refuse to join the Constituent Assembly of either Hindustan or Pakistan. However, it was agreed that state departments should be created within both India and Pakistan to control the relations of those governments with the princes. Corfield objected very reasonably that: 'Whatever the safeguards or precautions, these Ministries will, if established under the aegis of the Crown, be looked upon and will behave as though they have inherited Paramountcy which the Political Department has exercised hitherto.' However, his objections were overruled.

In India (Hindustan), the Minister of State at the new department was the formidable Patel, assisted as secretary by that able civil servant V. P. Menon. Together, the two men were determined to bring the princely states into India. Walter Monckton, who was aware of this, commented gloomily that 'Patel's line can be summed up in a sentence. He intends, if he can, to inherit the rights, but not the obligations of the Paramount Power.'[13] And a fortnight later, Walter wrote in a still more depressed state to Leo Amery, who had been Secretary of State for India in Churchill's wartime Government, telling him that it was 'horrible that we should have encouraged the Rulers to believe in our promises up to such a short time ago and should then leave them without the resources to stand comfortably on their own feet. It is still worse that they should feel that, in spite of loyalty, they are being left to the mercy of those who have been proved in the past to be our enemies and theirs.'[14]

It was probably Walter who drafted the letter which the Nizam sent to Mountbatten on 9 July, in which he complained about the Indian Independence Bill (Clause 7), as reported in the press though not previously disclosed to him. 'I have always hitherto felt assured', he told the Viceroy,[15]

> that after more than a century of faithful alliance, during which I have reposed all my confidence in the British, I should certainly be able to remain without question within the family of the British Commonwealth. Clause 7 appears to deny me even that. I feel bound to make this Protest to Your Excellency against the way my State is being abandoned by its own ally, the British Government, and the ties which have bound me in long devotion to the King-Emperor are being severed.

Although the Nizam received no more than a formal acknowledgement of this letter, Mountbatten met the Hyderabad delegation in Delhi, when he did his best to convince them that accession to the new Dominion of India was their best way forward. Walter, who was present, pointed out that the Nizam would find it difficult to follow any route which might compromise his independent sovereignty and personal prestige. Would it not be better to talk of an 'agreement' than to press for 'accession'? To this Mountbatten retorted that Hyderabad had no military defences, and if, therefore, the Nizam truly had the interests of his state at heart, he would send representatives to the new Indian Parliament. Walter countered by suggesting that Hyderabad might consequently be driven to join Pakistan, but Mountbatten fully understood that geographical complications made this an empty threat.

Distasteful as he found the prospect of yielding to Congress, Walter now had to realise that there was no alternative. All that remained was to secure the best possible terms; and on 26 July he was able to write to the Nizam claiming that 'as a result of discussions I have had with the Viceroy and his staff, we have at the moment open to Hyderabad an offer of accession on terms more limited than could have been expected before, and more favourable to Hyderabad than we can expect after 15 August when the British have gone'.[16] The plan was that Hyderabad should accede to India by treaty, surrendering only defence, foreign affairs and communications; and should there ever be war between India and Pakistan, Hyderabad would have the right to remain neutral.

Unfortunately Syed Abdur Rahim, a member of an extremist Muslim sect in Hyderabad society, had been appointed to the Hyderabad Delegation; and Rahim began sending back messages from Delhi to the effect that Walter was in league with the Viceroy, and was throwing away the Nizam's case. These reports were telephoned to Hyderabad in an uncoded form, and so became generally known. The result was that, on his return to Hyderabad, Walter found himself the subject of severe and totally unjustified criticism. Once (with some difficulty) he had refuted this criticism, he felt it best to resign from the negotiating committee, though he agreed to stay on as the Nizam's personal adviser.

The Nizam tended to lean more and more on Walter, even though he altogether neglected Walter's advice on the crucial matter of accession to the Central Government. When, for example, the Nizam's birthday was ceremonially celebrated, Walter was the only non-Indian present, and as a mark of especial favour he was seated in the chair traditionally occupied by the President of the Executive Council. Those present included the Nizam's 15 illegitimate children, who stood up to greet him at their father's command. 'Sir Walter, meet my sons,' said the Nizam as they did so. 'Sir Walter, meet my daughters.' Walter sat with these children on each side of him, and the Nizam opposite; while the Nizam sat with his heir the Prince of Berar on his right, and his eldest (and only legitimate) daughter on his left. Behind the ruler stood an official in gold uniform whose duty it was to taste each dish when it appeared, as a precaution against poison. Apart from an occasional comment by the Nizam (who had procured some port for his guest which he assured him was 'good, very good'), the meal was eaten in complete silence. Since Walter had been accorded the President's chair, it was soon being rumoured in Hyderabad that he was to be the next President; but in fact the Nizam gave that post back to the same Nawab of Chhatari who had earlier resigned the position in despair.

Walter's daily meetings with the Nizam took place in the ruler's office, 'an excessively mean and squalid little room', in Walter's view, 'with two decrepit swivel chairs, two or three kitchen chairs, and two old tables which serve as desks'. The only other furnishings were several old wooden cupboards, an antique safe, a few boxes, and a pile of dusty letters and documents. The window looked into what Walter described as[17]

> a very small and smelly yard, and [it] lets in very little light because of the ramshackle buildings round the yard. There are cobwebs which always catch my eye hanging down from the dirty ceiling to the still dirtier wall near the window. At one end of the room, instead of a wall the space is taken up by one of the wooden cupboards, and there is a gap through which one can squeeze into a kind of dilapidated outer office crowded with papers, desks, files and cupboards.
>
> In this office two or three more dilapidated clerks sit and work, and overhear all the secrets shouted by the Ruler. It is a preposterous set-up, and the President tells me that the Nizam's private apartments, a bedroom (in which his daughter aged 40 also sleeps) and a thatched verandah outside, are even more untidy and inadequate. The bottles, cigarette-ends and odds and ends, he tells me, are only removed once a year on the Nizam's birthday.

By the end of July Walter was back in Delhi; and early the following month he and the Nawab of Chhatari met Menon and the Viceroy for further talks. Menon, much to Walter's fury, proved to be utterly inflexible. He made it clear that British promises to the states would be ignored, that there could be no special treatment for the Nizam, and that the only option for Hyderabad was accession, on whatever terms Congress dictated. Mountbatten then remarked that no doubt Congress would lay itself open to much criticism, 'but one had to face facts, and criticisms from the world would not deter them'. He added, most forcibly, that if the Nizam failed to join the Dominion, his state would be ruined and his throne lost.[18]

Subsequently Walter drafted a letter which he sent to London, intending that unless the pressure on Hyderabad were reduced, it would be sent to the leaders of the Conservative Opposition at Westminster: Churchill, Salisbury, Eden and Butler. In his letter, Walter explained that he had been reading the diary of Count Ciano, who had been Mussolini's Foreign Minister, and he was bound to say 'that the present exhibition of power seems an exact replica of those in which Hitler indulged. It may be,' he continued,[19]

> that you will not hear from me again upon this matter apart from a short message to let you know that the German tactic on the old European model has been adopted in India. But I rely on you in the name of our old friendship to see to it that if this shameful betrayal of our old friends and allies cannot be prevented, at least it does not go uncastigated before the conscience of the world.

There is no direct evidence that Mountbatten was aware of the existence of this letter, which he would have found most displeasing; but his adviser General Ismay certainly read it on 10 August, by which time it was clear that there was no hope of Hyderabad acceding to the Dominion before the transfer of power. In the circumstances, all that the Viceroy could do was to play for time; and this he did with considerable skill, obtaining from the Indian leaders an extension of two months so that further discussions could take place.

Then on 15 August 1947, as arranged, Mountbatten ceased to be Viceroy and Crown Representative. It had been hoped that he would become Governor-General of both the new Dominions of Pakistan and India, so that he could preside over the transition to effective independence; but Jinnah decided that he himself would be Governor-General of Pakistan, so Mountbatten's duties were now confined to India.

Meanwhile Walter had returned to Hyderabad where, now that he and Biddy had obtained their respective divorces, they were married on 13 August in the British Residency. That evening the Nizam's Prime Minister, known as the Dewan, gave in their honour a magnificent banquet to which all the Hyderabad nobles and notables had been invited; while the Nizam, who was not renowned for his generosity, increased the pleasure of the newly-weds by giving Walter £2,000 and Biddy £500 as wedding presents. Theirs was to be an unusually happy and successful marriage; and its immediate effect was to give Walter increased energy as he entered the closing stages of his struggles on behalf of Hyderabad and her Nizam.[20]

3

Intrigues by Kasim Razvi, leader of the fanatical Muslim 'Ittehad' which had spawned Syed Abdur Rahim, forced Walter Monckton to resign a second time from the Hyderabad Delegation; but at length he agreed that he would once again travel on the Nizam's behalf to Delhi. There, in late September, Walter told Mountbatten that he was confident that he could persuade the Nizam to accept the equivalent of accession, provided that the words 'Instrument of Accession' were replaced with some face-saving title such as 'Articles of Association'.

Unfortunately Patel strongly objected to this compromise on the grounds that the Indian Government could be accused of breaking faith with all those princely states which had already joined the Dominion on more stringent terms; while those who had so far failed to acceded, might decide that there were advantages to be gained from holding out for as long as possible. In fact by this time virtually all the princely states had acceded, and had also signed so-called 'standstill agreements' to facilitate administration during the transition period. Only Hyderabad, Kashmir, Junagadh and two small states in Kathiawar still continued to resist; and so things went on, with the Nizam continuing to demand a treaty, and Patel and Nehru insisting upon an Instrument of Accession. By the beginning of October Mountbatten, desperately casting about for some way forward, suggested that as the acceding states had standstill agreements, Hyderabad should have one too. In mid-October, therefore, Walter and the Hyderabad Delegation reappeared in Delhi with a draft standstill agreement, and a collateral letter from the Nizam; but these documents proved to be completely unacceptable to Nehru and Patel.

Mountbatten's next move was to suggest a standstill agreement which more closely resembled those which had already been agreed with the other princely states; and after considerable bargaining, a draft was agreed by Nehru and Patel, with Mountbatten's blessing. This differed from the rejected draft in that while the Nizam remained free to appoint trade representatives within the Commonwealth, he could no longer appoint political representatives. What he had wanted was the right to have his own political representative in Pakistan; but Walter eventually persuaded him to give way on this point.

Indeed, Walter believed that the new agreement was broadly favourable to the Nizam. For the year of its duration, it would enable him to retain his independence, his sovereignty and his rights. India would have no right to maintain armed forces in Hyderabad; it was recognised that the telegraph, telephone system and posts of Hyderabad should be distinct from those of the Dominion of India; and the same arrangements on communications, defence and foreign affairs which had existed between Hyderabad and the Crown would continue to exist between Hyderabad and the Dominion. The Hyderabad Executive

Council advised the Nizam to sign the relevant documents by six votes to three; and he agreed that he would do so and have them sent to Walter by eight o'clock on the morning of 27 October, so that Walter and the rest of the Hyderabad Delegation could leave for Delhi half an hour later.

However, the Nizam had no real intention of signing the standstill agreement, favourable though it was; and that night, with his advance knowledge and tacit consent, the Ittehad led by Kasim Razvi staged a *coup d'état*. At four in the morning, Biddy was woken by sounds of an angry crowd outside their compound at Lake View; and soon she was telephoning Brigadier Gilbert, Chief of Staff of the Hyderabad Army, who said that he already knew of the *coup d'état*, and promised to send help. He had already ordered the military guards at Lake View to fire at anyone attempting to enter the compound. Later that morning, Walter and Biddy were escorted to Gilbert's house by two lorry-loads of armed sepoys with their bayonets fixed.

There was no longer any question of Walter and the Hyderabad Delegation flying to Delhi, since the Nizam had not signed the agreement. There was some doubt in Walter's mind about whether this was because he had been frightened by the Ittehad, or whether he approved of their aims; but in any case he refused to disown Razvi; and Walter Monckton, Chhatari and another member of the negotiating committee were so annoyed by this refusal that all three resigned. Furthermore they refused to advise the Nizam on a letter which he was proposing to send to the Governor-General, in which he foolishly threatened that if he could not get what he wanted from India, he would come to terms with Pakistan.

Walter was deeply depressed by this turn of events; and soon afterwards he and Biddy set out for England. They were delayed first by transport difficulties, which held them up for a fortnight in Bombay; and then (at the Nizam's request) by discussions with Jinnah in Karachi. It was not until the last week in November that they finally left the sub-continent and returned to London, where Walter found that he had enough legal work to keep him occupied throughout the winter. However, he continued to keep a close watch upon the Nizam's affairs.

When, after further wrangling, a standstill agreement was signed on 29 November, it was essentially the same as the document which Walter had negotiated before the *coup*. Shortly before the signing, Mountbatten had sent Walter this generous tribute:[21]

I cannot refrain from writing to you on this great day, for in two hours' time (after the air mail has left) I am going to countersign on behalf of India the original Standstill Agreement negotiated by you and now signed by His Exalted Highness . . . I have made it clear that you have won all along the line.

This, therefore, is your day, Walter, and I shall be thinking of you as I sign your agreement.

The Nizam for his part wrote to Walter explaining (with a characteristic *volte-face*) that: 'In short, low cad Razvi has received a terrible defeat so that he cannot show his face to the world.' Shortly afterwards, however, the Nizam foolishly appointed as President of the Executive Council Mir Laik Ali, a businessman who had once represented Pakistan at the United Nations, but who was generally believed to sympathise with the Muslim extremists of the Ittehad.

During Walter's absence the Ittehad continued to cause trouble in Hyderabad, burning down Chhatari's house (though Chhatari himself was fortunate enough to escape the flames) and threatening the Nizam's palaces. Meanwhile the Indian Government had sent K. M. Munshi to Hyderabad as Agent-General to the state. Unfortunately the Nizam took an instant dislike to Munshi, who appeared to be trying to assume (or, rather, to the Nizam's way of thinking, to usurp) the rights formerly enjoyed by the British Resident. 'What I hear from other sources,' the Nizam told Walter, 'is that this fellow is someone of notorious character and also a dignified blackguard. He comes from Bombay and is a Gujerati by nationality and also, I believe, a lawyer. However, I shall be in a better position later on to form my judgment of this devil like Nehru and Patel.'

Munshi, who was a senior member of the Congress Party, was certainly an unfortunate choice as Agent-General, as he made no secret either of his scorn for the princely states, or of his conviction that Hyderabad was bound to become an integral part of India. Nevertheless he fully recognised that the Nizam had at least one outstanding adviser, as these passages from his book *The End of an Era* would later testify:[22]

Sir Walter Monckton was the most formidable instrument of the Nizam's policy. An astute diplomat, possessing immense foresight, he played the triple role of constitutional adviser, a roving ambassador with close contacts with the leaders of the British Conservative Party, and an intimate friend of Lord Mountbatten. To my esteem for his forensic ability was soon to be added respect for his flair in carrying out negotiations . . . Never had any client a more competent adviser than Monckton, and never was any adviser so recklessly flouted as he was to such complete undoing of the client himself.

The Nizam had become convinced both that the terms of the standstill agreement were being flouted by the Indian Government; and (as he told Walter) that Mountbatten was: 'no more a friend of Hyderabad' – though it was doubtful that he had ever really been one!

In January 1948 the Nizam cabled Walter with the news that Mountbatten had been intending to visit Hyderabad to make a personal appeal for accession to the Dominion; but that he had ordered his Agent-General in Delhi to put him off until the following month. Understanding from this treatment that the Nizam no longer trusted him, Mountbatten was in favour of further negotiations being postponed until the autumn, when he would have left India.

However, the Nizam had soon opened the doors to fresh discussion by begging Walter to return to Hyderabad. Walter did so; and at the beginning of March he was part of a small delegation from Hyderabad which had talks with Menon and Mountbatten. Afterwards, he had to return to England, from where he wrote to Mountbatten, telling him that he would be back in India by the end of the month. 'Both Biddy and I think that our presence might conceivably give [the Nizam] the courage to face up to extremists,' Walter explained to the Governor-General.[23]

> We do not either of us feel inclined to leave the ship for fear it will sink under us. The old man finished his letter to me rather pathetically: 'Do please come back as soon as possible, as without you our affairs cannot proceed satisfactorily; and this is absolutely true.'

Meanwhile the Nizam had continued to be his own worst enemy. For example, he breached the standstill agreement by making Indian currency illegal for everyone in Hyderabad but travellers from outside the state; and he also loaned more than 10 million rupees to Pakistan without consulting the Dominion.

Hyderabad's fate now appeared to be inevitable. It was out of the question, said Patel, that it should remain the only authoritarian state in India; and from this time (despite the denials of both Patel and Nehru) Hyderabad became subject to an economic blockade of mounting severity. In desperation the Nizam offered Walter Monckton a highly lucrative position as political adviser to his Government for the next two or three years. Walter had grown to like India so much that he was tempted to accept; but Hyderabad's prospects were now so bleak that he eventually declined.

4

As he had promised, by the end of March Walter Monckton was back in Hyderabad, where the situation greatly disturbed him. Not only had the economic blockade been tightened, but Hyderabad was being saturated with hostile propaganda and open subversion. 'With its overwhelming strength surrounding the state,' Walter observed at the time, 'India could have afforded to be generous and wait for its hopes to be fulfilled. But it has preferred power politics.' He could not help bitterly recalling Mountbatten's promise never to allow any undue pressure to be exerted on Hyderabad, and his assurance given to the Nizam that Hyderabad would never be subjected to an economic blockade. 'Whatever the next step,' Walter wrote, 'whether an open boycott is declared, or even a pretext discovered or manufactured so that Indian forces may enter the State, it is a shameful business.' Menon and members of the Indian Government denied that there was any blockade, while complaining in their turn about breaches of the standstill agreement, and about the Nizam's apparent inability to deal with the Ittehad.

Walter Monckton, furiously angry, stormed off to Delhi where, much to Mountbatten's discomfiture, he declined to stay or dine with him. 'H.E. was very upset,' Walter recorded in his diary,

> . . . after our fifteen years of intimate friendship. I told him I could not stay in his house and at the same time attack him publicly, as I should have to do if there was a show-down. I said that there was an economic boycott in spite of the assurances he had given me about improper pressure. These were the very methods against which we had fought two wars, and looked like fighting another. If after the assurances he had given, H.E. became a party to them, I would attack him publicly by every means in my power, and would go back to Hyderabad and fight such a policy to the end.

It seems that knowledge of the blockade had been kept from Mountbatten, who later protested to Walter's biographer Lord Birkenhead that

> Walter's failure to inform me of this boycott and ask me for an explanation before I received his refusal to stay or dine with me wounded me deeply. He actually thought that I had consciously broken my word and was a party to this blockade. He appeared quite dumbfounded when I told him that neither I, nor, on inquiry, any member of my staff had ever heard of this blockade. On further inquiry neither V. P. Menon, not Patel, nor

Nehru had heard of it. I can't believe these three trusted friends would have intentionally deceived me, thus involving me in dishonouring my word.

Quick inquiries did indeed reveal a blockade and boycott were being imposed locally, below our level and with the knowledge carefully kept from us. We were all equally upset and furious, and quick orders were given to put the matter right.

According to Mountbatten, he pointed out to Walter at their next meeting that he had given his assurances at a time when circumstances had been quite different. The Ittehad now controlled Hyderabad; and Muslim extremists such as Kasim Razvi had gone so far as to proclaim a *jihad* or holy war, and were ranting about 'ashes of Hindus' should there be an Indian invasion. 'Walter offered me,' Mountbatten recalled,[24]

a most handsome apology for ever having doubted me, but remained unconvinced that the others were in the same state of ignorance . . . This episode is the only misunderstanding in our long-standing friendship, and although I accepted Walter's apology and we resumed our friendship I was never able to understand his doubting my word. I would never have doubted his.

At a later meeting between Mountbatten and Nehru at which Walter was present, Nehru assured the Governor-General that Hyderabad would not be invaded. However, some weeks previously Mountbatten had discovered that plans for such an invasion already existed. When he tackled Nehru with this information, the latter said he was surprised that Mountbatten had not known of this for longer. It was a contingency plan, no more, and had been devised as a precaution against a massacre of Hindus by the Muslims of Hyderabad. Mountbatten was sceptical: 'I told him that it was my impression that Ministers were seriously trying to put this plan into effect . . . irrespective of any massacres and I said I would take an extremely poor view of any such action.' Absurd, replied Nehru, he would never be a party to such a move.

By 14 April, after a further visit to Hyderabad, Walter was back in Delhi for discussions with Mountbatten, Nehru and Menon. He listened patiently to demands for the suppression of the Muslim extremists in Hyderabad, and for the introduction of a government with a broader base (both of which he had been unsuccessfully recommending to his master), and said that he would advise the Nizam accordingly; but he also pointed out some of the difficulties which the Nizam faced. For example, now that there was a boycott of arms and ammunition, and petrol supplies were being withheld, the police could no longer ensure the safety of Muslims in outlying districts without the cooperation of the extremists.

Walter's law practice was suffering, and on 19 April he had to return to England. But before he set out, he received a letter from Mountbatten, who made it clear the he was aware of the 'immense debt' which the Nizam owed to Walter for his interventions during recent months, but suggested that Walter was now wasting his time on a lost cause. 'If he will not listen to your advice this time for God's sake go, Walter,' he urged him, [25]

> because it will mean that nothing you or I can do can save the Nizam from committing suicide . . . When I think how much you have sacrificed for him, and how we have worked to maintain the peace and secure him as a constitutional monarch in future, it sickens me to think that this should have been wasted if he doesn't prove himself worthy . . . But the sands are running out, and he won't listen to you this time, I wouldn't stay if I were you; history will record the true facts and there will be no difficulty in judging between you and him.

However, Walter would not abandon the Nizam; and before he left India he wrote to him pointing out the danger caused by the extremists and begging him to subdue them, and having done so to liberalise his Government. 'I can and do respect a determination to go down fighting if one must go down,' he concluded. 'But before deciding to die, the wise man first exhausts every chance of living honourably. I am sure that there must be some passage in the Holy Koran like that in the Bible: "See, I have set before you this day life and death, blessing and cursing. Therefore choose life that both thou and thy servant may live."'*

Mountbatten, due to leave India in the third week of June, hoped that it might be possible to reach a peaceful settlement in Hyderabad before his departure. However, the Nizam declined his personal invitation to meet him in Delhi; and he himself declined the Nizam's counter-proposal that they should meet in Hyderabad. Instead, Mountbatten sent his press officer, Alan Campbell-Johnson, who reported that although the Nizam was 'physically decrepit', he was

---

* The correct quotation is from *Deuteronomy* (xxx.19): 'I have set before you life and death, blessing and cursing: therefore, choose life, that both thou and thy seed may live.' Monckton uses 'servant' instead of 'seed'. There are several similar references in the Koran, particularly in Chapter 3 ('The Family of Imran').

'obviously mentally alert, and in full command of his faculties . . . He is a Prince of the old school – arrogant and narrow, but on his own ground formidable. His mood throughout was one of aggressive fatalism.'

The situation continued to deteriorate; and although he was weighed down with legal work in England, Walter responded to desperate appeals from both the Nizam and Mir Laik Ali by returning to India at the beginning of June. Campbell-Johnson met him at Bombay with details of the latest demands by the Indian Government. It was immediately obvious to Walter that the Nizam would never accept, as these 'Heads of Agreement' were the practical equivalent of accession to India, involving as they did the creation of a Constituent Assembly and an Executive Council both of which were to be elected on a 60 per cent non-Muslim basis; and the granting to India of the power of overriding legislation. Campbell-Johnson also told Walter that Patel and most of the Indian Cabinet had demanded that the Indian Army should immediately invade Hyderabad; while Mountbatten, Nehru and Menon, it seemed, still hoped that war could be avoided. On one occasion, for example, when Mir Laik Ali had dramatically declared that the Nizam would rather be shot than accede to India, Mountbatten had tried to lower the political temperature by retorting that 'if Hyderabad was occupied by an Armoured Division there would be very little shooting'. It would be a bloodless victory, in his view, and the Nizam would die only if he chose to throw himself under a tank. 'More probably he would end up living in a small house in straitened circumstances.'[26]

Patel at this time was lying ill in Dehra Dun after a heart attack; however, he found the strength to write to Mountbatten to express his anxiety that the Governor-General was still trying to find a peaceful settlement, and to urge that the only course was for India to break off negotiations, and to tell the Nizam bluntly that immediate accession was the only acceptable solution. Mountbatten, feeling indignant, sent for Nehru on 8 June, and later wrote the following third-person account of what he had told the Indian leader:[27]

The Governor-General said that he thanked God he would be free in a fortnight's time. He was also an honest man. He would be able to say what he liked and he would be able to say what he thought. If war came between India and Hyderabad this would be the result of Sardar Patel's deliberate effort against those which he himself, Pandit Nehru, Sir Walter Monckton, Mir Laik Ali and Mr Menon had been making. Such a war would bring about the slaughter of tens of thousands of innocent Muslims, beginning in Delhi. Everything that Mahatma Gandhi had stood for would be gone . . .

He never thought the day would come when he would be glad to leave India. He could be far more dangerous than people apparently thought. Surely Mr Patel and Mr Menon could not have imagined breaking off negotiations with Hyderabad as was advocated by Sardar Patel? A situation had now been reached where Pandit Nehru would have to make a straight choice between Sardar Patel and himself.

Instructed by Patel, Menon now informed Walter that no further compromise could be tolerated on this fundamental issue by the Indian Government; and on 10 June Walter travelled to Hyderabad with the delegation, taking with him a new set of proposals. Two days later he had returned to Delhi, where he was able to report that the Nizam and his Council had approved most of the proposals, but they could not possibly agree either to the Constituent Assembly having a majority of non-Muslims, or to the Indian Government having the power of overriding legislation; and if opposed on those points, they would have to terminate the current round of negotiations.

In the meantime Walter had drafted a new set of 'Heads of Agreement', and Mountbatten took these with him when on 13 June, accompanied by Nehru and Menon, he flew to Dehra Dun to say goodbye to Patel. Patel angrily dismissed the redrafted proposals as being far too generous, and Nehru agreed that they were unacceptable. Mountbatten waited until the moment had come for him to leave; and then, before doing so, he pleaded one last time for the proposals to be accepted. So persuasive was he that Patel began weeping. Through his tears, he declared that India owed Mountbatten so much that he deserved whatever he wished as a token of gratitude, and to Mountbatten's amazement he signed the documents.

More concessions were to come: when on 14 June the Hyderabad Delegation in Delhi asked for a further four amendments, the Indian Cabinet, hoping to conclude the matter once and for all, agreed. The following day, Mir Laik Ali set out for Hyderabad to report to the Nizam, having been personally assured by Mountbatten that after so much had been conceded it would be useless to press for further amendments. However, the Nizam's folly in this matter knew no bounds; and on 16 June he sent Mountbatten a telegram in which he demanded a number of changes which were both silly and unacceptable. It was now clear that the Nizam's advisers were determined to wreck the settlement; but Walter Monckton, who had been waiting anxiously in Delhi for the Nizam's response, decided to make one last effort on his master's behalf, and he flew to Hyderabad that night.

The next day, Walter saw the Nizam in the presence of Mir Laik Ali; but the Nizam would not sign the necessary documents, making the specious excuse that 'this was not what they had discussed'. Whereupon Walter telegraphed one word to Mountbatten, and that word was 'Lost'.

Many years later, after Walter's death, Mountbatten would write to Biddy Monckton about their troubles with the Nizam:

> I often wonder whether that silly old Nizam had any idea what a superlative genius was conducting the negotiations. And when Walter settled the terms with Laik Ali and I managed to get Patel and Nehru to accept them – this should have been his supreme triumph as a negotiator, and then that scoundrel Kasim Razvi threw it away.

The Nizam's behaviour was especially infuriating to the Indian leaders in view of the extensive concessions to which they had agreed, and which meant that Hyderabad was being treated in a very different manner from those princely states which had signed Instruments of Accession.

Although he now left Hyderabad, Walter remained utterly loyal to his irresolute master. On his way back to England he saw Sir Zafrullah Khan in Karachi and talked to him about the possibility of presenting Hyderabad's case to the United Nations; and he did his best to dispel the rumour that he had now decided to leave the Nizam to his own devices. No, there was no longer any possibility of negotiating with the Indian Government; but yes, he remained the Nizam's constitutional adviser.

On 25 June Walter Monckton summed up his feelings on the whole business at a press luncheon in London. 'I made it plain', he declared,[28]

> that in my judgment the British pledges, which enabled the Nizam to choose independence if he wished, were not being honoured. I pointed out that Lord Mountbatten had publicly admitted the legal right to make such a choice, and had stressed to the Princes that no pressure would be applied. I concluded that in these circumstances Hyderabad was being let down. Either the British had not seen to it that the obligations they had undertaken would be taken over by the Indian Government, or the Indian Government were repudiating the obligations they had assumed.

Walter had done more than anyone to convince the Nizam of the need to suppress the Muslim extremists; and journalists who asked why the Nizam had failed to deal with the Ittehad were given short shrift.

During the summer of 1948, as the blockade of Hyderabad tightened, Walter did his best to gain favourable publicity for the state by lobbying both Government and Opposition in Parliament, while at the same time he accumulated an enormous file of papers as he prepared Hyderabad's case for the United Nations. But all to no avail. Mentally and physically depressed – he became ill, and had to recuperate in the South of France – Walter observed the lead-up to the final reckoning.

On 13 September 1942 the Indian Army invaded Hyderabad in what the Indian Government would euphemistically describe as a 'police action'. So overwhelming was their strength that within four days they had compelled the Hyderabad army to surrender; and on the fifth day Major-General Chaudhuri and his forces entered the capital. There were few casualties, and the Nizam was allowed to live on quietly in King Khoti, his favourite palace near the townhall and the public gardens.* Thus was Hyderabad state forcibly incorporated in the Indian Union. Later it would be divided up between Bombay, Mysore and Andhra Pradesh, of which latter province Hyderabad city became the capital. The epitaph of the princely state was enunciated by Walter Monckton, who declared simply: 'India wanted Hyderabad, and took it by force. I always said they would. They ought to be ashamed of themselves, and so ought we!'[29]

---

* H.E.H. Sir Usman Ali Khan, Nizam of Hyderabad, died on 24 February 1967, aged 81.

Chapter 7

Law and Politics

I

WALTER MONCKTON'S work as legal adviser to the Nizam of Hyderabad, and his visits to India adversely affected his practice in Paper Buildings; and although he continued to make a substantial income, averaging £30,000 a year, he would have made considerably more but for these extra-mural activities. Nevertheless the cases which he handled were of considerable importance: two in particular were so complicated that they could only have been conducted by an advocate of profound experience; while two more were of great popular interest, concerning as they did murder and gaming.

In the first of the two more demanding cases, Monckton appeared for the Church of Wales in *Representative Body of the Church of Wales v. Tithe Redemption Commission*.[1] This involved an appeal to the House of Lords on a matter arising from the disestablishment of the Welsh Church back in 1914. At that time, certain of the tithe rent charges which had formerly been vested in the Ecclesiastical Commissioners of England, had become vested in the Commissioners of the Church Temporalities in Wales, and had been subsequently transferred by statute to the University of Wales. The Representative Body claimed that the University, as 'lay impropriator' had become liable to repair the church chancels. Although this bizarre outcome cannot have been what was intended, legally Monckton's arguments were impeccable; and his claims on behalf of the Church of Wales were upheld by five Law Lords led by the Lord Chancellor Lord Simon.

Hickman v. Peacey (1945), the second demanding case, involved Walter in another appeal to the House of Lords.[2] What had happened was that four persons, two of whom had made wills benefiting some of the others, were killed when a bomb exploded in an air-raid shelter in London in 1940 during the Battle of Britain. In these circumstances, and in the absence of any evidence rendering it certain that some of them survived the others, how should section 184 of the Law of Property Act 1925 be interpreted? A lower court had decided that the deceased had died simultaneously; but Walter argued that the deaths should be presumed to have occurred in order of seniority, with the younger being deemed to have survived the elder. This was agreed by a majority of three to two (Macmillan, Pooter and Sumner against Simon and Carson); and so, once again, Monckton was successful.

The murder case was the most notorious of Monckton's career, and involved a memorable trial presided over by the recently appointed Lord Chief Justice Lord Goddard. Walter's client was Thomas John Ley, an Englishman who had emigrated to Australia where he had become a lawyer and a politician and had risen to be Minister of Justice in New South Wales. At the age of 66, disappointed at not having become Premier, Ley had returned to England, accompanied by his wife, and followed by a certain Mrs Brook, his mistress.[3] Mrs Brook was as old as Ley, and there had been no sexual intercourse between them for ten years; but he was insanely jealous of her, and before long had developed the absurd idea that she was having an affair with a young barman who worked at the Reigate Hill Hotel in Surrey. In fact Mrs Brook had only seen the young man once, when they passed each other on the stairs of the lodging house where they both happened to be staying; but their accidental proximity was more than enough for Ley, and before long he had decided that John Mudie must die.

The affair became popularly known as the Chalk Pit Murder, since Mudie's body was discovered near Woldingham, another Surrey town, in a chalk pit. Around the neck of the corpse was the loose cord which, from the deep mark that was visible, had evidently been pulled tight enough to cause death by strangulation. Two other men had been involved in the murder: Lawrence Smith, a joiner, and John Buckingham, a car-hire driver; but Buckingham turned King's Evidence and therefore avoided being charged.

Buckingham explained that he had been introduced to Ley by a hotel porter of his acquaintance; and that he had then agreed to help to dispose of Mudie for a fee of £200. After an initial attempt to kidnap Mudie had failed, a woman friend of Buckingham's asked the unfortunate barman whether he would like to earn some extra money by running the bar at a cocktail party which she said that she was planning to give at 5 Beaufort Gardens in Chelsea, where both Ley and Buckingham had flats. When Mudie agreed, it was arranged that she should pick him up in Reigate on the evening of 28 November 1946. She did so, and the two of them were chauffeur-driven to London by Buckingham's son, shadowed all the way by another car containing Buckingham and Smith.

On the previous day, Buckingham and Smith had used the same vehicle (which Smith had hired for a week with Ley's money, and which bore the registration number FGP 101) to view the chalk pit in which it was planned to hide Mudie's body once he had been killed.

When Mudie arrived at Beaufort Gardens, he was taken down to the basement which Ley used as offices. There, in Ley's presence, he was shortly afterwards seized by Smith and Buckingham. A carpet was thrown over his head, cloth was stuffed into his mouth, and he was then asphyxiated through the tightening of a rope around his neck by what would later be described in court as 'the exertion of sustained upward pressure'. Once Mudie was dead, Ley paid Buckingham £200 in £1 notes; and that same night Mudie's body was dumped in the chalk pit.

However, the murderers had bungled their job. Not only was the body discovered the very next day; but the police also found a car which contained both Mudie's clothes and his name and address; while a search at the Reigate Hill Hotel soon brought to light some letters from Ley giving his address in Beaufort Gardens. There they found some green cloth exactly matching the cloth with which Mudie had been gagged; while two landscape gardeners remembered seeing a frightened man looking over the chalk pit on the day before the murder, and then speeding away in a car whose registration number included the figures 101. All this was quite enough for Ley and Smith to be charged with murder; and their trial took place at the Old Bailey on 19 March 1947 before Lord Goddard and a jury. Anthony Hawke, later Recorder of London, led for the Crown; while the defence was in the hands of Walter Monckton, for Ley; and of Derek Curtis-Bennett, for Smith.

Defence counsel had a hopeless task. Walter wished his client to plead guilty but insane, which would reduce the charge against him from murder to that of manslaughter; but Ley refused to do this, and so Walter was thrown back upon the unlikely defence that Mudie had committed suicide. In an effort to establish his case he called upon the eminent pathologist Dr Keith Simpson as an expert witness. According to Simpson, he had only been able to deduce from his examination of Mudie's body that death was due to asphyxia by suspension. There was nothing to indicate whether this had come about as the result of accident, suicide, or wilful strangulation.

'But this body was lying in a trench in a chalk pit?' asked the Lord Chief Justice in a tone of astonishment.

'Yes, my Lord,' answered the witness. 'I am describing the conclusions I draw from this mark [on the corpse's neck]. One could *imagine* a great deal, but there was nothing to show *how* the body had been lifted in some way at the side of the neck.'

Lord Goddard then questioned the witness most vigorously as to whether Mudie had been conscious or unconscious at the time of his death, and whether by that time he had suffered any appreciable violence. These were crucial matters. If it could be shown that there had been either unconsciousness or violence before death, that would virtually rule out the possibility that Mudie had committed suicide. How serious, in this context, was the bruise which had been found on Mudie's head? Dr Simpson, an admirable expert witness who confined himself to the limits of his scientific knowledge of the case, characterised this bruise as trivial; while the Crown pathologist (who could hardly be expected to agree with Dr Simpson) described it as deep.

When Ley himself was called to the witness box he stonewalled and denied everything. Later, when his mistress Mrs Brook was being cross-examined, it seemed that he had an alibi, as she declared that she had been playing gin rummy with him on the fatal evening. Answering the judge, however, she had no explanation for her failure (if the story was true) to inform the police on first hearing of the murder that she could account for the movements of one of the accused men.

Ley and Smith were both found guilty by the jury, and sentenced to death. They both appealed and their appeals were dismissed. However, three days before the date fixed for their execution, the Home Secretary Chuter Ede announced that Ley had been pronounced insane and was being sent to Broadmoor, the asylum for criminal lunatics. At the same time Smith's sentence of death was being commuted to one of penal servitude for life.

'I have no doubt the prisoner [Ley] was insane,' Lord Goddard said three years later, when he was discussing the Chalk Pit Murder with members of the Royal Commission on Capital Punishment;

but he refused to allow his counsel to raise the defence of insanity, and would have been horrified at such a suggestion . . . I had no doubt that Ley was what you may call a pathological case, by the way he gave evidence, in which he simply denied everything flatly . . . The whole thing was planned in the most elaborate way, and he was a very wicked man.

Asked by one of the medical commissioners whether he thought that Ley should have been hanged, despite his insanity, the Lord Chief Justice showed that in all circumstances he was resolute on the noose. 'I should have thought it very proper,' he replied, 'that he should have been hanged.' In other respects Lord Goddard was a most humane judge; and yet he would greatly deplore Parliament's 1967 abolition of capital punishment.

The gaming case, *Hill v. William Hill (Park Lane) Ltd*,[4] in which Monckton was involved in 1949, was to become the leading case on the interpretation of Section 18 of the Gaming Act of 1845. This section provided first that 'all contracts or agreements, whether by parole or in writing, by way of gaming or wagering, should be null and void'; and second, that 'no suit shall be brought or maintained in any court of law or equity for recovering any sum of money alleged to have been won on any wager'. In this case the appellant, Tom Hill, was a racehorse owner who regularly placed bets with the bookmakers William Hill Ltd. In April 1946 William Hill reported him to the committee of Tattersall's for saying that he could not pay the £3,635 12s 6d which he then owed them; and the committee devised a schedule of payments beginning with a sum of £635 12s 6d which was due within 14 days. Any loser who failed to agree to such an arrangement would in due course be reported to the Jockey Club, barred from Newmarket Heath, and publicly exposed as a defaulter. This would mean that he could no longer enter any horse for a race in his own name, or attend any race meetings which the Jockey Club controlled; and no bookmaker would be foolish enough to accept any further bets from him.

Despite knowing of these penalties, Tom Hill protested that he could not comply with the schedule of payments. Instead, in August 1946, he offered William Hill a cheque for £635 12s 6d post-dated to 10 October, and said that he would then pay the remainder of the money as directed. His offer was accepted; but when October came, the post-dated cheque bounced. The following month, Tom Hill paid the bookmakers £335 12s 6d, which they accepted 'without prejudice to the legal position'; and that was the last payment they received. The result was that in February 1947 William Hill issued a writ claiming £700; in his defence, Tom Hill pleaded Section 18 of the 1845 Gaming Act.

Mr Justice Hallett, who heard the case, gave judgment for the bookmakers. Tom Hill's subsequent appeal to the Court of Appeal was unsuccessful; and he then appealed to the House of Lords, where Walter Monckton appeared on behalf of the bookmakers.

Tom Hill's counsel argued that the contract in this case, although it was not a contract 'by way of gaming or wagering' as specified in the first part of Section 18 of the 1845 Act, definitely fell within the second part of the Section, as the money paid was 'alleged to have been won on any wager'. And the provisions of that section clearly stated that 'no suit shall be brought or maintained in any court of law or equity for recovering any sum of money alleged to have been won on any wager'. His client was therefore under no obligation to pay.

In reply, Walter Monckton relied on the 1908 precedent of *Hyams v. Stuart King*, a similar case in which it had been decided that if the loser of a wager agreed for a fresh consideration to pay what he owed, this was a distinct transaction which fell outside the scope of Section 18. Tom Hill was therefore liable to pay.

Walter's arguments failed, but only just. By a majority of 4 to 3, the Law Lords held that the payments did indeed fall within the second part of Section 18, and so were not recoverable. Accordingly Tom Hill's appeal succeeded, and the bookmakers lost.

2

Walter Monckton's years at the Bar would end in 1951, when he accepted office in Winston Churchill's last Government. But before then he appeared in three more cases which attracted considerable public interest. The first of these, *Braddock v. Tillotson's Newspapers Ltd*,[5] arose out a libel action brought against the *Bolton Evening News* by that bizarre and controversial Labour MP, Bessie Braddock.

It was on 1 April 1947 that an article entitled REVELRY BY NIGHT appeared in the *Bolton Evening News* describing what had happened in the House of Commons during the report stage of the Transport Bill. The Conservative Opposition had left the chamber in protest, after the Labour Government used the guillotine procedure to ensure that numerous amendments to the bill could be dismissed without debate. According to the article, what had happened next was that:

In the middle of this unlovely burlesque, Mrs Braddock, who represents the Exchange Division of Liverpool, danced a jig on the floor of the House, finishing in the seat vacated by Mr Churchill, our greatest House of Commons man. The whole performance was nauseating, a sorry degradation of democratic discussion, the nadir, let us hope, of this Parliament.

Mrs Braddock, claiming that her reputation had been damaged, and that she had been held up to ridicule and contempt, sued for libel. The case was tried by the Lord Chief Justice Lord Goddard; and Mrs Braddock's action was dismissed, since the jury accepted a defence of fair comment on a matter of public interest.

After the trial, however, Mrs Braddock's advisers discovered that the press reporter on whose report the article had been based, and who had been the principal witness for the defence, had been convicted of dishonesty a number of times during the past ten years, and had now been excluded from the House of Commons Press Gallery. Mrs Braddock therefore sought leave to cross-examine the witness to establish whether or not he was reliable; and Lord Goddard adjourned her application to the Court of Appeal, where it could be heard at the same time as her appeal against the jury's verdict.

In the Appeal Court, the defendant newspaper company was represented by Walter Monckton and Helenus Milmo, who later prosecuted Kim Philby at his secret trial, and afterwards became a judge. Walter and his colleague argued that in the past, when a witness had been recalled, it had been the practice to confine the fresh evidence to questions of fact which were relevant to the matter in hand. It could not be said that the witness's previous convictions were relevant to any part of the current case; and it would be a new departure for a witness to be recalled to establish his reliability. The judges in the Appeal Court (Tucker, Cohen and Singleton) agreed. Mrs Braddock's appeal against the verdict was dismissed, and her application for the admission of fresh evidence was refused, the Court holding that there was no certainty that the fresh evidence would have led to a different verdict; and that the Court of Appeal would not be justified in setting what might be a dangerous precedent.

The second case, *Kemsley v. Foot*,[6] was also a libel action in which fair comment was pleaded by the defence; and it affords a striking example of Walter Monckton's generous behaviour, even towards his opponents in court.

It was on 2 March 1950 that the London *Evening Standard*, under the sensational heading, FUCHS AND STRACHEY: A GREAT NEW CRISIS. WAR MINISTER HAS NEVER DISAVOWED COMMUNISM, launched an attack upon Mr John Strachey, the

Secretary of State for War. Klaus Fuchs had recently been convicted under the Official Secrets Act for giving nuclear information during the Second World War to the Russians, while officially working for the British; and the clear implication of the article was that Strachey might also be a communist and was not to be trusted. Just over a week later, on 10 March, the left-wing journal *Tribune* carried an article in which the Labour MP Michael Foot strongly criticised the *Evening Standard* for its behaviour in the matter, describing it as 'the foulest piece of journalism perpetrated in this country for many a long year'. Unfortunately Foot's article was headed LOWER THAN KEMSLEY, clearly referring to Lord Kemsley, a well-known news-paper proprietor.

Lord Kemsley (whose properties, incidentally, did *not* include the *Evening Standard*) brought a libel action in which he complained that the heading LOWER THAN KEMSLEY implied that he used his newspapers to bring about the publication of statements he knew to be false. Foot and *Tribune*, as part of their defence, stated that what they had written was 'fair comment'; but Kemsley sought to have this defence struck out, as it should only be available when a comment was based on fact. In this instance, the words of which he complained were all comment, and no fact! Parker, the trial judge in the King's Bench Division, agreed with Kemsley.

Walter Monckton represented Lord Kemsley when Michael Foot and *Tribune* took the matter to the Court of Appeal, which found in their favour; as did the House of Lords, where Kemsley took the matter, this time without Walter as his counsel. Both the Court of Appeal and the House of Lords believed that the comment could be argued to be 'fair comment', as it was based on 'a sufficient reference to Lord Kemsley's newspapers'.

Despite the defence of 'fair comment' being allowed, Lord Kemsley could easily have proceeded with his libel action; and had he won it, the costs would have been astronomical, and both Foot and *Tribune* would have been ruined. It was in these circumstances that Walter Monckton intervened and persuaded Kemsley not to proceed with the libel action, and even to pay some part of the defendants' costs. 'We, however,' as Michael Foot later explained to Lord Birkenhead, 'agreed that we would not celebrate this as a victory and on this basis the whole matter was settled. We were extremely grateful to Monckton, who had acted in the matter, partly, I believe, through his friendship with Aneurin Bevan.'

The third case, *Bolton v. Stone*,[7] was particularly close to Walter's heart since it concerned his favourite game of cricket. On its progress through the courts, it also caused considerable alarm to cricket clubs up and down the country.

What had happened in the first place was that on 9 August 1947 a certain Mrs Bessie Stone of Cheetham, near Manchester, had stepped from her garden gate onto the pavement skirting the adjacent road when she was hit between the eyes by a cricket ball. Luckily she was not seriously injured; but she was severely shocked. The ball had been hit over the fence which surrounded the nearby Cheetham Cricket Club ground; and Mrs Stone decided to sue the club, alleging nuisance and negligence.

The case was heard at Manchester Assizes, where it was established that the ball had been hit over the fence by a member of a visiting team; and that during the previous 30 years a number of other balls had been hit over the fence, though without causing injury. Mr Justice Oliver, the trial judge, rejected the plaintiff's claim that the defendants had committed a nuisance, but provisionally assessed her claim for damages for negligence at £104 19s 6d.

When Mrs Stone took the case further, the Court of Appeal also rejected her claim for nuisance (which legally involves a continuing wrong); but held, with one dissentient, that the defendants had indeed been guilty of negligence. Lord Justice Singleton stated that the defendants had failed to discharge their duty, which was to take reasonable care to reduce a foreseeable danger. Lord Justice Jenkins spoke more strongly, believing that the defendants were duty-bound to prevent a cricket-ball being hit out of their ground. However, the defendants were given leave to appeal to the House of Lords; and it was then, with every small cricket club in the country deeply concerned by the Court of Appeal's verdict, that Walter Monckton lent a hand.

Walter advised the defendants to appeal to the House of Lords. Otherwise Lord Jenkins's judgment in the Appeal Court might come to be regarded as authoritative; and it would be better and less costly to challenge the ruling immediately, than to wait for a later case, when the matter would have to be taken all the way up to the House of Lords before the Appeal Court ruling could be overturned. The cricket club therefore appealed to the House of Lords where Walter Monckton led for the appellants, while the respondent Mrs Stone was represented by Mr H. I. Nelson, KC. The appeal was heard by five Law Lords led by Lord Porter, the others being Lords Norman, Oaksey, Reid and Radcliffe.

Walter argued that the chance of a cricket ball being hit over the fence and striking a person in the road was so remote that the cricket club had no duty to guard against it. Anyone using a public highway, he believed, must accept that he might be at some slight risk from other people who were going about their lawful business; and it was important that such a risk should not prevent young men from enjoying healthy exercise. He agreed that the occupiers of any cricket ground owed some degree of care to the public; but there could be no absolute standard, as it would depend upon the nature of the risk, and that in turn depended upon such factors as the surroundings of the cricket club, and the volume of nearby traffic. Certainly any club had a duty to prevent balls from being constantly hit out of the ground: for that would constitute a nuisance; but no club could reasonably be expected to prevent balls from being hit out of the ground by an extraordinary and exceptional stroke. He concluded that cricket had been played on the appellants' grounds for 90 years, and this was the first time that anyone had been injured in such a manner.

Nelson KC commented that the appellants' case appeared to be that they were entitled to hit balls out of the ground, so long as no one was hurt! After all, it was no accident that balls were hit out of the ground, but the result of deliberate action by the batsmen, who knew that by doing so they would be awarded a 'boundary' of six runs! It must therefore be considered negligent of the appellants not to have taken proper precautions to prevent the escape of cricket balls from the ground. Supposing a bus-driver had been hit? The consequences could have been disastrous. In any case, once a ball had gone over the fence, anyone hit by it was entitled to compensation.

In his reply, Walter Monckton submitted that the authorities contained no case of nuisance which was remotely similar to the matter under discussion. It was only if the occupier of a piece of land allowed a nuisance to continue 'with actual or imputed knowledge of its existence' that they were under any legal liability. And in this case the appellants were anxious to prevent the opposing team from hitting boundaries! The batsman was not their servant, and they had no control over him. Want of care, therefore, could not be proved; without such proof neither nuisance nor negligence could be imputed; and in any case no fleeting event could legally constitute a nuisance.

After hearing Monckton's arguments, the House of Lords allowed the appeal. In his judgment, Lord Porter commented that it was clear that the appellants knew that cricket balls might be hit out of their ground, and that as a result of this someone might be hurt. However, this did not place them, as the Court of Appeal had ruled, under an obligation of care. If they were placed under such an obligation, then no one would dare to drive a motorcar, since in that case too the possibility of an accident was always there. It was not enough to be aware of such a remote possibility. The question was whether a reasonable man could be expected to anticipate it.

Mrs Stone's leading counsel later bewailed the fact that (as he put it) a cricketer might now deliberately hit cricket balls into the highway with impunity. 'Possibly at some future date,' he wrote to Lord Birkenhead,

> a cricket ball so hit may cause a major disaster, and the whole question of liability be reopened. The cricket ball case certainly made the headlines. To associate the sacred game of cricket with nuisance was regarded by many as something akin to blasphemy.

However, it would be unfair to describe Walter as one of those extremists; and it was appropriate that his last major case (which became a leading one in both nuisance and negligence) should have been associated with his favourite sport.

3

Apart from a short period as Solicitor-General in the Churchill Caretaker Government of 1945 (when there had been no time for him to find a constituency and secure election to the House of Commons as an MP), Walter Monckton had no experience of political office. From time to time before the war he had been asked to become a Conservative candidate (notably by both Sevenoaks and Maidstone in his native Kent); but the demands of his legal practice had always led him to refuse. By 1944, he had grown more interested in political life; and after being approached by the Chairman of a London Conservative Association, he had allowed his name to go forward as a possible MP. However, after reaching the shortlist he had a change of heart, and withdrew, apparently fearing that some of his political views might be an embarrassment to his Conservative colleagues once the wartime coalition had ended. However, Churchill, now the post-war Leader of the Opposition, hoped once again to become Prime Minister, and had his eye on Monckton for political office in a future Conservative Government. So when he heard in the spring of 1949 that the Conservative Association in South Oxfordshire were looking for a new candidate, he urged Walter to put his name forward for selection.[8]

The situation in South Oxfordshire was unusual. The sitting Member Sir Gifford Fox had represented the constituency for 20 years, but latterly had been the subject of so many complaints of neglect and inattention to local needs that the Chairman, Lord Macclesfield, had been persuaded to call an extraordinary general meeting. Sir Gifford (or 'Pam' as his friends called him) would have a chance to answer his critics. Either his candidature at the next election would be endorsed (most unlikely), or a new candidate would be chosen: almost certainly Sir Walter Monckton (who would come with Churchill's acknowledged backing); though a 38-year-old solicitor John Hay, Chairman of the local Young Conservatives, had also thrown his hat into the ring. The meeting (at which attendance was restricted to those who were registered members of the Conservative Party in the constituency) was to be held in the Oxford Union debating chamber, the scene of Walter's undergraduate successes.

Walter and Biddy drove down to Oxford from London, where they were now living at 12 Charles Street in the Temple. They were accompanied by their friend Lady Pamela Berry, daughter of the first Lord Birkenhead, and sister of the man who was to become Walter's biographer; and all three were in excellent spirits. In Oxford they lunched at the Mitre, where they found the author and landowner Peter Fleming sitting alone in the restaurant. Lady Pamela introduced the Moncktons to Peter, who told them that he detested political meetings, but would be coming to this one to support Walter. Then, during the course of a cheerful lunch at which there were many toasts to the future MP, Peter suggested that when the meeting was over they should all meet at Merrimoles, his house in Nettlebed, for a celebration drink. They all assumed that Fox would be dislodged, and that Walter was bound to be selected.

The meeting began with Sir Gifford Fox speaking to an audience of nearly 600. He pleaded for unity and loyalty 'to your Member in these difficult times'; and when he sat down there was some applause from his supporters, and a few shouts of 'Good old Pam!' The other two potential candidates were not in the chamber during his speech, but were brought in and introduced separately. First came John Hay, who was rapturously received (especially by a substantial phalanx of Young Conservatives), and who proceeded to address his audience in a manner which showed that he understood very well the particular concerns of each age-group and profession who sat in front of him. His speech was followed by a whole-hearted ovation.

Then Lord Macclesfield introduced Sir Walter Monckton, the candidate who had Churchill's support and who was warmly recommended by Conservative Central Office. He described Walter's success at the Bar, and the distinguished service he had rendered in India. However, just when Walter was beginning to seem the obvious choice, Lord Macclesfield sabotaged his chances in that highly traditional constituency by leaving a long pause, and then adding: 'Perhaps I should tell you that Sir Walter Monckton has been through the divorce courts.'

During the stunned silence which greeted this news, Walter and Biddy entered the chamber and were led up to the platform. Biddy, always a prey to nerves on public occasions, sensed an underlying hostility in the audience. Worse still, Walter confined his speech to international affairs, his legal work abroad, and the dangers of communism. As a speech, it was quite unsuitable for an audience in a largely agricultural constituency. As he realised that he had lost his audience, an unusual experience for him, Walter began to sound exhausted. His speech tailed away. Only slight applause greeted its end; and then he and Biddy left the chamber to the same deafening silence with which they had entered.

They joined John Hay and his wife in the Union library where they waited for the votes to be counted; and Walter, despite a sharp sense of impending failure, diverted the others by talking of the old days when he had been President of the Union, and showing them portraits and papers he thought might interest them. At last, after a seemingly interminable delay, the assistant agent opened the library door and announced that Mr Hay had been elected. Walter, showing no trace of resentment at what amounted, for someone of his experience, to a considerable public humiliation, turned to Hay and said in tones of evident sincerity: 'My dear fellow, I congratulate you with all my heart.'

There had been two ballots in the voting. The result of the first was:

John Hay	259
Gifford Fox	221
Walter Monckton	107

Walter, having received the fewest votes, was eliminated at this stage; and the result of the second ballot was as follows:

John Hay	312
Gifford Fox	259

So John Hay became the prospective Conservative candidate for South Oxfordshire; and he was duly returned as that constituency's MP at the General Election nine months later.

The Moncktons suffered a further disappointment that day, one that was comparatively minor but nevertheless disagreeable. Peter Fleming and Lady Pamela Berry, certain that Walter and Biddy would not wish to meet them for what had been planned as a celebratory drink, said goodbye to each other at the Union; and Fleming made no effort to hurry home to Merrimoles. When, many hours later, he did eventually return, he learned to his dismay that Sir Walter and Lady Monckton had waited for him for more than an hour, and had then left without having been offered any refreshment.

The Moncktons were naturally wounded by their experience at Oxford, and Walter determined not to go forward in any other constituency unless he were certain of selection. His chance came in 1951 at a by-election in Bristol West caused by the death of Mr Oliver Stanley. Churchill and the Conservative Central Office had seen to it that there was no rival Conservative candidate; and on 15 February 1951, two days before his 60th birthday, Walter was elected to Parliament with a majority of more than 17,000 over his Labour opponent. He was introduced to the House of Commons by Winston Churchill, and by the Conservative Chief Whip Patrick Buchan-Hepburn, later Lord Hailes. 'As we started our journey up the Chamber,' Walter later recalled, 'Mr Churchill said that he had never done this before, and we must lean inwards as he was no longer very secure on his legs. It was certainly not a well-drilled part, but it was an exciting occasion.'

Bristol West was convenient for Walter, as quite by chance he and Biddy had recently rented Priors Court, an attractive black-and-white house on the Madresfield estate of Lord Beauchamp in Worcestershire; and it was an easy drive from Priors Court to the heart of his constituency. Representing Bristol West also brought Walter the benefit of meeting the Rev. Mervyn Stockwood, then a local parish priest, later Bishop of Southwark. Walter's spiritual life had been distorted by his divorce, which, much to his distress, prevented him from receiving Holy Communion; but Stockwood, in whom he confided, consulted the Bishop of Bristol on his behalf, and was able to arrange for Walter to receive Communion at a local church. This was an enormous relief to Walter, who later presented the church with a beautiful chalice. Stockwood also endeared himself to Walter and Biddy by holding a service of blessing to give a religious element to their marriage, hitherto an entirely civil affair; and many years later, when Stockwood became a bishop, he married them privately with the full rites of the Church.[9]

At the General Election of Thursday 25 October 1951, Walter Monckton was opposed by a Liberal as well as by a Labour candidate; but although the Liberal candidature cost Walter some votes, he was still returned to Westminster with a comfortable majority of more than 14,000; while in the country as a whole, Churchill and the Conservatives came to power with a majority of 14 in the new House of Commons. Two days later Walter was relaxing at Priors Court when he received a message from the Cabinet Secretary Sir Norman Brook, to the effect that the Prime Minister wished to see him as soon as possible at his London house in Hyde Park Gate, where he was interviewing prospective Government Ministers.

Walter hastened up to London by car, and found Churchill in bed. The Prime Minister told him that he had a job for him. Did he know what it was? Walter, who had been expecting to be asked to be Attorney-General, a post which carried a salary of £10,000 per annum, replied that he very much hoped it was a law office, since that was his ambition. 'Oh, my dear,' Churchill answered, 'I cannot spare you for that. I have the worst job in the Cabinet for you!' To his surprise and alarm, Walter learned that this was the Ministry of Labour. When he pleaded his inexperience (it may also have crossed his mind that the salary would be half what he had hoped for), the Prime Minister replied that it was his lack of a political past which made Walter so suitable. However (according to Churchill's friend Brendan Bracken), the Prime Minister also gave Walter an assurance that if and when Lord Goddard resigned, he would become the next Lord Chief Justice. In the circumstances, Walter accepted, albeit with some reluctance and misgivings.

When on Monday 29 October Walter Monckton went to Buckingham Palace to kiss hands on his appointment as Minister of Labour, he was asked by King George VI whether he could carry on as Attorney-General to the Duchy of Cornwall. Walter replied regretfully that he no longer had the necessary qualifications to be Attorney-General, as he could not now continue with his Bar practice. Some weeks later, when recommending a successor, Walter wrote to the King:

> I think I have held the appointment in all longer than any of my predecessors in the whole history of the Duchy and I want to tell Your Majesty how deeply grateful I am for your invariable kindness and forbearance during the last fourteen years. If I may be permitted to say so, Your reappointment of me in 1948 [Walter had resigned on account of his divorce] gave me more pleasure than any honour I have received in my life.

Walter later recalled his visit to the Palace and his brief conversation with George VI, how ill the King looked – a few months later he

would be dead – and how pleased he appeared to be that Walter had
been given the ministerial job.

That very afternoon, Walter went round to his new department in
St James's Square, where he[10]

> met for the first time Sir Godfrey Ince, who was Permanent Under-
> Secretary of the Department through the 4½ years during which I was
> Minister. We started with a useful personal link. We were both madly keen
> on cricket and Surrey cricket at that. I was President of the Surrey County
> Cricket Club and he was on the Committee, though we had hardly met at
> the Oval.
>
> It is impossible to think of the Ministry of Labour without the shadow
> of the spirit of Ernest Bevin. I was always told that he thought Godfrey
> Ince the most able civil servant he had come across. I certainly never met
> anyone abler or a more loyal friend and supporter. The Department in
> those days must have been nearly 40,000 strong. When I left it, it was
> down to 27,000 or thereabouts.

4

Walter Monckton's time as Minister of Labour was characterised by a
constant series of industrial disputes, which his conciliatory manner
had the effect of alleviating, and usually resolving. The situation he
faced was one in which the bargaining power of labour had been
progressively strengthened; and shortly before Walter's appointment
the Trades Union Congress had expressed its belief in wage claims in
these terms: 'It is apparent in the present situation [that] the trades
unions must endeavour to maintain the real wages of their members
by demanding wage increases.' The comparative success of this strategy
contributed to a sharp increase in inflation. From October 1950 to
May 1952, for example, wage rates rose by 16 per cent and prices by
17 per cent; and it was clear that further increases would adversely
affect exports, and therefore the balance of payments. A shortage of
skilled labour was also damaging exports; and the Government had
little knowledge of what was happening in this area, as relatively few
skilled workers used the Labour Exchanges, choosing instead to make
their own employment arrangements direct with the employers. The
Cabinet therefore decreed that workers could not be employed except
through the Labour Exchanges, and the Minister was entrusted with
carrying this out through the Notification of Vacancies Order.[11]

At first the unions were suspicious of Walter, but he soon won them over not only by his conciliatory manner, but also by his actions. 'I am a firm believer in government by consultation and consent,' he told them at the Birmingham Union Festival Exhibition shortly after he took office, 'and I shall do everything I can to carry out that principle in the conduct of my Ministry.' He added that he would be 'sorry to see party politics enter the factory gates and embitter our industrial life'.[12]

In May 1952, when the Chancellor of the Exchequer R. A. Butler attended a meeting of Sir Walter Monckton's Joint Advisory Council, he too tried to place party politics to one side, and instead spoke plainly about the dangers to the national economy of inflation arising from excessive wage increases; and the result was that during the following months most wage claims were rejected by the employers and referred to arbitration.

It was particularly important to the Government to control the wages of those in the engineering and shipbuilding industries; since, with some three million workers, their influence upon the national economy was considerable. Indeed, by 1953 as many as 39 unions would be affiliated to the massive CSEU, the Confederation of Shipbuilding and Engineering Unions; and it was a worrying factor that several of those 39, including the Amalgamated Engineering Union, were dominated by communists.

In 1951 the CSEU claimed £1 extra a week, and were given 11s 6d; and then in 1952, emboldened by this measure of success, they claimed an extra £2. The employers could not possibly agree to such a large increase, and the Ministry of Labour was called in. Eventually, after prolonged negotiations, the CSEU agreed to an increase of no more than 7s 6d; and for this excellent result the Minister of Labour was congratulated by Churchill and lauded by the press. 'Sir Walter Monckton's reputation at the Ministry of Labour and among the trade unions has been growing steadily,' wrote the *Daily Mail* on 9 October 1952,

> but this is his greatest success so far. It is a double success, for not only has he kept the peace in industry, but he has stalled the extremists in the engineering and shipbuilding industries who would have been glad to see their industries plunged into chaos.

The following year, however, militancy in the CSEU increased; and a claim for 15 per cent led to a 12-month dispute, which involved at various times a stoppage involving a million workers, a threatened ban on overtime and piecework, and the institution by Walter of two separate Courts of Inquiry. Eventually the long industrial struggle was ended in April 1954, when an increase of just over 5 per cent was agreed for unskilled, and just over 6 per cent for skilled workers. These prolonged negotiations seriously impaired Walter's health; and his absences from the office through illness became more and more frequent.

Another communist-controlled union with which Walter Monckton had to deal was the ETU, the Electrical Trades Union. Its officials had imposed a remarkable constitution upon the union, by which the Executive Council could, whenever it wished, order its members either to cease or to resume work. After a claim for a substantial increase had been met in November 1952 with an award of only 2d an hour, and further negotiations had led nowhere, the ETU began organising strikes at selected construction sites. Several months later, in August 1953, the Ministry of Labour intervened, and an informal meeting of both sides was followed by the summoning of the National Joint Industrial Council. The strikes were halted temporarily; but the ETU became dissatisfied when the employers asked for time to consult their member firms, refused the employers' suggestion that the claim should go to arbitration, and organised more strikes to begin from 1 September.

Two days later Churchill, who was in bed at Chequers recovering from a stroke, was seen by his physician Lord Moran. 'I don't like this strike,' he told Moran. 'It is surely a new technique. Certain key electricals are called out, while the rest go on working; they pay the wages of those on strike.'

He rang for a private secretary. His call was answered by David Pitblado.

'Is electricity nationalised?' the Prime Minister demanded. Pitblado thought it was. 'Make certain,' said Churchill impatiently. 'Find out the exact position.' (In fact it had been nationalised by the Labour Government back in 1948.)

To Moran's query about whether the strike would hold up everything, Churchill replied: 'Oh, no, it can't go on for long. It would cause too much annoyance and interference with people's lives.' He added that he 'meant to take a hand' in the affair. 'Walter Monckton has gone for a holiday,' he added with a grin. 'He is worn out giving way. His deputy* is coming down after luncheon.' The Prime Minister

---

* Harold (now Viscount) Watkinson, parliamentary secretary to the Ministry of Labour.

went on to tell Moran that Walter had been making £60,000 a year at the Bar before joining the Government.

The strike was temporarily lifted when Walter set up a court of inquiry; but when this court reported on 6 October it did no more than suggest further discussions within the industry; strike action began again on 10 January 1954, and did not end until 8 April, when the Industrial Disputes Tribunal, meeting in Walter's Ministry, awarded an extra ½d to the unconditional twopence which the employers had granted in March. Although the talks were ultimately successful, the strikes had by this time caused enormous damage both to industry and to the national economy, damage for which the communist elements in the ETU were largely responsible.

5

From time to time there were rumours that Walter Monckton was slated for another job. Following Anthony Eden's illness in April 1953, the result of jaundice and gallstones, Walter lunched with the Prime Minister; and the press speculated that he was to succeed Eden as Foreign Secretary. However, Churchill personally assumed command of the Foreign Office until Eden had recovered from his operations, and Eden stayed on. A year or so later Lord Goddard sold a good many of his law reports which led to rumours that he was about to retire as Lord Chief Justice; but in fact he had only sold the reports because they were dilapidated, and he wanted a new set! In any case, Lord Goddard knew that Walter Monckton hoped to succeed him, and was determined to prevent this. He told a colleague that he opposed Walter for not knowing enough criminal law; but Goddard's hostility seems more likely to have been rooted in his straitlaced views on divorce, and his knowledge that Walter had been the guilty party in a divorce suit.

Meanwhile the Labour Minister was constantly beset by industrial disputes. The railways were perhaps his biggest headache. Until 1951, strikes had been illegal under the Conditions of Employment and National Arbitration Order, which the unions had accepted. But this was replaced by the Industrial Disputes Order which made strikes legal, and encouraged arbitration by independent tribunals. Under these new conditions, Monckton's brief from Churchill was that he should do his best to preserve industrial peace. The Labour Party had foretold serious industrial troubles if the Conservatives were elected,

and it was up to him to smooth things over. The fact that Monckton
did his job so well brought reproaches from those who felt that a
sterner line was necessary. Churchill's private secretary John Colville,
for example, expressed a view held by a sizeable minority when he
wrote:[13]

> The trouble with Monckton, almost the only trouble, was that he could
> not bear to make anyone unhappy. He was thus a natural appeaser and it
> has to be admitted that by 1951, when he was appointed Minister of
> Labour, Churchill was on the way to becoming one too. [In December
> 1953] there was a threat of a rail strike which would have dislocated the
> Christmas holidays. Monckton was advised by his Ministry to stand firm,
> though the thought of an unhappy Christmas for many who had hoped
> to visit their aged parents filled him with distress. Churchill was a prey to
> similar sloppy sentiments. He sent for Monckton and conjured him to avert
> the strike by whatever measures were required. Monckton did as he was
> told: the railwaymen were given what they demanded; and poor Monckton
> earned the reputation as the architect of slippery slopes.

The strike was averted only when the Minister persuaded the
employers, the British Transport Commission, to agree to an immediate increase of 4s a week, pending a review which would decide on
what further increases were to be offered. Such an increase breached
the financial constitution of the Transport Commission, since it meant
going into deficit. Nevertheless the prevention of the strike was ap-
plauded both in the press and in the House of Commons as an
outstanding political success for Sir Walter. The present writer, who
was an Ulster Unionist MP at the time, remembers the unprecedented
ovation which Walter Monckton received in the House on 16 December
1953 when he announced the settlement. Indeed, some members of
the Opposition actually crossed the floor of the House and patted him
on the back. 'Was this a *Conservative* Minister,' asked the *Daily
Telegraph* next morning, 'earning the heart-felt plaudits, without
exception, of Socialist ex-Ministers and MPs?' Among Walter's Ministerial predecessors was the Labour politician George Isaacs, who
also paid him a glowing tribute. Others felt with John Colville that
Monckton should not have given way; but in this crisis Walter was
merely the agent of Government policy, which was to capitulate rather
than run the risk of a national rail strike.

In any case, industrial troubles were far from over. Early in 1954
there were prolonged electricity strikes; and later that year the railwaymen again threatened to strike. The NUR had reached a wage settlement which it then repudiated, refusing at the same time to go

to arbitration by the Railway Staffs National Tribunal. Monckton therefore set up a court of inquiry, which recommended (in an interim report of 5 January 1955) that the railwaymen should be paid a 'fair and adequate wage', and implied that the Transport Commission (already in deficit) should be subsidised to pay those fair wages. Walter had promised that he would impartially support the Court's findings, and did so; but they were widely criticised, and it was argued that the Government was once more using the Ministry of Labour to capitulate to the unions. It was felt by some that the real problem in the railways was one of gross overmanning; and that although Monckton had succeeded in ending the dispute, it was at the cost of a pay settlement for which the British Transport Commission had inadequate funds. However, the strike had been called off; and the Queen sent Sir Walter a personal message of thanks for 'his patience and power of persuasion'. Or, as the *Star* newspaper put it:

> Once again the Monckton magic has worked. Sir Walter, prince of industrial peacemakers, has brought at least temporary harmony from discord in the railway wages dispute. The Nation heaved a sigh of relief, but was not surprised when news came that the railway strike had been called off. Sir Walter is such an expert at reconciling industrial and labour differences that it had pinned its faith to his skill as a performer of miracles, and he has succeeded.

It was unfortunate that Churchill's last days in Downing Street, and the news of his retirement, should have been clouded by a newspaper strike. This was due to complaints by the maintenance workers (members of the ETU and the ATU) that they were denied proper negotiations with their employers, the Newspaper Proprietors Association; and that they were always expected automatically to accept the terms of any settlement reached by the NPA with the printing unions.

It was on 5 April 1955, when the court of inquiry was still in session, and the strike was still on, that Churchill resigned. There were no newspapers to pay tribute to him, or to welcome Anthony Eden as his successor. The editorial staff of the *Daily Telegraph* were particularly disappointed not to be able to comment, since Churchill was their oldest living correspondent, having written his first article for them back in 1897. Churchill's last Cabinet was held at noon in the Cabinet Room at 10 Downing Street, when the Prime Minister announced that he would be tendering his resignation to the Queen that afternoon. To mark the occasion a composite photograph was taken, showing Walter Monckton among the other members wishing Churchill a fond political farewell.

6

Before resigning the Premiership, Churchill asked his successor Anthony Eden to keep as many Ministers as possible in their own posts, and to avoid any general overhaul of the Government until after the forthcoming General Election. Hence the only immediate changes of any significance were that Harold Macmillan replaced Eden as Foreign Secretary; that Selwyn Lloyd replaced Macmillan as Minister of Defence; and that Lord Home became Secretary for Commonwealth Relations.

The election which took place on 26 May 1955 resulted in the Conservative majority being increased from 17 to 60. In Bristol West, Walter Monckton had only a single opponent, a Labour candidate; and despite the fact that Labour disputes kept him working in London for almost the whole of the run-up to the election, he increased his majority by more than 2,000. It was the first time for almost a century that a political party had gone to the country and been returned with a substantial increase in their majority; and the Conservatives had polled nearly a million votes more than Labour. It was also the first General Election in which television played a major part.

Industrial strife was the greatest problem facing the new Prime Minister. During May, workers on strike had included miners, busmen, lightermen and dockers; by the time that the nation went to the polls, the dock strike was already causing serious damage to the economy; and within three days of the election, an inter-union dispute had led to a railway strike. A state of emergency was declared; and Eden broadcast to the nation, praising Walter Monckton's efforts to avoid the railway strike, and calling on the unions concerned, NUR and ASLEF, to negotiate.

The various disputes were eventually settled: the railway strike was over by 14 June, and the dock strike by 4 July. Walter had managed to attend most of the more important negotiating sessions; but sadly his health was being seriously undermined by the constant pressure. Typically, having settled the railways dispute, he found himself being blamed by the Chief Industrial Commissioner Sir Wilfred Neden for being too conciliatory, and for seeing the TUC and the Transport Commission without him. Still more typically, Walter apologised for this, and then effected a reconciliation in his office by opening a cupboard and producing a bottle of port.

The rash of strikes naturally provoked widespread discussion as to what, if anything, could be done about it. Many people wondered about the possibility of using the call-up to national (military) service as a strike-breaking weapon; but should such a weapon be used against official strikes ordered by trade unions, or should it be applied only to unofficial strikes? When on 21 June questions were asked in the House of Commons on this sensitive issue, Walter replied that the issue of call-up notices was a routine procedure outside his control. When asked why, on previous occasions, routine call-up notices had not been despatched to coalminers when they were on strike, he replied that the routine in that industry was different. In fact he parried these difficult questions with his usual efficiency.

Two days later there was a House of Commons debate on industrial relations; and despite feeling exhausted and ill, Walter opened with an excellent speech which was praised by both sides of the Chamber. He declared that the responsible leaders of the trade-union movement were as much troubled as the Government by the increasing signs of irresponsibility in industry. What was wanted – and he had made this point before – was a more human relationship between employers and employed, and a shared sense of responsibility to the larger community. His speech concluded, Walter listened to most of those who followed him; but then a splitting headache forced him to leave while his able parliamentary secretary wound up the debate.

Later in the year there was a Cabinet reshuffle; and this gave Eden the chance to transfer Monckton to what he considered a less arduous post, that of Minister of Defence. 'He is the best of coordinators', Eden explained,

and has never lost interest in Service matters since his brave military career in the First World War. I thought that the Ministry of Defence which, for all its urgent tasks, normally does not carry a heavy Parliamentary charge, would fit him admirably and he welcomed the change.

Monckton was succeeded as Minister of Labour by the rising young Conservative Iain Macleod; while, as part of the same reshuffle, the former Minister of Defence, Selwyn Lloyd, became Foreign Secretary; and the former Foreign Secretary, Harold Macmillan, went to the Treasury, from where 'Rab' Butler was moved on to become Lord Privy Seal and leader of the House of Commons. At the same time Attlee was succeeded as Leader of the Opposition not, as many people had expected, by Herbert Morrison, but by the much younger Hugh Gaitskell.

Walter Monckton's new duties, which he assumed on 20 December 1955, proved more onerous than Eden had expected. His first task was to secure Cabinet approval for a series of measures intended to make a substantial reduction in the £1,500 million spent each year on defence. Selwyn Lloyd had already devised a scheme (based upon paying more money to anyone who was prepared to sign on for a long-term engagement) by which the armed forces could maintain their effectiveness with fewer numbers; and in February 1956 Monckton introduced the new pay codes which this scheme entailed. However, he soon found that Macmillan, as Chancellor of the Exchequer, was hoping for annual cuts of as much as £300 million. This figure, in Monckton's view, might have been attainable if Britain had not been committed to the nuclear deterrent. Since the Americans would not share their nuclear secrets, that commitment, as Walter pointed out, meant

> making our own experiments and tests, and our own nuclear weapons, and arranging for their delivery by air or missile. This was inevitably most expensive. I always wanted to reduce our subscription to the nuclear club, and confess to our reliance upon the US. This was difficult in circumstances in which we wanted to have an important voice in decisions of policy as to the use of the weapons.

Since he could not persuade the Prime Minister or the Chancellor of the desirability of cutting back on nuclear research, Walter was left with the task of seeing where cuts could be made in our conventional forces; and at length he wrote a controversial report in which he stated his belief that he was being asked to make cuts that were simply not possible without jeopardising our national security.

The Suez crisis would soon lead to Walter Monckton disagreeing not merely with the Prime Minister and the Chancellor, but with almost the entire Cabinet.

It was on the evening of 26 July 1956, while the Prime Minister was entertaining the King of Iraq and his Premier to dinner at 10 Downing Street, that a private secretary interrupted their meal with the dramatic announcement that the Egyptian leader Colonel Nasser had proclaimed the nationalisation of the Anglo-French Suez Canal Company. Next day the Cabinet met in formal session, and heard the Chiefs of Staff state that, if it was decided to use force against Nasser, they would need time to prepare for action. They were therefore sent away to begin making provisional plans; and the same day Eden despatched a telegram to President Eisenhower in which he stated that: 'My colleagues and I are convinced that we must be ready, *in the last resort* [author's italics], to use force to bring Nasser to his senses. For our part, we are prepared to do so.' The italicised words seemed to the American President to leave the way open for some diplomatic solution; on the other hand, had Eden sent an ultimatum to Cairo (in the manner of Mrs Thatcher when dealing with the Argentine invasion of the Falklands in 1982), Nasser might well have climbed down.

7

Walter Monckton's department was heavily involved in drawing up plans for military intervention, and he took part in the lengthy debates which led up to the decision to use force. However, he felt deeply unhappy about the prospect of military intervention, and made his views clear to his colleagues. On 24 August 1956, for example, he spoke with particular vigour at the relevant Cabinet Committee (the so-called Egyptian Committee), as a result of which both the Commonwealth Secretary Lord Home, and the Colonial Secretary Lennox Boyd wrote protesting to the Prime Minister.

Walter restated his position on 28 August in Cabinet when (according to the minutes) he agreed that Britain could not afford to allow Colonel Nasser to succeed in his attempt to seize control over the Suez Canal and that, if all other methods proved unavailing, force would have to be used. However, he was adamant that the Cabinet must consider the serious disadvantages of using force. If, together with the French, Britain took military measures against Egypt, her action would be condemned by a substantial body of public opinion in countries overseas, countries which would include several independent members of the Commonwealth. Within the United Kingdom itself opinion would be divided. Her vital interests in other parts of the world would also be affected; she must, in particular, expect sabotage against oil installations in other Arab countries. Moreover, once she had sent military forces to Egypt, it would not be easy to extricate them, and she might find herself saddled with a costly commitment. It was therefore essential, in his view, that no opportunity of securing a peaceful settlement should be allowed to pass.

When therefore John Foster Dulles, the American Secretary of State, proposed a meeting of all countries interested in the Suez Canal, who would form the SCUA, or the 'Suez Canal User's Association', Walter expressed the hope in a Cabinet meeting on 12 September that the establishment of such a body would not be regarded as a step towards the use of force. Instead, they should be looking to 'the possibility that, if the Canal could be brought under effective international control, the present regime in Egypt might be overthrown by means short of war'. Any premature recourse to force, especially without the support and approval of the United Nations, was likely (in Monckton's view) to precipitate disorder throughout the Middle East, and to alienate a substantial body of public opinion both in Britain and elsewhere throughout the world.

In the event, SCUA met in London between 19 and 21 September 1956, with delegates from 22 nations under the chairmanship of the British Foreign Secretary Selwyn Lloyd. Of those countries who were invited to attend, only two had declined: one of those, not surprisingly, was Egypt; and the other was Greece, which at that time contained a great many Egyptians. The SCUA conference led to an appeal to the United Nations, but its effect upon Nasser was negligible. He knew that a number of countries including the Soviet Union had refused to subscribe to several important resolutions; and he may also have been aware of American opposition to the use of force. At this time President Eisenhower was repeatedly informing Eden both by letter and by telegram that he was against the use of force unless Nasser gave further provocation.

According to Walter Monckton's own account, he was the only member of the Cabinet who openly advised against invasion, though he was aware that the Leader of the House 'Rab' Butler and the Agricultural Minister Heathcoat Amory had doubts; while outside the Cabinet a number of junior ministers were also unhappy, and indeed two of them, Anthony Nutting and Sir Edward Boyle, resigned on the issue. Walter himself was tempted to resign, though he was aware, as he later wrote, that:[14]

> Resignation at such a moment was not a thing to be lightly undertaken. I felt that I was virtually alone in my opinion in the Cabinet and that I had not the experience or knowledge to make me confident in my own view when it was so strongly opposed by Eden, Salisbury, Macmillan, Head, Sandys, Thorneycroft and Kilmuir; for all of whom I had respect and admiration. I knew that if I did resign it was likely that the Government would fall, and I still believed that it was better for the country to have that Government than the alternative. What the Labour people had in mind was a kind of rump of the Tory Government led by Butler, which they would support. This could not last. Moreover, far more than I knew at the time, the ordinary man in the country was behind Eden.

In the event Walter wrote to Eden on 24 September telling him that he was far from fit and did not feel that he could continue in his office as Minister of Defence. He made it clear that he would not have contemplated resignation but for his differences with his colleagues both over the size of the armed forces and over Suez; but he added that:

> As you well know, the military preparations which we have had to take in consequence of the Suez crisis have been planned and taken. I have done my best to prepare the way for the vital decisions in many fields of defence which have to be made in the weeks and months which lie immediately ahead of us. They are not short-term decisions but involve adopting policies which must be pursued and implemented over the next few years. I feel sure that it is essential that the Minister who makes these decisions should be prepared to continue in his office until the end of this Parliament. After more than four years as Minister of Labour and the constant and mounting strain which my political office has entailed I do not feel able to carry on for as long as that. If I am right in this, though I shall be personally sorry to leave the Ministry, I think that the moment has come for me to go.

Eden accepted that Walter would not go on as Minister of Defence; but, in a gesture which Walter felt was very generous, he retained him in the Cabinet as Paymaster-General, 'thus preserving', as Walter noted,

> the unity of the front. I had in fact been ill at the beginning of August so that Antony Head [the War Minister], who believed in the political wisdom of the enterprise, had more to do with the planning of the operations than I had myself and it was easy for him to succeed me as Minister of Defence.

The last Cabinet which Walter attended as Defence Minister was on 18 October, after it had been decided that Head should succeed him. On this occasion Eden indicated that the Israelis might be about to attack either Jordan or Egypt. Britain, he said, would have to defend Jordan; but despite the Tripartite Declaration of 1950 (by which Britain, France and the United States were pledged to come to the aid of either Israel or Egypt, should one of those countries be invaded by the other), despite that declaration, defending Egypt was out of the question. Indeed, the Prime Minister believed that it would be 'far better from our point of view that Israel should attack Egypt rather than Jordan', as in that case 'the issue might be brought more rapidly to a head'.

On Sunday 21 October, Eden summoned to Chequers a number of Ministers and advisers including Butler, Lloyd, Macmillan and Head, who was now acting as Defence Minister, although it was not until the following day that he would formally take office. Monckton was not present, and therefore knew nothing of the decision to send Selwyn Lloyd incognito to Paris where on the following day, in the suburb of Sèvres, he met first the French and then the Israeli leaders. The result was approval for a conspiracy against Egypt: Israel would attack Egypt, which would give Britain and France the excuse to intervene to separate them, and in so doing to regain control of the Suez Canal.*

Monckton was, however, present on 25 October (three days after he had been sworn in as Paymaster-General) at the Cabinet meeting called to consider the situation which would arise if hostilities broke out between Israel and Egypt, and to decide whether in those circumstances Anglo-French intervention would be justified. Eden (according to the Cabinet minutes) said that:

> The French Government were strongly of the view that intervention would be justified in order to limit hostilities and for this purpose it would be right to launch the military operation against Egypt which had already been mounted. Indeed, it was possible that if we declined to join them they would take military action alone or in conjunction with Israel. In these circumstances the Prime Minister suggested that, if Israel mounted a full-scale operation against Egypt, the Governments of the United Kingdom and France should at once call on both parties to stop hostilities and to withdraw their forces to a distance ten miles from the Canal; and that it should at the same time be made clear that, if one or both Governments failed to undertake within twelve hours to comply with these requirements, British and French forces would intervene in order to force compliance. Israel might well undertake to comply with such a demand. If Egypt also complied, Colonel Nasser's prestige would be fatally undermined. If she failed to comply there would be ample justification for Anglo-French military action against Egypt in order to safeguard the Canal.
>
> We must face the risk that we should be accused of collusion with Israel. But the charge was liable to be brought against us in any event, for it could not be assumed that, if an Anglo-French operation was undertaken against Egypt, we should be unable to prevent the Israelis from launching a parallel themselves; and it was preferable that we should be seen to be holding the balance between Israel and Egypt rather than appear to be accepting Israel's cooperation in an attack on Egypt alone.

Subsequently, Walter attended Cabinet meetings (including those at which on Eden's orders no minutes were taken) throughout the brief and ill-fated Suez campaign. This began on 29 October with the

---

* Selwyn Lloyd saw the Israelis (led by Ben Gurion) after the French; and according to his own account (Lloyd, p.183) he pointed out the dangers of the military operation they were planning against Egypt, and advised restraint.

Israeli invasion of Egypt, was followed on the night of 31 October by the Anglo-French attack and the bombing of Egyptian airfields, continued with the airborne assault on Port Said and the seaborne landings, and ended on 6 November when the Egyptian forces surrendered and fighting ceased. On the following day, Walter made this note of his feelings:[15]

> I have remained in the Cabinet without resignation because I have not thought it right to take a step which I was assured would bring the Government down. The view which I have always expressed has been against the armed intervention which has taken place on the grounds:
>
>   (a)   that we should have half our country and 90% of world opinion against us;
>
>   (b)   that it was difficult to justify intervention on behalf of the invader and against the country invaded;
>
>   (c)   that it would inflame opinion against us in the Middle East and upset the whole of the Arab world;
>
>   (d)   that it would jeopardise our relations with the US which were the foundation of our international and defence policy.
>
> I have not changed my opinion on these matters, but I have always felt that, inasmuch as my opinion was not shared by any of my colleagues, a certain measure of humility demanded restraint in action on my part . . . In all these circumstances I have never been able to convince myself that armed intervention was right, but I have not been prepared to resign. I have lived on from day to day, and am still so living on, in the hope that I could contribute towards a settlement as soon as possible.

Walter also appreciated other risks: for example, that the United States might impose oil sanctions; that the British currency might decline or even collapse; and that Nasser might make a successful appeal for military help to the Russians.

During the Christmas recess of 1956–7, Walter and Biddy spent 'a few quiet days' with the Anglo-American journalist and man of letters Whitney Straight and his wife Bin at their house in Majorca. It was while he was here that Walter made up his mind that he must leave the Government. The first Cabinet which he attended on his return was that of 8 January 1957, which was marked by Eden's announcement that he was resigning on health grounds, and would tender his resignation to Her Majesty the Queen later that day. Eden was succeeded as Prime Minister by Harold Macmillan, who immediately set about forming a new Government, and asked to see Walter. By this time (as Walter noted) Macmillan 'knew of my wish to go, and only said that he was sad that he could not offer me the Lord Chief Justiceship because Goddard had not resigned'.

As we have seen, Walter had long wished to become Lord Chief Justice, and both Churchill and Eden had promised him the reversion of that office when it came. But by this time Walter was 66. He had come to the conclusion that he did not wish to return to the strain of a large Bar practice, and that in a year's time, when Lord Chief Justice Goddard was likely to go, it would be too late for him to start afresh with such a heavy job. However, a new opportunity had suddenly opened up. 'It so happened by great good fortune,' wrote Monckton, 'that on the very day I was to see Macmillan I was offered the Chairmanship of the Midland Bank, which was exactly the sort of job which offered me new opportunities, but not the same mental and physical struggle.'

Chapter 8

Banking and the
Beginning of the End

S IR WALTER MONCKTON tendered his resignation to the
new Prime Minister on 12 January 1957, and arranged to meet
him at 10 Downing Street. 'It is nearly 45 years since we first
became friends at Oxford,' Harold Macmillan wrote to him the next
day, 'and I think that friendship has never ceased. To have your good
wishes means a great deal to me.' As well as leaving the Government,
Walter resigned his Parliamentary seat. He was at once raised to the
peerage, choosing to become Viscount Monckton of Brenchley, that
place in Kent which had long been associated with his family.

Other honours came in Walter's direction. From 1950 to 1952 he
had been President of the Surrey County Cricket Club; and now he
was invited to become President of the MCC, a position which crowned
and rewarded his life-long devotion to cricket.

Another equally strong devotion was rewarded when in November
1957 Walter was appointed Visitor to Balliol. Sir David Lindsay Keir,
who was Master of Balliol at the time, was certain that the Fellows
had appointed the right man. As an experienced lawyer, Walter was
able to deliver an expert opinion on any legal problems which arose,
without the need for outside assistance. The Visitor traditionally acted
as a final court of appeal for any don or undergraduate who felt that
he had been badly treated by the college; and here Walter's sympathetic
approach and unvarying kindness were as valuable as his legal experience. That sympathy and kindness made him extremely popular; and
he was soon a firm favourite at the Gaudy nights and other college
functions which he attended with such obvious pleasure.

Another prestigious appointment came four years later in 1961, when Lord Monckton was made Deputy Treasurer to the Duke of Edinburgh at the Inner Temple. This particularly pleased him, because it continued his long association with the Royal Family.

Meanwhile Walter and Biddy had moved into the Old Rectory, Folkington, a comfortable country house in Sussex looking towards the South Downs, where they went on long, happy walks together. Biddy also spent much time in surrounding their new home with an exquisite garden; and later, as Walter's health deteriorated, this became the place where he liked to sit and reflect upon the past.

But before then, there were fresh challenges to be met. On 1 February 1957 Lord Monckton joined the Board of the Midland Bank; and only 14 days later (the *Daily Express* described it as 'the fastest piece of promotion in banking history') the Chairman of the Board Lord Harlech announced that he would be retiring on 12 July, and that Monckton would succeed him as Chairman. During those intervening five months Walter busily applied himself to learning as much as he could about banking. As a professional lawyer, he was used to assimilating new information very rapidly; and he had expert help in his studies from men such as W. F. Crick, the Bank's General Manager for Research and Statistics.

Walter's appointment had been an exciting one; partly because of his fame, and partly because despite that fame he was in many respects an unknown quantity. 'There were few of us on the staff at that time,' one of his new colleagues later recalled,[1]

> who did not recognise immediately that we were to be led by someone of national and international repute – not so much as an experienced politician (he had entered politics late in life, in 1951 when he was already 60 years old) but rather as a man of the humanities whose genius lay in industrial mediation . . .
>
> To a great extent Walter Monckton was to us then a mystical figure. His name was a household word, yet, by the very nature of his confidential work, we knew little of his achievements in detail.

From the beginning, much to everyone's pleasure, Walter showed every intention of being an active Chairman. All matters of day-to-day administration, he learned, were delegated by the Board to a management committee. That committee, consisting of the two chief general managers and the joint general managers, met each day to discuss the immediate position. After the meeting, the two chief general managers would then report to him as Chairman; and if there was any particular problem, Monckton would discuss it with one or both of the deputy chairmen, and decide whether or not the matter should be taken before the Board of Directors.

It was soon noticed that, thanks to his intensive preparations, Monckton never found himself at a loss in understanding what was required of him. Before making any public appearance he would always make doubly sure of his ground by insisting upon a detailed briefing from his staff; and he was totally in command of his facts both when he was conducting shareholders' meetings, and when he was giving addresses to professional audiences. The result was that within a year Monckton had made so strong an impression as Chairman of the Midland Bank that he was also appointed Chairman of the Iraq Petroleum Company and its associates.

The first major task which Monckton had to deal with at the Midland Bank was the modernisation of its capital structure. When it had first been registered in 1880, as the Birmingham and Midland Bank, the only people to hold shares were those of considerable wealth. The capital then consisted of 40,000 shares of £60 each. £12 10s of that sum was paid up on each share, an equal sum could be demanded at any time, and the remaining £35 was reserve capital to be called upon only if the bank were to be wound up. These arrangements were in line with the capital organisation of most of the joint-stock banks of that day.

Over the years, the capital was increased many times, and the shares were reduced in size. However, partly paid shares had become unpopular with investors who disliked facing the risk, however slight, that they might one day be called upon for more cash; while at the same time there was a marked preference for shares whose nominal value was no more than a pound. The difficulty was that converting the partly paid into fully paid shares meant writing off the notional reserve; and legally, this would constitute a reduction of capital, and would require formal permission from the Court. In such circumstances, the Court would usually ask for the approval of all creditors – an impossible task in the case of a bank – though they had the power to waive that requirement.

Detailed preparations had been made to overcome these difficulties, and to move ahead with modernising the capital structure, under the chairmanship of Lord Harlech. This meant that within three weeks of Lord Monckton becoming Chairman, it was possible for him to sign a preliminary circular to shareholders on the subject; and two months later, he presided with great authority and panache over the Annual General Meeting of the Company and over subsequent meetings of all three classes of shareholder. All the necessary resolutions were carried; the reduction of capital was approved by the Court; and from 11 November 1957 the capital consisted entirely of £1 shares, fully paid.

This change in the Midland Bank made a great impression upon the City; and before long it was realised that Walter's reign would continue with all the excitement with which it had begun. Everything that he did was news, and was fully reported: hardly surprising, in view of the innovations which he steered through the Board of Directors! These included such revolutionary services as a personal loans scheme requiring no conventional security from customers, with the bank itself providing against the risk of the customer's death; long-term loans to farmers; loans for developing small businesses; and personal chequebook accounts. In these ways banking facilities were brought within the reach of the man-in-the-street as never before; and by December 1958 the *City Press*, writing about Lord Monckton, would declare that he had[2]

> injected competition and vigour into the banking world, and destroyed at a blow the Socialist cry of monopoly and vested interests. It was he, too, who gave the lead, which the Government followed, in easing credit. Look again at some other of Lord Monckton's innovations, notably his drive to bring the small man and wage earner to the banks' counters. Doubtless it is long-term good business for the banks. But it is also of immense social and political importance.

With his deeply held belief in the paramount importance of human relationships, Walter also set himself to establish close links with the management, staff and customers of the bank. In this he was highly successful: 'His staff,' said his secretary Miss Dunton, 'thought the world of him'; and by the winter of 1957 he was already on tour, meeting hundreds of branch managers at dinners given by the Board and management throughout the country. Walter also became a most welcome figure at the Midland Bank's sporting fixtures held in their ground at New Beckenham. He took a keen delight in presiding over these events. When appropriate, Biddy would join him to hand out prizes; and occasionally he would arrange for a team of nationally famous cricketers to play against the Bank's XI.

Such moments of relaxation were unfortunately rare. Monckton allowed himself little respite from his duties, and in his very first year at the Midland he accepted the Presidency of the Institute of Bankers, following which he became Chairman of the Overseas Bankers Association, President of the British Bankers Association and Chairman of the London Clearing Banks.

During the next few years Walter Monckton also steered the Midland Bank successfully through numerous changes in the field of overseas business. In the course of extensive travel for meetings of the World Bank and the International Monetary Fund, he formed personal contacts with bankers all over the world; and on behalf of the Midland Bank, he formed a consortium which included the leading banks of Belgium, Holland and West Germany. Known as the European Advisory Committee, this was chiefly intended for the exchange of information rather than of capital; but it opened the way to future cooperative ventures. Another important step in extending overseas business was the formation of a new bank of which he was the first Chairman. Called the 'Midland and International Banks', it was formed with the Midland Bank, the Toronto Dominion Bank and the Commercial Bank of Australia.

Walter seemed to remain perennially enthusiastic through all these changes and developments; but as the years passed his health, which had been seriously over-taxed during his years in Government, began to fail. In January 1963, when he was entering his seventy-third year, Walter made a statement to the shareholders in which he debated with his usual incisiveness the knotty problem of competition between banks for deposits; but this was the last public occasion on which he seemed to be in reasonably good health. A few weeks later came a kidney operation which kept him in hospital for a month, and left him feeling weak and exhausted when he was finally allowed home. His doctors insisted that he should convalesce in some warmer climate, so Biddy took him to Montecatini, where he regained enough strength to go for gentle strolls around the hotel gardens; but when they came back to England in June he was still very frail, and clearly required more time to recuperate.

However, Walter was not the man to submit to medical advice when it clashed with what he considered to be his public duty; and within a few days of his return to England, he insisted on travelling to Brighton where he was to be installed as the first Chancellor of Sussex University. This involved him in an exhausting schedule of events. Arriving in Brighton on the evening of 10 June, he attended first a mayoral reception at the famous Brighton Pavilion; and then a dinner at the Corn Exchange, at which both he and the Prime Minister Harold Macmillan made speeches.

The following day, wearing his official robes of heavy gold and black brocade, Monckton scorned the use of a wheelchair, and walked in procession under a blazing sun all the way to Brighton Dome. On one side he was supported by Biddy, on the other by her grand-daughter

Lady Jane Howard, while his train was held by his beloved grandson Christopher. Walter still looked remarkably well, with his hair as thick and dark as it had been when he was an undergraduate; but at times he was seen to lean heavily upon his stick, and this was only the start of a lengthy round of duties. Once he had been installed as Chancellor, and had accepted an honorary Degree of Laws, he had to confer degrees on many others, including such old friends as the Bishop of Southwark, Lord Mountbatten of Burma and Harold Macmillan. Each of these distinguished figures made speeches in which they dwelt at some length upon their high regard for the new Chancellor; and at one point Biddy, growing anxious about the strain that Walter was undergoing as the ceremony went on and on, left her seat and moved to one just below the platform; but fortunately this was an unnecessary precaution.

Walter's health had not been improved by this ordeal; and very soon he faced another of similar magnitude. In July 1963 there were to be celebrations for the 700th anniversary of the foundation of Balliol. A lesser man would have pleaded illness; but both as Visitor, and as one of the trustees of the special Anniversary Fund, Walter felt that he had a duty to be there, and nothing could prevent him.

On his arrival, the sickness of this frail but determined old man was so apparent that the King of Norway and his son moved out of their rooms in the Master's Lodgings to accommodate him. After a brief rest, he attended a service in the college chapel, a reception in a tent set up in one of the college quadrangles, and then a formal dinner at which he rose to his feet to make a speech.

The following day Walter was fully prepared for similar exertions; but, fortunately for once, rain effectively stopped play. The main celebrations, for which 2,000 people had arrived, were ruined by a tremendous rainstorm which lasted all day; and the guests, who had been expecting supper in the grounds followed by fireworks, were instead confined to a marquee. The Master of Balliol, seeing how ill Walter was, would not allow him to be exposed to this crush, but arranged for his immediate party to have supper in one of the college houses nearby.

Two months later, as a great concession to his doctors, who had vainly suggested complete retirement from the Bank, Walter reluctantly agreed to take a short holiday; and he went to Italy where he spent three weeks in the sun. However, on his return, feeling guilty about his long absence from the Bank, he rapidly undid whatever good his holiday had done him, by arriving far too early each day, and then staying far too late. By now, his declining health could no longer be concealed from the Bank staff; and when he struggled to attend some of his official dinners he was obviously in considerable pain, and his powers of concentration were also failing.

Amazingly, March 1964 found Walter planning to travel to Abu Dhabi, where he intended to open a new pipeline in his capacity as Chairman of the Iraq Petroleum Company. Everyone knew that a journey of this kind was madness in his appalling state of health. No one could stop him, but he was persuaded to take one week's holiday in Tripoli on the way. Sadly, Walter hurt his back while getting out of the bath on what was only his second day in Tripoli. He was instructed to lie quite still for several days, which did him further harm as his liver and kidneys became disordered; and then Biddy was shocked to notice a curious change in his face. She called in a neurologist from Beirut, who diagnosed a slight stroke. Walter's speech had not been affected, but he was ordered home at once; thus he had to return to England without even a glimpse of Abu Dhabi.

Back in London, Biddy learned from the doctors that Walter was suffering from arterio-sclerosis, and that this accounted for the decline in his health. Walter himself was compelled to face the fact that he could no longer cope with his enormous workload; and in June 1964 he resigned the Chairmanship both of the Midland Bank, and of the Midland and International Banks. The *Midbank Chronicle*, organ of the Midland Group, would one day write of their former Chairman:[3]

> . . . he applied his energies to the Chairmanship of the Bank, enterprisingly in its business development – yet with deep-rooted concern for the fortunes and welfare of those thousands of us whose daily work is also the Bank's.
>
> Humanity and humility were endearingly and endurably a part of him, manifested in a nature so warm and friendly, so sincere and so responsive to sincerity, that he drew nothing but affection from those who, by the order of things, were beholden to him.

Walter remained a director of the Midland Bank, which he had come to love so greatly, and where his qualities were so fully appreciated, for the rest of his life.

Chapter 9

The Monckton Commission

I

EVEN during the period of his most active Chairmanship of the Midland Bank, Lord Monckton had remained open to the call of public duty; and had undertaken another diplomatic mission abroad, just as taxing as his earlier duties in India. However, he was no longer acting for the Nizam of Hyderabad, but for the British Government; and the scene had changed to Africa, where the matter in question was the future of the Federation of Rhodesia and Nyasaland. The Federation had been established in 1953, as an experiment to see whether black and white people could co-exist and co-operate within the same land; and since it was clear that difficulties would arise, it had been laid down that a review conference would re-examine the Constitution after a trial period of between seven and nine years.

It was in the summer of 1959, a year before the review conference was due to meet, that the British Government decided to convene a prior Commission of Inquiry into the Constitution; and Walter Monckton accepted the Prime Minister Harold Macmillan's invitation to be Chairman.

The principal problems lay in the differing backgrounds of the three territories concerned. Nyasaland, for example, had been proclaimed a Protectorate of the Crown back in 1891, the year of Walter's birth, with the object of stamping out the Arab slave trade. Both Southern and Northern Rhodesia, on the other hand, had long been controlled by the British South African Company, formed by Cecil Rhodes; but were now very different from each other. In 1923 the inhabitants of Southern Rhodesia, which contained a growing European population, had voted to become a self-governing colony under the Crown; while in 1924 Northern Rhodesia had become a Crown Protectorate like Nyasaland.

The status of a Protectorate is of course given to countries which are not considered far enough advanced to be politically responsible for their own Government, so that another country needs to be appointed to administer the backward one for the benefit of its native population: a condition far from that of a conquered country, which can expect to be run for the benefit of the conquerors. After the 1914–8 War, Protectorates had been placed under the supervision of the League of Nations, which could issue directions to the countries in charge, and receive reports of their administration. For this reason, the natives of Northern Rhodesia could always expect that in the event of any dispute with European settlers, the British Government would take their side; whereas in Southern Rhodesia, the Europeans deeply distrusted both the Matabele and the Mashona who had revolted in 1896, and intended to avoid giving the natives any political power whatever.

The Zambezi River, which winds for 2,000 miles from Angola to the sea, effectively cut these three territories in two. To the south of the Zambezi lay Southern Rhodesia, controlled by its European population, with their dairy-farming, their tobacco plantations, and their developing industries; while to the north lay Nyasaland, with only a few white settlers among a predominantly native population; and Northern Rhodesia, where copper, zinc, lead and gold were already being mined, and there was the prospect of further mineral wealth.

Those in favour of a permanent Federation of all three states argued that it would be of mutual economic benefit, would tend to encourage a multi-racial society, and would have the added benefit of preventing Southern Rhodesia from joining the politically distasteful Union of South Africa. From the beginning, however, the Africans of both Nyasaland and Northern Rhodesia were totally opposed to the idea of Federation. They saw that it might mean increased prosperity; but that counted for little in their eyes when set against the severe electoral disadvantages under which it was proposed that they should labour.

Sir Godfrey Huggins, Prime Minister of the Federation, and for ten years Prime Minister of Southern Rhodesia, and Sir Roy Welensky, the leading figure in Northern Rhodesia, did nothing to allay their doubts. Unrest grew, and a new extremist element calling itself the Nationalist Congress began to appear everywhere, ready to foment trouble. Indeed, the Africans came more and more to disbelieve the propaganda directed at them in favour of Federation. On all sides, they could see their fellow-Africans gaining political independence. From 1957, when the Gold Coast became Ghana, Macmillan's 'wind of change' was blowing through Africa; by the end of 1960 there were no fewer than 25 independent states; and the natives of the Federation felt bitterly that they had been left behind, and that the Federation would permanently deprive them of political independence.

2

The announcement that an Advisory Commission would be appointed was made by Harold Macmillan, on 21 July 1959. These were its terms of reference:

> In the light of the information provided by the Committee of Officials and of any additional information the commission may require, to advise the five Governments,* in preparation for the 1960 Review, on the constitutional programme and framework best suited to the achievements of the objects contained in the Constitution of 1953, including the Preamble.

That Preamble stipulated that the colony of Southern Rhodesia should continue to enjoy reasonable government; and that separate Governments under Crown protection should continue to exist both in Nyasaland and in Northern Rhodesia for as long as their inhabitants desired. It also stated what it took to be the advantages of a Federation between the colony and the territories: it would be to their mutual benefit, in that it would foster partnership between their inhabitants; and it would enable the Federation to move confidently towards becoming a full member of the British Commonwealth.[1]

Macmillan's hope had been that Lord Forster would chair the Commission; and when he declined to do so, Lord Monckton was summoned to Downing Street in his stead. Following their meeting, Macmillan wrote to Monckton on 22 August 1959 as follows:[2]

> I want to thank you for listening to me about Central Africa . . . I am sure that this is one of the most important jobs in our long history for, if we fail in Central Africa to devise something like a multi-racial state, then Kenya will go too; and Africa may become no longer a source of pride and

---

* These were the Governments of the United Kingdom, the Federation of Rhodesia and Nyasaland, Southern Rhodesia, Northern Rhodesia, and Nyasaland.

profit to the Europeans who have developed it, but a maelstrom of trouble into which all of us will be sucked. The cruder concepts, whether of the left or of the right, are clearly wrong. Africans cannot be dominated permanently (as they are trying to do in South Africa) without any proper opportunity for their development and ultimate self-government. Nor can the Europeans be abandoned. It would be wrong for us to do so, and fatal for the African interests.

If you could steer the work of this Commission in the period before the end of 1960 when the Governmental Review takes place, you would be doing a great work. This is not just a matter of writing a report. It is a matter of creating a climate of opinion and calling into being all the best feelings of all sides. You have a particular position and reputation which fits you specially for this work. I told you frankly that I had asked Lord Forster, chiefly because of his previous connections with inquiries in Africa; but I know of nobody else except you two who commands the necessary   authority.

Monckton accepted the Chairmanship on condition that his wife Biddy should be allowed to accompany him on his travels. However, he was not to leave for Africa without a severe setback. The Labour Party refused to have anything to do with the Commission, arguing that its terms of reference should have included a consideration of the right of secession.

This question of secession was to bedevil the whole work of the Commission. The Government did not want secession to be discussed at all; but the individual members of the Commission were well aware that it could not be ignored if they were to have any chance of success. Lord Home, the Secretary of State for Commonwealth Relations, did his utmost to change the Labour Party's attitude, but to no effect. Without clear all-party backing from the British House of Commons, it was doubtful how effective the Monckton Commission could be; but since it seemed to be the only hope of preserving the Federation, Home decided to let it proceed as planned.

Sir Roy Welensky resented the Commission from the start, considering that its members were being asked to adjudicate on matters which were none of their business, and which should be left entirely to the Governments concerned in the 1960 Constitutional Review. Welensky was also worried that the African Nationalists might believe that the Commission had been formed in response to their own violence, a belief which could only encourage them to continue along that road. However, after a secret message from Harold Macmillan, reassuring him that Britain had no intention of allowing secession to be included

within the Commission's terms of reference, he reluctantly agreed that
it should go ahead.[3]

The Commission met for the first time on 15 February 1960 at the
Victoria Falls Hotel. There were 26 members, speaking a variety of
languages, and each with their own apparently irreconcilable aims and
beliefs. In the event it was generally agreed that Lord Monckton was
the man who somehow welded these disparate groups into an effective
committee. Lord Crathorne (one of the British Parliamentarians on
the Commission) later recalled that all through the inquiry, Monckton[4]

> showed himself conscientious, authoritative, prepared to show surprising
> firmness when necessary, but softening every enforcement by his incom-
> parable charm. [He was] essentially a directing chairman, in full control
> throughout, dominating operations and permitting no bickering or intrigue.

The Secretary-General of the Commission, Sir Mark Tennant, would
particularly remember[5]

> the extraordinary personal respect in which he was held by all his colleagues,
> whatever their colour and opinions . . . the words 'I do not want to
> embarrass the Chairman' were often on the lips of both white and African
> members.

Even the white Rhodesian members, who to begin with were totally
opposed to any discussion of secession, were eventually prepared to
consider it; and of them all, only two signed a minority report.

During the three months that the Commission spent in the Federation, Monckton frequently carried the debate outside the normal
constrictions of the conference chamber by organising its members
into several small groups, and sending them out into the country to
find out for themselves how the Federation and its problems appeared
to those on the ground. Walter himself was flown from group to group
in a small aeroplane, accompanied by Biddy, Mark Tennant and a
press officer. This was a brilliant arrangement. Walter met a large
number of people from all areas of the Federation; while the members
of the three groups found that their preconceived ideas and prejudices
melted away in the face of personal experience.

In particular, they realised that dislike of the Federation in the
northern territories was not of recent origin, fostered by the various
African Nationalists, as many of them had believed, but was both
long-standing and profound, and owed much to a deep-seated prejudice
against Southern Rhodesia as a white man's country. The Africans
were highly indignant that the Federation had been foisted on them

against their will; and they feared that, in time, it would lead to their own subjugation by the whites.

Members of the Commission also realised that much harm had been done by the British Government when they instructed British officials and District Officers to adopt a neutral attitude towards the Federation. The Africans looked up to these men for guidance in all their affairs; and their apparent lack of enthusiasm for the Federation had been more than enough to outweigh the increased prosperity which it had undoubtedly brought in its wake.

With the aim both of allaying groundless fears and of dealing with real grievances, the Monckton Commission therefore proposed drastic changes. The central authority should have fewer functions; an equal number of seats in the federal Assembly should go to Africans and whites, regardless of education or wealth; cooperation between the states should be improved; there should be safeguards against racial discrimination; and minority groups should be protected. The Commission also hoped that the review conference should find a name to replace that of 'Federation', which was so deeply hated in the northern territories; and Southern Rhodesia was warned that the only way to achieve close relations with her northern neighbours was immediately to remove all traces of unfair discrimination from her laws.

A further suggestion was that attention should be directed to the organisation of the public services, with special training centres in each country for civil servants of all races; and then they moved onto what had proved to be the nub of their discussions: the question of whether there should be a right of secession.

3

The Monckton Commission had been established at a time when the chances of preserving the Federation of Rhodesia and Nyasaland were already extremely slight. It was already inevitable that when the time came for the Review Conference to be convened in 1960, the right to secede would be a major issue. In those circumstances, the Commission could have produced no worthwhile report without examining that right, even though such an examination formed no part of its terms of reference. Indeed, by the time that work began on drafting a set of proposals, even the white Rhodesians on the Commission had been convinced by their experiences in the field that they must make recommendations about secession, both to postpone that evil, and to

persuade the Africans to give the Federation another chance. As the
Monckton Commission saw it, at that late stage the only other way to
preserve the Federation would have been by using armed force.

First they made the legal position absolutely clear. The Federation
had been established, and its Constitution defined,

> by an Order in Council made by Her Majesty under the authority of an
> Act of the United Kingdom Parliament (the Rhodesia and Nyasaland Act,
> 1953), section 1 (2) of which expressly reserves the right of Parliament to
> revoke or amend the Order in Council. Thus Her Majesty's Government
> retain unfettered power to make provision for the future of the Federation
> in any manner they may think fit.

They added that:

> The present Constitution does not confer on any of the Territorial Legis-
> latures any right, express or implied, to secede from the Federation . . .
> The attainment of responsible government by any one of the Territories
> does not import any such right . . . In these circumstances, there is no
> legal right on the part of any Territory to secede from the Federation. To
> create a right of secession an Act of the United Kingdom Parliament would
> be required.

However, the Commission went on to say that there could be no legal
justification for excluding from discussion at the review conference
any part of the Constitution. Indeed, they suggested that, paradox-
ically, the survival of the Federation might depend upon the provision
of a right to secede in certain specified circumstances, or after a stated
time. If, for example, secession became allowable upon the attainment
of an agreed stage of constitutional development, this should encourage
those of moderate views, and ease the tension in Northern Rhodesia.
Again, the right to secede after a stated time could be seen by the
whites of Southern Rhodesia as a safeguard against the possibility that
the Africans might come into power in the North.

When the Report of the Monckton Commission was published in
October 1960, it was favourably received by the British press; while
the Labour Party felt that the Report fully justified the line they had
taken earlier on the need to include secession in the Commission's
terms of reference. However, in Salisbury there was outrage that the
Commission had dared to mention secession. Sir Roy Welensky in
particular protested loudly and angrily about what he considered to
be a breach of faith; and his rage seemed to some extent justified
when the leaders of the African Nationalists, overlooking everything

constructive in the Report, fastened joyfully upon the word 'secession', and demanded it at once.

Walter Monckton had always feared that no solution could be found which was acceptable to all the disparate elements of the Federation, and had to be satisfied with knowing that he had done his duty. Indeed, he had done it at some personal cost: the burden of the work had seriously over-taxed his health, leading to rheumatic pain in his wrists and ankles of such intensity that for a while he was frightened of being touched, and would cry out to Biddy telling her not to come too close to him. However, a few weeks before publication of the Report, he could write philosophically to Sir Lionel Heald, a fellow-Commissioner:

> I expect our Report will be badly received and violently attacked . . . I only hope that the Report, though unpolished and necessarily without precise references to evidence, may do some good. Anyhow, it was work honestly done, and we must bear the blows as best we may.

Chapter 10

Crossing the River

HAVING resigned as Chairman of the Midland Bank in June 1964, Walter was now too ill to undertake work of any kind. It was a sad task which Biddy shouldered, to support him through his declining months; and she decided to move him from London to the peace and quiet of their country house in Folkington. It was a warm summer, and for a time Walter practically lived amongst the sweet-smelling flowers and shrubs of Biddy's beautiful garden, walking a little when he was able, and mostly eating his meals outside.

There were long periods when, apart from a loss in energy, Walter seemed almost normal for a man of his years. But sometimes he could not speak coherently, and found it difficult to write; and for someone whose brain had always been so keen, and who had always hated to show any sign of physical weakness, such a decline must have been particularly hard to bear. Yet he retained his consideration for others to the last, and frequently apologised to his doctor, Anthony Churcher, for being such a troublesome patient.

Walter was fortunate in finding an excellent male nurse, the young Dr Halliday, who was his constant attendant. Under Halliday's care, he became somewhat better, and was able to visit Dr Churcher's house for tea. His first act there was to apologise to the doctor's wife for taking up so much of her husband's time, and keeping him from his family. Dr Churcher later commented that: 'It was remarkable to me, that the kindest and most appreciative patient I ever had was the one I considered the greatest joy to look after.'[1]

Even now, Walter still clung to the hope of recovery and a return to work. His children, close to him all their lives, were now constant in their attendance and a great source of comfort. When Biddy had to go away for a short break, his daughter Valerie came to stay and keep him company. As for his son Gilbert, he now had five children: Christopher, Rosamund, Anthony, and the twins Timothy and Jonathan. He had been promoted Major-General the previous year at the comparatively early age of 48; and had delighted his father still more with the news that his sons were to go to Harrow. In the meantime Gilbert's wife Marianna, always a great favourite, had become an unstinting visitor; she lived not far away at Bearsted, and Walter particularly enjoyed it when she brought the twins over from their private school at Seaford. Indeed, he adored all his grandchildren: he never talked down to them but had the knack, which they much appreciated, of treating them as equals.

In November, only two months before he died, one of Walter's last remaining wishes was granted. Both his first wife, Polly, and Biddy's first husband, Lord Carlisle, were now dead; and on 1 November 1964 Walter's great friend Mervyn Stockwood conducted a very private marriage service for Walter and Biddy in the tiny parish church of All Saints near their home. Walter was so moved by the ceremony that he stood by the altar rails with tears running down his cheeks.

Towards the end of December, Biddy went to the home of her friend Lady Alexandra Metcalfe for a short rest; but on 31 December Walter had a sudden relapse. When Biddy reached home, she saw that the end was near. Dr Churcher asked for a second opinion, and Dr James Dow of St George's Hospital came down from London. A bulletin was issued each day until the end.

When Walter had become very weak, he asked to see Mervyn Stockwood; but the Bishop was away in Zurich, and while he was being contacted, the Bishop's chaplain Michael Mayne asked if he could help. Biddy was sure that Walter now knew that he was dying, and wished to receive Communion, so on Wednesday 6 January Mayne administered that sacrament. Gilbert and Valerie were there to see their father for the last time.

On Thursday, Walter seemed much more peaceful. Mayne read to him the passage from *Pilgrim's Progress* where Christian crosses the river and reaches the Heavenly City. On Friday, Mervyn Stockwood took his place at his friend's bedside, and continued reading to him. Then Walter lapsed into a coma. Biddy sat with him all night, but there was no change in his condition. Finally, at some point in the early afternoon of Saturday 9 January, Walter stopped breathing. The Bishop put his pectoral cross in Walter's hand, and Dr Churcher confirmed that he was dead.

The *Midbank Chronicle* recorded his passing as follows:[2]

Lord Monckton was interred on January 13 at All Saints, Brenchley in Kent where many of his forebears are buried. It was a day of gale-force wind and driving rain that drenched the mourners yet could not disperse the heady perfume from the wreaths (one of them was from the Duke and Duchess of Windsor) that banked the paths round the church. A poignant sight were the groups of villagers huddled in the doorways of shuttered shops to watch the cortege pass.

The following day (still windy and cold, but sunny) came the memorial service at Southwark Cathedral, attended by the famous . . . At Brenchley the lesson was read by Earl Alexander of Tunis, and at Southwark by Mr Harold Macmillan. Sir Archibald Forbes, Lord Monckton's successor as Chairman of the Bank, was at both services with Mr Thackstone, chief general manager; at Southwark they were joined by other directors and very many of the staff, active and retired.

To Lady Monckton, who was so devotedly at her husband's side while he was with us, we offer the deep sympathy and regard of the staff. We have all been the richer for having known him and worked with him; his influence will endure. In the words of Mr G. F. Wakeford, one of the Bank's pensioners:

Not for his high honours honourably earned,
Nor the esteem for which he was regarded
In high places,
But for the humanity he brought to the high office
He held among us,
We, the staff of the Midland Bank,
Will remember him.

Walter Monckton's had been a life of service, informed ever since his days at Balliol by the highest Christian ideals. A sense of duty can be a cold thing: but combined with Monckton's warmth of heart, keen intelligence, and genuine interest in people of every rank and race, it made him into that rare person: someone who is formidable, and yet well-loved. A keen advocate, with a highly paid career at the Bar, he might have been still more formidable had victory been his only aim. But he cared more for justice than for victory; and by nature, though not a pacifist, he was a peacemaker. When he thought of conflict, he could remember only too clearly the misery of the trenches in the First World War. Men of the calibre of Churchill, Mountbatten and Macmillan recognised that his supreme gift was to reconcile the apparently irreconcilable. Whether he was steering an uncrowned King through the difficult waters of an abdication crisis, attempting to guide a Nizam through a series of major constitutional changes, reconciling warring unions, or hammering out the form of a possible agreement between native Africans and white settlers, his personal gifts were such that he frequently achieved more than anyone could reasonably have expected.

In his own private life, Monckton suffered two great tragedies: a disastrous first marriage, and, equally distressing to one of his convictions, years of alienation from the Church. These events, far from making him bitter, enlarged his human sympathies and deepened his sense of what was spiritually important; and before the end came, not only had he found personal happiness, but also his long years of faithful service had been crowned by a complete reconciliation with the Church. 'Blessed are the peacemakers,' runs the exhortation, 'for they shall be called the children of God'; and as his mortal remains were laid to rest in a Kentish churchyard, his Christian friends had no doubt that Walter Monckton, like the hero of *Pilgrim's Progress*, had crossed the river and reached the Heavenly City.

A Note on Sources

THE principal source is the Monckton Papers, which were deposited in the Bodleian Library Oxford in 1974. They come as two separate collections and as the ownership of each collection is different it has not been possible to integrate the papers.

1. *Dep. Monckton Trustees 1–89*. These papers were the property of the Literary Trustees of the late Viscount Monckton of Brenchley and were deposited in Balliol College, Oxford, in 1974. Balliol College later deposited them in the Bodleian. The bulk of these papers relate to Monckton's life prior to 1950, although there are some papers after that date. A section of the papers (14–24) relating to the Duke and Duchess of Windsor (1976–1981), other members of the Royal Family (1939–41) and confidential files and correspondence (1940–1956) are restricted and will not be made available until 1999.

2. *Dep. Monckton 1–63*. These papers were given by Viscountess Brenchley to Balliol College, and by them deposited in the Bodleian Library in 1974. Most of this collection dates from after 1950, although there are some earlier papers as well. Some of the more recent correspondence and papers have been closed for a period of 30 years from the date at which they were written.

Notes

CHAPTER 1
Early Years and the Great War

1 DMT 77. Birkenhead pp.171, 179
2 *Ibid.* Birkenhead p.175
3 D. H. Monckton, *The Family of Monckton* (privately printed 1887):
   DMT 88
4 Birkenhead p.8
5 DMT 1
6 *Ibid.* 23 November 1902
7 *Ibid.* 2 August 1904; see Birkenhead p.13
8 *Ibid.* 2 August 1904
9 Birkenhead p.15ff
10 DMT 1
11 Birkenhead p.21. Bowen's name here is incorrectly spelled Bower.
12 Christopher Hollis, *The Oxford Union* (1965) *passim.*
13 DMT, cited Birkenhead p.34.
14 Robin Barrington-Ward, quoted in Donald McLachlan, *In the Chair:
   Barrington-Ward of* The Times (1971) p.35
15 The present Lord Monckton to H. Montgomery Hyde, n.d.
16 DMT 1
17 *Ibid.*, cited Birkenhead p.47
18 Birkenhead p.49
19 Birkenhead p.50
20 Birkenhead p.54

CHAPTER 2
The Bar and India

1 Birkenhead, pp.56–8
2 Robert Jackson, *The Chief* (1959) pp.161–2

3 Birkenhead pp.60–61
4 Lord Boothby, *Recollections of a Rebel* (1978) p.29ff
5 DMT 1
6 DMT 1, cited Birkenhead pp.77–8
7 *Re Boundary between Labrador and Canada in Labrador Peninsula*, 137, *Law Times*, 187 PC.
8 Law Reports, 1927, AC 354
9 *Ibid.*
10 DMT 1
11 Law Reports, 1930, 1 KB 467 CA, 1931, AC 331 HL
12 *Fisher v. Oldham Corporation*, Law Reports, 1930, PKB 364
13 *Bishop of Norwich v. Davidson*. See Rupert Furneaux, *Great Issues in Private Courts* (1964) pp.28–50
14 On the Office of Works see Sir Lionel Earle, *Turn Over the Page* (1935) *passim*.
15 Cited Birkenhead pp.65–6
16 Birkenhead p.76
17 *The Times* 4 and 8 Nov, 1933
18 A. P. Herbert *Independent Member* (1950), p.1ff
19 DMT 53
20 DMT 44
21 *Horse and Hound*, 25 Jan 1965
22 Birkenhead p.67
23 *Ibid.* p.71
24 For Monckton's relations with the Indian princes, and his visits to India, see Birkenhead pp.93–120
25 DMT 44
26 *Ibid.*
27 *Ibid.*
28 Cited Birkenhead p.68

CHAPTER 3
The Abdication

1 On the *Nahlin* cruise, see Frances Donaldson, *Edward VIII* (1974) p.211
2 Lord Beaverbrook, *The Abdication of King Edward VIII* (1986) p.31
3 DMT cited Birkenhead p.123
4 *Ibid.* p.128
5 Keith Middlemass and John Barnes, *Baldwin* (1969) p.98 note
6 DMT cited Birkenhead p.128
7 DMT cited Birkenhead p.129
8 DMT cited Birkenhead p.128
9 J. Bryan III and Charles J. V. Murphy, *The Windsor Story* (1979) p.139ff.

10   DMT cited Birkenhead pp.132–3
11   H. Montgomery Hyde, *Norman Birkett* (1964) p.454ff.
12   DMT cited Birkenhead p.175
13   HRH The Duke of Windsor, *A King's Story* (1951) p.329
14   The Duke in his memoirs claims that it was Mr Baldwin who brought up the subject of his possible marriage; but this may well be due to his misreading of the account which Mr Baldwin gave to the House of Commons, an account upon which the Duke, writing many years after the event, appears to have relied. Baldwin's private account, as given to his wife the same evening, would appear to be more reliable.
15   H. Montgomery Hyde, *Baldwin: The Unexpected Prime Minister* (1973)
16   DMT cited Birkenhead p.135
17   Baldwin Papers, cited Hyde, *Baldwin* p.46
18   Bryan and Murphy *op. cit.* p.260
19   Baldwin Papers, cited Hyde, *Baldwin* p.46
20   Rhodes James and J. C. C. Davidson (eds), *Memoirs of a Conservative* (1969) pp.416–7
21   Hyde, *Baldwin* pp.175–6
22   Charles Higham, *Wallis: Secret Lives of the Duchess of Windsor* pp.1–5
23   *Ibid.* pp.11–12
24   *Ibid.* pp.18–23
25   *Ibid.* p.36
26   *Ibid.* p.72. See also R. von Krafft-Ebing, *Psychopathia Studia* (Eng. trans. 1893) p.124
27   Private information. China dossier on Mrs Simpson compiled by the British Secret Service during the Abdication Crisis.
28   Higham p.45
29   Higham p.39
30   Higham p.72. Consuelo Thaw (née Morgan) was married to Benjamin Thaw of Pittsburgh, a cousin of Mary Copley Thaw, whose dissolute son Harry had shot and killed New York's most prominent architect, Stanford White, in 1906. Thaw was found criminally insane at his trial for murder but was later freed. See Gerald Langford, *The Murder of Stanford White* (1963).
31   *Ibid.* p.78
32   Robert Sencourt, *The Reign of Edward VIII* (1962) p.160
33   Monckton's account of the Abdication, cited Birkenhead p.157
34   Sir Henry Channon, *Chips*. Diaries edited by R. Rhodes James (1967) pp.30, 34–5
35   *Ibid.* p.76
36   Lady Leslie ('Beloved Leo') had been the Duke of Connaught's mistress for many years. See Anita Leslie, *Edwardians in Love* (1972) pp.200–18
37   Monckton, cited Birkenhead p.125
38   *Ibid.* p.41

39 *Ibid*.
40 Hyde, *Baldwin* pp.483–4
41 Monckton, cited Birkenhead pp.142–3
42 *Ibid*. p.144
43 Monckton, cited Birkenhead pp.145–6
44 *Ibid*.; and see Hyde, *op. cit.* p.493
45 Duke of Windsor, p.393
46 Hyde, *Baldwin* p.497. The King's Proctor would later conduct his own investigation of Stephenson's application.
47 *Ibid*.
48 Monckton, cited Birkenhead pp.148–9
49 Hyde, *Baldwin* pp.500–1
50 Duke of Windsor, p.409; G. M. Young, *Stanley Baldwin* (1952) p.241
51 Birkenhead p.150
52 Monckton, cited Birkenhead p.251
53 *Ibid*.
54 Lord Boothby, *Recollections of a Rebel* (1978) p.124
55 Monckton, cited Birkenhead p.151
56 Birkenhead p.152
57 J. W. Wheeler-Bennett, *King George VI* (1958) pp.287, 295
58 Bryan and Murphy, pp.287–8
59 Monckton, cited Birkenhead pp.153–4
60 Hyde, *Baldwin* p.511

CHAPTER 4
Royal Affairs and Other Duties

1 Cited Birkenhead p.164
2 *Ibid*. p.164
3 Cited Birkenhead p.165
4 Michael Bloch (ed.), *The Secret File of the Duke of Windsor* (1988) p.51
5 Higham p.175
6 Cited Birkenhead p.166
7 Duchess of Windsor, *The Heart Has Its Reasons* (1956) p.298
8 *New York Daily News*, 12 December 1966
9 See *Secret File* pp.70–1; and Higham p.188
10 Birkenhead p.167
11 Cited Frances Donaldson p.525
12 Cited Birkenhead p.162
13 Higham pp.191, 192
14 *Cole v. Police Constable 443A* 1937 1 KB 316 DC
15 *Read v. Croydon Corporation* 1938 44 AER 631
16 DMT 77: Notes for autobiography
17 DMT 54, *The Almanac de Gotha* (1941) p.175

18 Paraphrased Birkenhead p.168
19 Cited Birkenhead p.168
20 *Secret File* pp.126–9
21 Cited Birkenhead pp.169–170
22 Cited Birkenhead pp.170–1
23 *Ibid.*
24 Donaldson p.349
25 Cited Birkenhead p.172
26 Birkenhead p.172
27 Lord Moran, *Winston Churchill* (1966) p.466; and Birkenhead p.176
28 Duff Cooper, *Old Men Forget* (1953) p.285
29 Cited Birkenhead p.178
30 Reynolds *op.cit.* (1942) pp.187–94
31 Sir Robert Bruce-Lockhart, *Diaries 1939–1965*, ed. Kenneth Young (1980), pp.45–6
32 *Ibid.* p.103
33 Cited Birkenhead pp.185–6
34 Cited Birkenhead p.186
35 Cited Birkenhead p.179
36 Walter Schellenberg, *Memoirs* (1956) p.139
37 Duchess of Windsor, 342–3
38 Bloch, 126–7
39 Cited Birkenhead p.180
40 Schellenberg p.142
41 Bloch, p.212
42 *Ibid.* p.213 note
43 *Ibid.* p.213

CHAPTER 5
The Ministry of Information

1 Birkenhead p.184–5
2 *Who's Who in the Theatre (passim)*.
3 DMT 4
4 Andrew Boyle, *Poor Dear Brenda* (1974) p.266
5 *Ibid.* p.270
6 MP 187
7 'How is our big broadcasting station, which is to override foreign broadcasts, getting on?' Churchill wrote to Bracken on 31 August 1941. 'There was a long delay in setting about it, but I understand the fullest priorities have been given.' Winston Churchill, *The Second World War* (1950) III, p.731
8 MP 187
9 *Ibid.* p.188

10   Birkenhead p.188
11   MP 89
12   Quentin Reynolds, *Only the Stars are Neutral* (1942) p.196ff
13   *Ibid.* p.200
14   MP 192; extract cited Birkenhead p.192
15   Reynolds, p.213
16   Reynolds, p.214–5
17   Cited Birkenhead p.193
18   Lord Chandos, *Memoirs* (1962) p.240
19   MP, cited Birkenhead pp.196–7
20   Birkenhead p.197
21   A letter in a private collection from 'Barbara', who served under Mary
     Newall, to Sir William Charles Crocker MC, 30 May 1969
22   MP cited Birkenhead pp.198–9
23   Chandos p.276
24   Birkenhead p.201
25   *Ibid.*
26   Chandos p.280
27   Cited Birkenhead p.203
28   *Ibid.* p.204
29   Bloch, *op. cit.* p.278
30   Cited Birkenhead pp.205–6
31   DMT 49 (partly cited Birkenhead p.207)
32   Cited Birkenhead p.211
33   *Ibid.* p.210ff

CHAPTER 6
The Fate of Hyderabad

1   MP cited Birkenhead pp.220–1
2   *Ibid.* p.221
3   Martin Gilbert, *Winston Churchill: Never Despair* (1988) p.233
4   *Ibid.* p.234
5   Philip Ziegler, *Mountbatten* (1986) p.404
6   Birkenhead pp.223–4
7   MP cited Birkenhead p.224
8   DMT 13 cited Birkenhead p.225
9   DMT 28 cited Birkenhead p.225
10   *Hansard*, 20 February 1947, cited Birkenhead p.225
11   MP cited Birkenhead p.226
12   On Mountbatten in India, see generally Ziegler, p.363ff
13   MP cited Birkenhead p.229
14   MP cited Ziegler, p.415 (27 Jan. 1947)
15   Cited Birkenhead p.229

16 *Ibid.* p.230
17 *Ibid.* p.232
18 *Ibid.* p.233
19 MP cited Ziegler p.413
20 Birkenhead p.234
21 Broadlands Archives, cited Ziegler, p.453. MP cited Birkenhead p.240
22 K. M. Munshi, *End of an Era* (Bombay 1957) pp.34–5, 173; cited Birkenhead p.242
23 Birkenhead p.243
24 *Ibid.* pp.245–6
25 MP cited Birkenhead p.247
26 Broadlands Archives (25 May 1948) cited Ziegler p.454
27 *Ibid.* (8 June 1948) p.455
28 MP cited Birkenhead p.251
29 *Ibid.* (16 Sept 1948) p.254

CHAPTER 7
Law and Politics

1   1944 AC 228 HL
2   1945 AC 304 HL
3   *Rex v. Ley*, Fenton Bresler *Lord Goddard* (1977) p.139 ff.
4   1949 AC 530 HL
5   1950 1 KB 47 CA
6   1951 2 KB 34 CA
7   1951 AC 850 HL
8   Birkenhead p.268 ff
9   MP dep 49
10 *Ibid.*
11 For information here, the author is indebted to the following works: Anthony Eden, *Full Circle* (1960); Selwyn Lloyd, *Suez 1956* (1978); and David Carlton, *Britain and the Suez Crisis* (1938).
12 Lord Butler, *The Art of the Possible* (1971) p.164
13 John Colville, *The Churchillians* (1981) pp.182–3
14 Cited Birkenhead p.308
15 Cited Birkenhead pp.309–10

CHAPTER 8
Banking and the Beginning of the End

1   Quotation from the *Midbank Chronicle*, organ of the Midland Group, by courtesy of Edwin Green, Group Archivist, Midland Group.

2   Cited Birkenhead pp.319–20
3   As 1 above

CHAPTER 9
The Monckton Commission

1   Birkenhead p.340
2   MP cited Birkenhead pp.340–1
3   Roy Welensky, *Welensky's 4000 Days* p.141
4   Birkenhead p.345
5   *Ibid.*

CHAPTER 10
Crossing the River

1   Birkenhead p.362
2   *Midbank Chronicle.* Quotations by courtesy of Edwin Green, Group Archivist, Midland Group.

Index

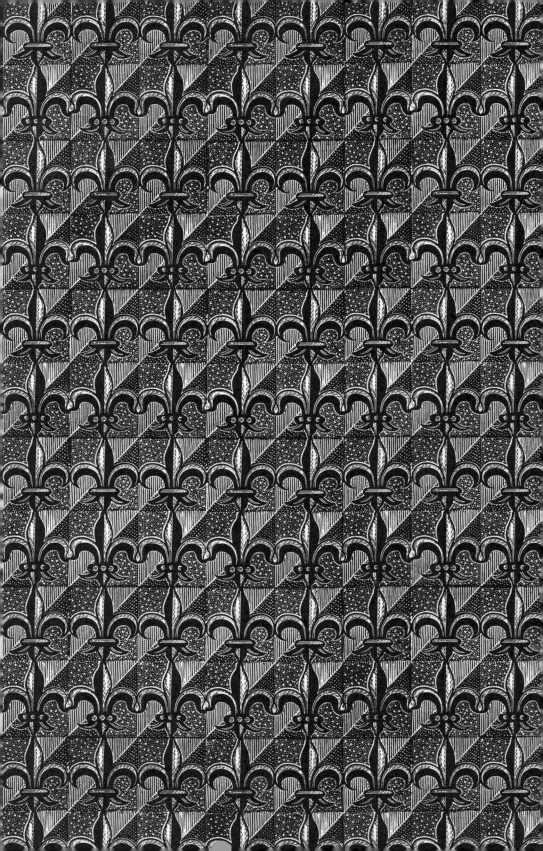